Stitching Identities in a Free Trade Zone

Gender and Politics in Sri Lanka

SANDYA HEWAMANNE

D0075277

PENN

University of Pennsylvania Press

Philadelphia

Published by
University of Pennsylvania Press
Philadelphia, Pennsylvania 19104-4112

Printed in the United States of America on acid-free paper

10   9   8   7   6   5   4   3   2   1

A Cataloging-in-Publication record is available from the Library of Congress
ISBN-13: 0-978-0-8122-4045-0
ISBN-10: 0-8122-4045-6

For Neil
Navathanpola obayi mata

Contents

Chapter 1

Introduction

December 2005

I stood at the edge of the dancing women and peered into the swirling faces and colors in front of me. Twilight was just beginning to fall over the factory grounds and the revelers on the dance floor. Standing at the edge of the steel and tar sheet party tent, looking for a familiar face in the dancing crowd, I felt lonely and somewhat scared. There was no need to feel scared. This was the same Suishin garment factory where I had roamed almost freely for seven months in 2000, getting to know workers and letting them get to know me. True, their annual Christmas party was of a much grander scale this time, with an outdoor stage decorated in red velvet curtains, a better-known band, beer and Coca-Cola fountains for unlimited drinks, and several games, including a beer-drinking competition. But there were familiar sights too, such as the women's brightly colored, glittery party dresses, gold jewelry, and high heels and the animated dancing. All seemed so incongruous in the background of the stark concrete factory structure and the enormous shipping containers, which were placed on the edge of the party grounds in readiness to ship the garments that these women workers produced earlier in the day. I had just finished taking a photograph of a young woman in a purple and gold *shalwar* suit dancing near a corroded shipping container when someone tapped me on the shoulder. It was my dear friend from 2000, Rena.

It was after about an hour of hugging, kissing, and exchanging information with old friends and being introduced to numerous new workers that Sanuja came to greet me. He had put on a little weight around the midsection of his body and in his face. Maybe it befit his new position as the factory manager. He had come a long way from 2000, when he was the Floor 1 production coordinator. When he took his leave, I turned back to Bhagya and Deepika, who were being entertained by my husband with tales of my fieldwork woes from those days.

"Things have changed a lot since I was here," I said as a way to turn the conversation away from my fieldwork mistakes.

"Things have not changed as much as you think, miss. When I started sewing here 10 years earlier, Sanuja sir was a production assistant. Then he became the floor coordinator, and look where he is now. *Ane*, ten years later we are still sewing in the lines," Bhagya said while gesturing with both hands to indicate "no gains."

"*Ane*, true, miss. I just received this gold coin as a gift for completing ten years of service here. But my basic salary is Rs. 6,500 (65$)," Deepika agreed while offering the gold coin with the Suishin logo for my inspection.

"I am so mad that they have not promoted you to at least an assistant supervisor position," I said while balancing the coin on my palm to ascertain the quality of gold.

"*Apoi*, miss, even if given, we would not have accepted. You know by now that we don't want to shout at our fellow workers. How can we get them to hurry up and produce more when we as workers know that it is absolutely impossible to work faster . . . ," Bhagya said. The last part of her statement was drowned by a loud wail of laughter that emanated from a circle of women jostling by the entrance to the factory building. It was the somewhat chaotic line formed to pose for photographs with Sanuja, the newly appointed factory manager.

"Sanuja sir was talking to miss and some other people. So now the line is really thick. We knew that was going to happen, so we went ahead and got our photos with him early," Bhagya said in her usual leisurely accent. I turned to look at her closely, and she looked back at me with her big, drooping eyes, which rarely reflected how she felt. Then her lips curved a bit at the corners and a thin smile lit her face. Still smiling sweetly, she added, "No, truly, I took a photograph with him. Each year I do. At least I can see how he is getting fatter and fatter each year and I am getting thinner and thinner." Bhagya was right. Things have not changed much since I spent seven months at Suishin in 2000.

It is this ambivalent way female migrant workers responded to free trade zone (FTZ) factory discipline and capitalist patriarchy that fascinated me in 2000 and prompted me to explore their lives in detail. My quest to learn more about their lives began when I started hanging out with a group of FTZ workers in a boardinghouse in August 1995 for a short-term research project. Four years later, with that many years of graduate-school education behind me, I came back in August 1999 to Katunayake for an in-depth study of their lives. I again started spending time with workers at their boardinghouses and eventually started staying at two boardinghouses. Five months later, I got one of those lucky breaks that rarely occur in fieldwork when an FTZ factory agreed to let me conduct research on its shop floor. In addition to the shop floor, my fascination with these workers' lives took me to beaches, musical shows, movie theaters, temples, and shops where they spent their leisure time; to their family homes in rural Sri Lankan villages; and to an activist organization where I volunteered my time to improve workers' labor and human rights. This intensive involvement in their lives gave me insights into how Sri Lankan rural women created a "space to maneuver" under such unfavorable conditions. It also allowed me to see how important identity games were for these workers, who were positioned in an awkward intersection of multilayered marginalization.

They were poor women from rural areas who migrated to do garment work in transnational factories of a global assembly line. Their difficult work routines, sad living conditions, sickness, and tears had been examined and written about in detail. When I was with them I often wondered whether anyone noticed the smiles; winks; smirks; gestures; tones of voice; words they chose to speak, sing, joke, and parody; and the films they saw, songs they sang, and dancing they may do. I also wondered whether anyone connected those with the clothes they wore, accessories they craved, colors they chose, and shoes they balanced themselves on. Had anyone thought about why they sometimes spoke with words and other times with symbols and even more times with their silence? I wrote this book because my answer to most of these questions was no. I wrote this book because I want the readers to get a glimpse at a part of these women's lives that had not been told. I want the readers to feel the human spirit that allowed these women to deal with power and violence in the best way they could: through creativity, through everyday poetics and politics, and through developing differential consciousness that allowed them identity moves. It is the story of their lives in all its complexity: its vibrancy, its violence, its laughter, and the very depths of despair that I present in the pages that follow.

In the Enemy Camp

I first entered Suishin garment factory[1] in January 2000, on a day the government imposed a twenty-four-hour curfew over the city of Colombo. Suishin's finance manager had obtained a curfew pass and kindly offered me a ride to the FTZ. It was 4:00 P.M. when the van reached the guard gates at the entrance to the FTZ's barbed-wire fence. The van crossed the heavily guarded gates and sped along the concrete road dotted on both sides with enormous square structures made with concrete and tar sheeting. There were flower bushes and young trees, but the abundance of concrete and the heat generated from it gave one a feeling of being in a desert. Still, when the van entered the Suishin factory compound, I heaved an involuntary sigh of relief. Four months of letter writing, telephoning, e-mailing, and meeting middle-level managers at various FTZ factories was finally over.

It had taken me four months to find a garment factory that would permit me to spend as much time as I wanted on its premises. But the process did not exactly end the way I wanted. In the first two months, I asked the factories to give me an assembly-line job as a machine operator or at least an office job. Many factories did not even respond, whereas managers in several others granted me interviews, interrogated me about my research, and then sent me home saying they would let me know when they got approval from their foreign owners. I often did not hear from them or received short, sympathetic notes about company rules that did not allow outsiders on the shop floor. It was after such frustrating experiences that I called friends and family seeking help. Several friends offered opportunities to observe the shop floor for a week or two. Many said they could help me find jobs or observing opportunities in non-FTZ garment factories in Katunayake and outlying areas. All these leads, however, quickly fizzled. Therefore, when Suishin's finance manager, Shanil, one of my sister's friends, said that I could do a few months of participant observation at Suishin, I was overjoyed. But the happiness was vitiated by the realization that I was reaching the shop floor through managerial connections, which was not exactly a position that feminist ethnographers would fancy.

My introduction to the shop floor on that first day was quick and short. The factory building was located a few yards away from the single-story office building, to which it was joined by a concrete walkway with a roof. Although much larger with many sections, the factory building was single storied and housed seven different assembly lines and the workers' meal hall. Just before 6:00 in the evening, Shanil took me across the walkway to the factory for a short tour, and this indicated the daunting task ahead of trying to familiarize myself with the numerous machines and human beings that passed before my eyes. Two days later, a Monday, I was at Suishin by 8:00 A.M. Everybody offered their support, and several officers helped in clearing a desk for me so that I could carry out participant observation at the office. Kasun, Suishin's shipping manager, wanted to know whether I needed a computer, as he could move one onto my desk. Mr. Perera, the human resources manager, asked me not to bring lunch to work because the factory was going to provide lunch for me. Ando san, Suishin's Japanese managing director, asked whether it was still winter in Texas.[2] It was in this peculiar position through the "enemy camp" that I first entered the lives of Suishin factory workers.

The incessant clash of different noises combining to make one big din attacked my ears as soon as I entered the Suishin shop floor for the first time in January 2000. Machines grinded, music played, supervisors shouted, and women responded. "You will not notice the noise in a few days. Ears learn to ignore it," Sanuja, the Floor 1 coordinator who ac-

companied me, said when he noticed how disoriented I was. It was difficult for me to find a place to focus. Each assembly line was busy producing different garments. Line C looked colorful with pink satin material
at each machine as women produced a pink pajama top for a well-known
company.[3] Line H, in the other corner, produced the bottom half of the
pink pajama. Line E also looked cheerful, with lime-green satin material
gleaming in the florescent light at each machine. In contrast, the
women seemed tired and tense. "Satin is slippery and hard to sew. Girls
do not like it when these orders come to their line. They like to sew
pants or blouses in cotton or polyester material," Sanuja explained. The
two lines producing dress jackets in black and dark blue looked even
gloomier, with the thick material in murky colors dominating their lines.

When I started work at Suishin, I had been staying with FTZ workers
in a boardinghouse for about four months. The first few very difficult
days at Suishin I often wondered how women could laugh and be lighthearted after such hard work. But then gradually I realized that factory
work was not just about hard work and gloomy lives. It was also a space
where women found ways to express their changing sense of self, be this
through everyday resistance to immediate supervisors, connections to
big bosses, socialization with peers, attachments to tools of their trade,
or excelling at what they do. Even their minute maneuverings to subvert
rules and finding a moment to tell a joke or perform a prank gave them
much satisfaction. I felt that an epistemic violence had been committed
on their lives as study after study chose not to focus on the complex and
contradictory ways they dealt with everyday challenges. It was the overwhelming need that I felt to fill this gap that prompted me to focus on
these very contradictions that made the workers who they are and illu-
minated us on numerous issues of identity stances and moves.

With that intention, I explored four interrelated areas of migrant
women workers' lives: (1) negotiation of identity, resistance, agency, and
"respectability" as embedded in their everyday expressive practices (personal narratives, jokes, gossip, and material display) and in performative
acts; (2) conditions of embodiment as they mediated the opportunity to
explore intimate desires and sexuality and responded to varied forms of
violence against them; (3) material conditions of their factory work and
life in the FTZ as they affected the possibilities for class and feminist politics; and (4) ways and means of strategically shifting identification in
the specific power relations they faced. It is by exploring these areas that
I explicate the ways in which migrant women workers negotiate and perform situational identities and move back and forth between identifications as the situation demands.

When Sri Lankan rural women started migrating to urban areas to
work in transnational factories, intense anxieties were aroused about

female morality and cultural degradation. The dominant Sinhala Buddhist image of the ideal woman constructs women as passive and subordinate beings who should be protected within the confines of their
homes and thus stigmatizes women living away from their families. At
the urban FTZs, women come into contact with global capitalist patterns
of production and consumption as well as global discourses on labor
and human rights, Marxism, and feminism. My research focused on
workers' everyday social interactions and expressive practices at multiple
sites, and it enabled me to show the ways workers create and negotiate
their identities—resisting, appropriating, transforming, and re-creating
the images constructed for and about them in these varied discourses.
In the following chapters, I show how women respond to the intense
contradictions and ambivalences surrounding their migration and industrial employment by expressing an alternative identity that is between the subject positions prescribed by the dominant Sinhala cultural
discourses and those propagated in global discourses.

Multiple Sites, Multiple Voices

These findings are based on preliminary research conducted among
FTZ workers in 1995, 1997, and 1998 and on a year of ethnographic field
research conducted in Katunayake during 1999 and 2000. In 2003 and
2004, I visited some of the FTZ workers who had left the factory to see
how they were negotiating their reintegration into village life. In the
summer and winter of 2005 and the summer of 2006, I continued
the study on former FTZ workers while reentering Suishin for further research. Some of this material is included as introductory pieces to several chapters.

During the 1999 and 2000 research, the fieldwork centered on four
intertwined but separate sites, the combination of which allowed me to
draw a complex picture of FTZ workers' lives. For much of the research
period, I conducted participant observation in a transnational garment
factory at the Katunayake FTZ and stayed in a local boardinghouse with
more than fifty workers. I visited several other boardinghouse clusters in
the area and also volunteered my time at the Dabindu Center (a grass-
roots organization active among FTZ workers). I accompanied several
workers to their native villages during four-day vacations. I collected personal narratives and case histories and conducted in-depth interviews
with the workers, factory officials, boardinghouse owners, neighbors,
workers' parents, and people in neighboring villages, as well as non-
governmental organization (NGO) officials and officers belonging to
various state institutions that concern themselves with women, development, industrial labor, and foreign investment.

Because identity formation as FTZ workers occurs within existing discourses on women, class, and culture, an examination of these discourses is important. There are numerous speeches and writings by government officials, ministers, social workers, politicians, factory officials, and scholars on FTZ working women. I explore how these multiple layers of meaning create subjectivities for workers. Neighbors, boardinghouse owners, and the mass media also construct images of working women. I examine the way in which FTZ workers were represented in different media—from newspaper reports and mainstream expressive cultural forms such as serialized television dramas to poems and songs. I examine the sources from which these contemporary discourses derive their notions of women and sexuality and the way they become a part of the "panopticon" surveying women at the intersection of gender, class, and sexuality. I trace the constant flow of ideas and images between different discourses and the ways this interchange contributes to tropes of victimhood and moral degeneration.

The major part of the research focused on workers' negotiation of identity in everyday social interactions and expressive genres. Language is a critical locus, for both the reproduction of identities and the production of alternative identities (Kondo 1990). I investigate the FTZ women workers' everyday lives and expressive practices at the FTZ area as a space where ongoing negotiations of alternative identities took place. During the FTZ workers' occasional four-day vacations and their two long vacations (Sinhala/Tamil New Year in April and Christmas), I accompanied several workers from different regions of the country to their native villages. This gave me an opportunity to investigate how, away from the anonymity of the FTZ, they recentered their identity, strategically responding to the tighter patriarchal control and surveillance of village life. I studied the way they performed social rituals of accommodation and subtle forms of resistance. I interviewed family members, village elite, and older women from economically and socially marginalized groups who had not had a chance to find formal employment. Based on these interviews, my work explores the way men and women construct their images of the "other" according to their own multiple positionings while reflecting the dominant constructions of women's purity as a symbol of family honor.

My Travels and Travails

My travels, experiences, and relationships with migrant FTZ workers were shaped by identification and disidentification that depended on relations of power. At the beginning of my research, I was driven by my desire to identify with women workers most of whom were of the same ethnicity, religion, and marital status as mine. I also identified with their oppression and the discipline they endured in industrial patriarchies at the FTZ and in their native villages through my own experiences of discipline and domination in the hierarchical university system and in my middle-class home. It took me only a short time, however, to discover that my identity among them was also flexible and situational. My study, therefore, is based on the premise that gender identification obscures different experiences of oppression and the workings of power. It also recognizes that contextual identification helps expose the operation of power and influences effective action. Awareness of feminist theorizing on situated knowledge, multiple standpoints, politics of location, and strategic essentialism further propelled me to engage in strategic identification according to the given form of power relations at a specific moment as well as to work toward coalitional politics.

Uncritical notions of "native" anthropologists can also make researchers blind to class, caste, and other power differences. As Kirin Narayan writes (1993), every author is at least minimally bicultural, and therefore it is only by situating ourselves as subjects, simultaneously touched by life experiences and swayed by professional concerns, that we can acknowledge the "hybrid and positioned nature of our identities" (672). While at one level my experiences as a Sinhala-speaking Sri Lankan woman allowed me to identify with the FTZ women workers, at another level my different life experiences set me apart from them. This complex and shifting character of my positionality provided for a more dynamic understanding of the research relationships formed during the research period. My constant entrances, departures, and returns shaped my relationships with the women workers at these different sites. This required continual reconstruction of my identity according to the specific power relations we confronted.

I did not try to hide my background during the research, and the workers recognized me as someone from a middle-class family who had a university education. Despite my fears, workers welcomed me and from the first day onward assumed that I was on their side even though I clearly had good relations with the factory managers and boarding-house owners. On a general level, they understood my need to have such good relations and typically were not wary of me; they confided in me and made me a special partner in some of their daily struggles. In such moments, they resolved contradictions presented by my class background by assuming the roles of educator and guide to a world that they had the courage and strength to master and I was struggling to negotiate. There were tense moments when they did not know where to place me, but these situations resolved quickly and my position as a dear friend among them was restored. Those tense situations notwithstanding, I was fortunate enough to enjoy a general sense of acceptance, kindness, and affection at all the spaces in which I associated with them.

It is also interesting how I was addressed differently at each site according to where I stood in the network of power. At the factory, the workers always called me "Sandya miss," despite my repeatedly asking them to use my first name alone. They sometimes paired this with common endearments such as "*sudhu*" (fair one) or "darling." I got quite used to requests such as "Sandya miss, come here for a minute, darling." At the factory I made some very close friends, whom I still visit and correspond with via mail. They still insist on addressing me as "miss" while repeatedly affirming in conversations and letters that I am like a sister to them. Perhaps this is not surprising considering the many markers that noted our difference within the factory. As I was helping with Line C work on a volunteer basis, I did not have to report to work at a certain time even though I tried to be there on time. I was also allowed to rest on a sick-room bed if I felt tired. The most notable detail that marked our difference was my frequent time-outs when I sat at Sanuja's table located by Line C to write field notes.[4] Both the workers and the supervisors used this time to comment about their fears and anxieties about what I might be writing, consequently providing even more fodder for my purposes. While one of the workers' major concerns was obtaining leave, I was allowed to be absent from work if I wanted. However, it was rare that I missed work at Suishin. Even when I was in Colombo on university business or for a family matter, I somehow traveled back to Katunayake for a few hours at the factory. These afternoon travels allowed me to observe overtime work into the night and notice the different dynamics as tiring workers became more vocal and combative. It was at these times I felt an overwhelming sense of guilt for my ability to break free when I needed to. Perhaps it is the memory of those privileges that still prevents my factory friends from calling me by any other name but the class- and gender-specific title "miss."

In contrast, the workers I got to know at the boardinghouses easily started calling me "Sandya *akka*" (elder sister) after a few visits. In the same way, the boardinghouse friends felt it more deeply when I took breaks to visit my family home or to spend more time with my colleagues at the University of Colombo. They would call my home and urge me to come back, as they were planning to cook a special dish or go see a movie that I should not miss. My family members got used to their calls, and it was not uncommon for my mother or my cousin to call me to the phone by somewhat sarcastically noting that "one of your FTZ sisters is on the phone."

It is the fluctuating nature of each of our identifications as women that led me to focus on the importance of coalitional politics and strategic essentialism. According to Bernice Reagon (1983), political coalition is the only way to find cross-cultural commonalties of struggle. A political coalition requires one to have the wisdom to know when to engage and when to withdraw, when to break out and when to consolidate (explicated in Martin and Mohanty 1986:192). Gayatri Spivak calls for strategic essentialism, in which one takes women as a universal category in order to advance a feminist political agenda. According to Spivak (1988), between imperialism and patriarchy there is hardly any space in which the "third world gendered subaltern subject" can speak. However, without falling into the common trap of political silence, she stresses the need for representation as long as subaltern women lack the language and technologies to represent themselves. Her call for learning to "speak to" rather than "speak for" the subaltern is of great significance for feminist political projects.

My work and relationships among the FTZ workers were informed by these perspectives. The politics of location and engagement, in particular, is an important part of my commitment to feminist research and struggle. Although I was unable to initiate any political activities with the FTZ workers during 2000, I was part of day-to-day struggles as well as several political actions taken by the NGOs with which I associated. The form and intensity of alliances that women workers sought varied depending on power relations they faced at the time. They struggled over labor issues and against sexual exploitation, social and cultural constraints, and media representations. The dynamics of shifting alliances informs my current political and educational activist work among them as well as for them through NGOs.

Free Trade Zone, Migrant Workers, and Dominant Values

Sri Lanka set up its first FTZ in Katunayake (near the capital city of Colombo) in 1978 as a part of the structural adjustment policies adopted in 1977. Establishing FTZs in Katunayake, and later in Biyagama and Koggala, fulfilled a campaign promise by the United National Party (UNP), which came to power in 1977 by pledging to initiate free-market and open economic policies. Located about 29 kilometers northeast of Colombo and opposite the country's only international airport, the Katunayake FTZ spans over 190 hectares (469.5 acres) of flat land. The Board of Investment (BOI) of Sri Lanka oversees this FTZ along with the others that were later established. In its attempt to attract foreign investment, Sri Lanka offered numerous incentives—such as duty-free imports of machinery and raw materials, duty-free exports, preferential tax, double taxation relief, unrestricted repatriation of dividends, and up to 100 percent foreign ownership. One major attraction cited by the BOI in its advertising pamphlets is the "availability of a low-cost, easily trainable workforce." In interviews with foreign factory managers, the BOI identified Sri Lanka as "a highly favorable place to invest" (Mann 1993:24).

The Katunayake FTZ houses around a hundred multinational industries that practice a distinctively late-capitalist form of gendered working relations. Garment factories, which constitute the majority of all the industries within the FTZ, recruit large numbers of young rural women from economically and socially marginalized groups to work as machine operators (Dabindu Collective 1997:17).[5] In 1986, between 85 and 90 percent of these women were unmarried, young, and well-educated, often with 8 to 12 years of schooling (Rosa 1990). In 1995, more than 70 percent of the workers had attended school up to grade 10 (Fine and Howard 1995). The vast majority of these young women are Sinhala in ethnicity and Buddhist by religion.[6] I met only a handful of FTZ workers belonging to minority communities. When asked for a plausible reason, a BOI official speculated that Hindu and Muslim parents were reluctant to send their female children to live alone in the city. However, the protracted civil war between the Sinhala-dominated government and the Tamil militants and the resultant tensions between the two ethnic communities seem a major reason for this imbalance.[7] The location of the FTZs in Sinhala-majority areas discourages Tamil women from seeking employment, suggesting that the Sinhala-dominated government designed the FTZs to provide jobs for Sinhala women from the south who will ultimately help Sinhala politicians win elections.[8]

However, very few state- or factory-run hostel facilities are available even for Sinhala women who flock to the FTZ each year. People living in the area have rented hastily built rows of rooms to these young women, resulting in extremely poor living conditions. When coupled with physically and mentally arduous working conditions, the problems associated with these makeshift boarding facilities make life in the FTZ more difficult (Voice of Women 1982; Dabindu Collective 1989, 1997; Fedric Ebert Stiftung 1997; Hewamanne and Brow 1999).[9]

It is their status as young women living alone and without male protection, however, that receives the most public attention. Popular accounts of widespread premarital sex, rape, prostitution, abortion, and infanticide simultaneously portray these women both as victims of labor and sexual exploitation and as victims of their own loose morals. Workers are identified in everyday discourse as "garment girls" and "Juki pieces"[10] and are said to be recognizable by their dress, hairstyle, and language. Having so many young women congregating in one place is such an unusual phenomenon that people call the FTZ *Sthri Puraya* (city of women), *Prema Kalape* (love zone), and *Vesa Kalape* (whore zone).

Their neighbors in the FTZ area liken the "free-living women [*ayale yana*]" amid them to a great (cultural) disaster (*maha vinasayak*).

The reasons for such fear derive from an ideal image of the Sinhala Buddhist woman that was formed in the late nineteenth and early twentieth centuries. Primarily constructed as a response to colonial discourses on women and culture, this ideal projects women as passive and subordinate beings who should be protected within the confines of their homes. As a result, women leaving their parental homes to live alone in urban, modern spaces arouse intense anxieties about cultural degradation and female morality. These fears also emanate from a discursively constructed rural/urban divide that corresponds to binaries such as traditional/westernized and good/bad. According to this understanding, rural women who have been raised with a deep sense of shame-fear (*lajja-baya*) become westernized in urban spaces and consequently become bad or immoral women.

According to Gananath Obeyesekere (1984), practices of *lajja-baya*—to be ashamed of subverting norms of sexual modesty and proper behavior and to fear the social ridicule that results from such subversion—is instilled into Sinhala children through early childhood training (504–5). When rural women from mostly lower-income or lower-status groups migrated to work in the FTZ (and started to occupy public spaces), it was the effects on women's shame-fear that the mostly urban, middle-class commentators focused on. Many commented on the *lajja nethi kama* (shamelessness) or *lajja-baya nethi kama* (lack of shame-fear) in FTZ workers' behavior and identified them as symptomatic of the decline of dominant Sinhala Buddhist culture.

A discursively constructed notion that claims that the village is morally superior and is the locus of tradition has put another burden on rural women. The belief in superior morals and undisturbed traditions is superimposed on women, creating expectations that village women are naïve, innocent (in the sense of being sexually ignorant), and timid and are the unadulterated bearers of Sinhala Buddhist culture.[11] Therefore, when these women migrated to the city and started enjoying their time away from patriarchal control, fears about their morality became a major preoccupation for urban, middle-class nationalists. Like nationalists in many other postcolonial societies, they considered any threat to women's morality as a threat against the cultural purity and survival of the nation (Chatterjee 1993; McClintock 1995).

This focus on migrant women's morality and the subsequent exaggerated reports and rumors of their sexual misadventures further stigmatizes them (Hettiarachchi 1991:56–59; *Sirikatha* October 30, 1995). Their reputations are tarnished by speculation about their "respectability." Protestant Buddhist traditions and discipline construct "decent and correct" manners and morals, as well as a proper attitude toward sexuality, for middle-class women.[12] Although the socioeconomic circumstances of lower-class or lower-caste women are not conducive to following these rules, in rhetorical and written expressions all Sinhala Buddhist women are measured by this unitary notion of respectability. FTZ garment factory workers, rural women now living in the city away from their villages and freely moving around, came under harsh criticism, and their conduct became the space where deep anxieties and ambivalences over notions of development, modernity, and sexuality were played out.

In the FTZ, rural women encountered new global cultural flows and acquired new knowledge. As they migrated from rural agricultural communities and became subject to the discipline of capitalist industrial production, young women underwent a change in their cognitive, social, emotional, and moral dispositions. It is this change that was resented by the family members, neighbors, factory managers, and government and NGO officials with whom I talked. This resentment also figured heavily in the speeches of politicians. While parents and neighbors focused on the economic benefits of FTZ employment, politicians and officials representing a variety of institutions couched such benefits in terms of development, progress, and modernity. They all, however, mused over the cost in moral and cultural terms and expressed hopes for development and modernity with moral reins intact. I discuss these ambivalent desires as well as the hegemonic cultural formulations that initiated such contradictory desires and meanings in Chapter 2.

The major focus of this work, however, is the way migrant FTZ garment factory workers themselves understood and responded to the new cultural discourses they encountered in the FTZ and how they also developed a new sense of themselves within and against the dominant cultural discourses. The articulation of their new sense of self as industrial workers living in the city in the apparently incompatible position of being the young, unmarried daughters of patriarchal villages enabled viable spaces for creativity, tactics, and strategies. These spaces, where the clash of contradictory discourses played a central part in shaping the women's responses to specific situations, figure prominently in the following six chapters. The chapters show the way garment factory workers creatively combined elements from varied discourses to narratively construct new identities. Refusing to accept identities crafted for them within various dominant discourses, the women situationally negotiated alternative identities within shifting relations of power.

The focus on identity formation in this study is twofold. First, it traces the ways in which the new cultural world that women workers encounter in the FTZ influences new individual identities; second, it describes the

ways in which migrant workers create an overarching identity for themselves as a gendered group of migrant industrial workers who are different both from other women and from male industrial workers. In fact,
this study is concerned with the links between the construction of difference and identity. It analyzes interconnected aspects of gender, sexuality, taste, and class that construct the FTZ workers as different. The
gender and class stigma attached to the women workers' particular way
of life plays a major part in creating difference and in the subsequent
formation of a new group identity. The study weaves through the formation of work identities, class relations, and feminist consciousness at a
transnational FTZ garment factory; the processes of migrant women becoming desiring subjects; and the violence that follows their refusal of
embodying shame-fear; as well as the creation of a gendered class culture within and against the dominant culture. After mapping this complex picture of women's social worlds in the FTZ, the study sketches the
way the workers reconcile their newly fashioned identities with already
constructed identities imposed on them in their native villages.

Identity, Subjectivity, and Consciousness

I had two reasons to title this work *Stitching Identities in a Free Trade Zone*.
The first was to acknowledge the extent to which Dorinne Kondo's
(1990) excellent work on women workers crafting selves at a Japanese
confectionary had inspired my work.[13] The second was to evoke Stuart
Hall's notion of identity as a suturing (stitching) of the subject into discursively constructed subject positions (2000:6).

As people encounter multiple cultural discourses, they are confronted
with numerous contradictory but possible identities that they could
choose to adopt at any given time. According to Stuart Hall (1996), "The
very process of identification, through which we project ourselves into
our cultural identities, has become more open-ended, variable and
problematic" (598). From this perspective, the sense of a coherent, unified identity is a fantasy, and the only reason for its existence is humans'
capacity to construct a coherent identity narrative for themselves. It is in
these narratives that people combine elements from the dominant cultural world they inhabit and other extant systems of meaning. My work
focuses on multiple and situational identities and the narrative construction of the self within shifting fields of power relations.

According to Foucault (1973; 1978; 1979), subjectivities are produced
as an effect through and within discourses. It is the power of knowledge
that ties an individual subject to his or her own identity by conscience
and self-knowledge. Individual subjectivities are shaped considerably by
the numerous discourses that construct positions for them. Foucault's

notion of subjectification, in which individuals uncritically accept the subjectivities to which they are being summoned, has been critiqued by several scholars (among them McNay 1994; Hall 2000). Foucault's discursively constructed subjects are docile bodies, and he neglects the psychological mechanisms through which individuals might resist the interpellation. My study attempts to avoid this weakness by focusing on agency, strategy, and intentionality in migrant FTZ workers' actions as they negotiate varied discursive constructions, at different times, and by analyzing how they sometimes simultaneously accept, transform, resist, and reject those constructions.

Hall (1995) writes that identity is the meeting point between ideological discourses, which attempt to interpellate us as social subjects, and psychological processes, which help us develop as subjects who can speak (65). According to Hall, identities should be understood as points of suture or points of temporary attachment to already constructed positions. But effective suturing requires not only that the subject is "hailed" but also that the subject maneuvers through other potential positions and chooses and invests in the position (2000:6). My work traverses such processes of suturing among FTZ garment factory workers that result in situational identification with certain constructed positions such as "migrant garment girl" or "innocent village girl." My account, however, also notes the specific ways in which workers act within such positions, highlighting the experiences that fall outside the domain of the docile subject. Focusing on the situational and moving nature of their celebration and performance of identities, it also highlights the importance of analyzing the shifting matrices of power in each instance.

Hall asserts that identities are "sliding" and "fictional" (1995:66)—sliding because they are assumed after the fact and fictional because personal identities are narratives that "we tell ourselves about ourselves." Situational identification can be used as a strategic tool by developing differential consciousness, which enables individuals to recenter subjectivities according to shifting fields of power. According to Chela Sandoval (1991), differential consciousness enables movement among positions and in that sense operates like the "clutch of an automobile: the mechanism that permits the driver to select, engage and disengage gears in a system for the transmission of power" (14). Although articulated as an oppositional stance for the feminists of color against the hegemonic feminist praxis, Sandoval's conceptualization of differential consciousness has had far-reaching effects on later theorizing on the formation of differential identity within complex networks of power. What this theorization calls for is a "tactical subjectivity with the capacity to recenter depending upon the kinds of oppression to be confronted" (14). The differential mode of oppositional consciousness depends on an ability to read power relations and consciously choose the most-suited position to challenge that power relation.

I use Sandoval's conceptualization of tactical subjectivity (shifting/sliding identity) to theorize the way FTZ working women develop oppositional consciousness through living in the FTZ and the way this consciousness facilitates movement among identity stances. However, Sandoval's notion of self-conscious subjects who can freely choose to break away from ideological subjugation or discursive constructions poses certain problems. This formulation allows much space for agency and resistance within different relations of power. However, we may lose sight of how not just relations but structures of power impose identities on the social subject, including that the so-called "shifting of gears" between identities may be imposed by social structures and institutions and that the internalized doxic common sense could also constrain agency. The power of the subject to shift gears to another identity may be extremely limited, curtailed, and constrained, again by both social and psychological structures and institutions. FTZ workers certainly excel in identity games for the duration of their employment, but when the very structure of this employment forces them out of their jobs after a few years there is only an extremely slim chance for them to do anything other than go back and reassume their identities as village daughters. So, while I agree that identities are dynamic and that they shift because of one's own agency, I also hold that they are shifted for us, that there may be serious obstacles to holding onto a favorite identification, and that some identities may be less dynamic and have a greater propensity toward fixity than others. Therefore, while focusing on differential consciousness, decentered subjectivity, and agency, I also pay attention to the way identities and subjectivities are constituted for us above and beyond our limited social agency.

Subject positions are discursively created slots that individuals can assume for themselves as best suits their situation. At times, individuals can carve out unconventional positions for themselves. Usually the carved-out positions are somewhat ambiguous and therefore are allowed to exist together with positions accorded by the social, cultural structures. New and shifting positions, which contain an explicit oppositional character, often entail a social cost to the individuals who carve out or assume such positions. In this study, I focus on the way FTZ garment factory workers manipulate different subject positions at the workplace, at boardinghouses, and in their narratives. They creatively maneuver among conventional subject positions and newly crafted, often oppositional positions within constantly changing matrices of power to negotiate situational identities.

My work focuses not only on the way workers develop oppositional consciousness within the FTZ but also on the multiple and contradictory consciousness that the workers grapple with daily. As Gramsci (1971) theorized, the everyday consciousness of the masses, or common sense, is typically incoherent, disjointed, and contradictory. It is modified and transformed over time by the different philosophical currents that enter everyday lives (362). By focusing on the plurality of identities enabled by the multiplicity of consciousness, I trace the ways in which FTZ garment factory workers move between identity stances, depending on the ideological current that achieves primacy in a given moment. Women workers expressed class and feminist consciousness at one moment, yet at the next moment expressed duty and obligations to "fatherly managers" and performed nurturing roles toward male supervisors. It is in narratives about themselves that people resolve contradictions and construct a coherent identity. I focus on their narratives to show the way FTZ workers emerge as "self-controlled, talented women" who enjoy the perks of modernity within the constraints of Protestant Buddhist moral standards.

Road Trips and Road Maps

> *We will bring Anura sir //*
> *Will show the* maligawa *[temple of tooth relic/vagina] //*
> *Lalai, lilai, la—*
>
> *We will bring Weere uncle //*
> *Will show Anti's that thing //*
> *Lalai, lilai, la—*
>
> *We will bring Sandya* akka *//*
> *Will show Saman's* sthupe *[Buddhist pagoda/penis] //*
> *Lalai, lilai, la—*

The dancing women rhythmically pointed their hands in my direction while singing that last verse. I was seated near the front of the van that the women at Saman's boardinghouse hired to go visit Buddhist temples at Varana and Atthanagalle. Women dancing in the middle aisle of the van enormously enjoyed their song parodies to make fun of people who held power over their lives—factory bosses, boardinghouse owners, and even the researcher. I was also fascinated by how frequently they used Buddhist sacred places as symbols for sexual organs and functions. The same women who engaged in these extreme transgressions displayed deep devotion while they worshiped and meditated at the temples we visited. During their return journey, they again picked up transgressive song parodies and jokes with sexual innuendos.

This is not the only occasion when Sri Lanka's Katunayake FTZ factory workers transgressed dominant cultural values. It would not have been surprising for them to, individually, in narrative assertions, show allegiance to dominant cultural values even while engaging in clearly transgressive behavior such as singing those verses. It is this complexity I try to capture in the following chapters.

All the chapters traverse borderlands—the critical spaces created when disparate discourses clash in a contested domain—and analyze moments of transgression as they are expressed and performed in multiple but intertwined sites. Chapter 2, which discusses discourses on women, morality, and FTZ workers, is followed by chapters that trace FTZ workers' lives and the way they negotiate identities at different sites. These chapters, covering their work in factories, their lives in boarding-houses, their public recreational activities, and their return journeys to villages, demonstrate how these sites are not isolated entities but ones that are deeply affected by the surrounding world. Women's experiences and responses at each of these sites were highly influenced by their experiences at other sites, and thus the chapters represent the complex interweaving of different social worlds in their everyday lives.

In Chapter 2, "Nation, Modernity, and Female Morality," I analyze the construction of an ideal image of the Sinhala Buddhist woman during the late nineteenth and early twentieth centuries and its influence on contemporary discourses. Examining contemporary media representations (newspapers, television, and movies), I show the way contemporary discourses on female morality, national culture, development, and modernity have been variably influenced by earlier discursive formations and the way they present migrant FTZ factory workers with deeply ambiguous situations.

Chapter 3, "On the Shop Floor," traces the ways in which FTZ garment factory workers respond to such ambiguous situations and negotiate situational identities on the shop floor. Everyday social interactions and expressive practices are spaces where ongoing negotiations of alternative identities take place. Analyzing such spaces on the shop floor, I demonstrate the way workers create and negotiate their identities—resisting, appropriating, transforming, and re-creating the images constructed for and about them in varied discourses.

Chapter 4, "Loving Daughters and Politically Active Workers," analyzes workers' political activities (collective and otherwise) that create the conditions of possibility for transformational politics. While the everyday acts of resistance discussed in Chapter 3 go on to create an oppositional culture on the shop floor, the activities analyzed in this chapter contribute toward building solidarity and alliances around specific situations or sequences of events. These political activities consist of culturally meaningful responses to specific situations at the workplace that facilitate the development of oppositional political consciousness. By analyzing such practices, I assert that class interests and solidarity are an integral part of cultural struggles and negotiations at Sri Lanka's FTZ factories.

Chapter 5, "Politics of Everyday Life," discusses the way the boarding-houses are organized around patriarchal values and the way the workers create and negotiate new positions within and against these forces. By examining the workers' narratives of changing values, violence in their daily lives, and everyday cultural struggles, I demonstrate how the FTZ area provides a transformative space for the workers and aids in the process of women becoming desiring subjects who nevertheless strategically move back and forth between subversion of cultural codes and an expressed loyalty to existing discursive constructions on women's lives.

Chapter 6, "Performing disrespectability," highlights the way the workers created alternative cultural practices as a critique of existing socioeconomic inequalities. By creating new preferences in clothing, body adornment, language, and mannerisms, as well as different tastes in reading matter, music, film, dance forms, and religious practices, the women perform a different lifestyle and a specific identity as migrant industrial workers. The chapter shows that while FTZ workers' participation in stigmatized cultural practices was explicitly transgressive and critical at some levels, their demonstrated acquiescence to different hegemonic influences marks the inseparability of resistance and accommodation.

Chapter 7, "FTZ Clothes and Home Clothes," focuses on the situational nature of women's identity as migrant industrial workers by showing how women resorted to a conscious process that visually narrated a different self to the curious onlookers in their home villages. When the women visited their homes, they took off their "FTZ clothing" and put on "village clothing." Women's changing narratives (through visuals, gestures, prosody, expressions, and so on) marked their response to social and cultural codes that sought to constrain them. Women protested against this suppression in their own locally relevant ways by smuggling "FTZ styles and knowledge" to younger village women. Manipulating differences in clothing and demeanor within the two different geographical spaces of the FTZ and their villages, women workers managed to move among a multitude of possible identities.

The epilogue contains details of several women's post-FTZ lives. They left the FTZ soon after I finished my research and were living either in their husbands' villages or with their parents and hoping to get married. In 2003–4 I spent eight months collecting narratives of past FTZ workers to see how they had negotiated their lives within increasingly globalizing Sri Lankan villages and thus spent time talking to them, their husbands, and their new relatives. The epilogue shows how, even though the workers were forced to select appropriate spaces (women's storytelling sessions) and appropriate audiences (younger women) to raise their voice even cautiously, they were not totally silenced. I assert, therefore, that FTZ employment could not be considered as a transitional space that had no effect on existing structures once the workers returned to their villages.

Needlework and Respectable Women

Christian missionaries and educators in colonial times laid heavy emphasis on teaching needlework to native girls and considered it crucial in constructing a particular moral demeanor and codes of decorum appropriate for women they sought to convert. Sewing required neatness, concentration, patience, and precision, qualities that colonial writers found so lacking in native women. Needlework at that time was considered central to molding respectable, decent, and moral women. Ironically, migrating to engage in the same profession brings stigma on today's young women. Although the association with modernity and the resultant nondomestic spaces daily threaten workers' reputations, they keep one foot firmly planted within domestic spaces such as boardinghouses and village homes even while resisting codes of behavior associated with shame-fear. It is again through "needlework"—stitching, unstitching, and restitching their selves to suitable subject positions—that they stretch and modify dominant notions of respectability, domesticity, and religiosity to accommodate themselves.

In this sense, my work is not only about identity but also about gendered discipline and sites of resistance from which FTZ workers express critical alternative perspectives and note how the intersection between global cultural flows and nationalist ideals of female morality and respectability shape new mechanisms of challenge and contestation.

Chapter 2

Nation, Modernity, and Female Morality

Intersection of the Modern and the Dangerous

The Colombo-Negombo highway runs past the entrance to the Japan-Sri Lanka Friendship Road, which leads both to the country's only international airport and to the Katunayake FTZ. This highway is considered one of the country's best and most dangerous arteries. The intercity buses speeding along this road almost always exceed the legal speed limit. One of my most difficult tasks during my stay in Katunayake was to cross this road at, what my friends laughingly called, untimely hours.[1] I often found myself standing by the yellow-striped crossings for long periods of time. Vehicles do not stop or slow down, forcing hapless pedestrians to find the right gap between two vehicles to cross.

One day in August 1998, several FTZ worker friends and I attended a wedding across the road from this intersection. One of my friends was suffering from stomach pains, and we were trying to cross the road to get to her boardinghouse so that she could drink something to ease the pain. We had to wait awhile at the pedestrian crossing before crossing the road. When we were well into the road, we spotted a van coming at breakneck speed toward us, almost as if willing us to stop crossing and let it pass. While my friends started to back off, I decided to show the driver that we had the right of way and forcefully pointed to the yellow crossing and stood my ground. The van skidded to a halt and the driver yelled at us in the worst filth I have ever heard. The only thing I remember is repeated references to "no-good whores." I was frozen in my tracks, but my friends urged me to run, and I took off a little after they did. While writing this, I realized that this was not the first time a group of FTZ workers, including me, were called no-good whores.

In March 1995, I accompanied a group of my FTZ friends to a boardinghouse to visit one of their friends. When we arrived, the owners, a middle-aged couple, started yelling at us, saying, "Those whores left this boardinghouse! They are just like you, nothing but whores!" After listening to their tirade for a few minutes, we left, shamed. Later we discovered that the women still lived there, but that the owners opposed any visits from outsiders for fear that the house's decrepit condition would be reported to the authorities. Although my friends forgot the incident in a day or two, it haunted me for quite some time as to how easily those owners vilified their tenants as whores.

My long-term field research in the area surrounding the Katunayake FTZ in 1999–2000 showed me that it is an everyday occurrence for working women to be called prostitutes by an angry vendor, a shopkeeper, a bus driver, or even a policeman. It is not uncommon for FTZ workers walking in groups near the main bus terminal, the shopping plaza, or the night bazaar to find men asking for sexual favors in the most graphic terms. This understanding that FTZ workers, as a group, are women with loose morals is related to their unique situation as young, unmarried women who live away from their families in an urban area. Their living in makeshift rooms with no clear male authority also contributes to the public's low image of the workers. The stigma attached to their living arrangements and relative freedom spills over into their lives away from the FTZ. According to Padmini Weerasekere, secretary of the Katunayake Women's Center, some of the marriage proposals advertised by the parents of prospective grooms in weekly newspapers specifically state that "garment factory workers need not apply."[2] The label, garment factory worker (garment *baduva* or *Juki kella*) sticks to a woman long after she stops working in the FTZ and goes back to her home village.

Not all FTZ workers are migrants from distant villages, and some young women from poor families surrounding the FTZ also work at the factories. One woman from a nearby village said that she was very careful not to work at a garment factory and, instead, chose a diamond-cutting factory. Even though diamond cutting is similarly marginalized industrial employment, she was able to escape being labeled a garment *baduva*, at least among friends and neighbors. The fact that she did not leave her familial home to go and live in another city also preserved some semblance of respect. Interestingly, she portrayed herself as a woman different from the garment factory workers and other FTZ workers who had come from rural villages. She said she admonished many of her male co-workers for talking badly about garment workers.

One reason for the negative image people accorded women who left their families and village communities for factory work in urban areas is grounded in the discursive construction of an ideal Sinhala Buddhist woman that occurred in the late nineteenth and the early twentieth centuries. Originally constructed as an ideal for middle-class women, this image quickly spread to every level of society through nationalist media and local nationalist leaders. This process was furthered during the postindependence era when the school system began to disseminate officially approved gender roles for women of all classes. As with the dom-

inance of Sinhala Buddhist elements in many other sectors of postindependence Sri Lanka, this image also dominated people's imagination of
the ideal woman. The male elite from minority groups also constructed
gender ideals for their communities that did not differ much from the
Sinhala Buddhist ideal, so they did not protest against official dissemination of such gender ideals. Thus, even though this image of the ideal
woman is presented in scholarly work as a Sinhala Buddhist–woman
image, it applies in general to other groups of women living in the country, such as Sinhala Christian, Tamil, and Muslim women.[3] However,
women of different ethnic groups and classes in postcolonial Sri Lanka
negotiate their everyday gender roles differently as they articulate this
ideal image with other factors such as regional differences, levels of mar-
ginality, and idiosyncratic traits. Nevertheless, agents of contemporary
discourses on women draw heavily from this image of the ideal woman.
The profound effect that such contemporary discourses have over FTZ
workers' everyday lives merits a deeper analysis of that earlier construction of ideal womanhood.

Nationalism and Ideal Gender Images

After staying for several months at one boardinghouse, I tried to find another place with fifty or more workers to enrich my research material.
One of my brother's friends put me in touch with an older woman who
owned a boardinghouse. When my brother and I visited her at the
scheduled time, she came out of the house shouting, "There are no
'couple rooms' here. We don't even let any man visit." And then she
apologized, saying that she forgot we were coming and thought that
we were a couple who were trying to get a room to "live in sin." Then she
launched into a monologue on how careful she is to avoid assisting any
nefarious activities that destroy the culture and how there are base people who would even sell their country and morality if they can earn
money. "Even if I were killed, I would not let this place be used for de-
base/outsider [*para weda*] behavior. The things we eat by betraying
country (*rata*) and nation [*jathiya*] do not digest."

These conversations display how deeply the intertwined discourses of
gender, sexuality, and nationalism have invaded people's everyday lives
and how those in turn shape people's attitudes toward women who became "the other" through these discourses. These everyday contributions in turn play a major part in shaping and reshaping the
already-existing discourses and become part of a complex process of
otherization of FTZ factory workers.

The stigma attached to working in an urban FTZ is rooted in the belief in an image of the ideal Sinhala Buddhist woman. An analysis of the

sociohistorical process through which the image of the ideal Sinhala Buddhist woman was constructed inevitably turns to an exploration of the link between orientalist discourses and the emergence of Sinhala nationalism as a response to colonialism. It is important to explore the way discourses of different agents, missionaries, travelers, educators, orientalist scholars, colonial government officials, and the response by local male elites remodeled the image of middle-class Sinhala Buddhist womanhood to one that fit the emerging nation state.[4]

Marriage and Chastity

Many nineteenth-century colonial writings on marriage customs, divorce, and women's status in Sri Lanka were framed in a language of accusation and horror. These writings were colored by the Victorian British ideal of marriage as a sacred lifelong commitment. They were also influenced by the Victorian view of women as mentally and physically inferior to men and the consequent belief that women should be protected and cared for at home. British writers were scandalized by the ease with which Sinhala people could divorce a spouse. According to Henry Charles Sirr (1850), Sinhala marriages were "unhallowed" and "horrible" unions from which a divorce could be "too easily obtained" (164).

The British sense of cultural superiority, closely linked to racism, initiated a patronizing gaze and, more often than not, sweeping generalizations were made about moral laxity based on the fact that Sinhalese found it appropriate to separate from a marriage partner just because one party wished it. The British Government Agent to Kegalle explained this tendency as follows, "To bind themselves to a lifelong union, which is sometimes found insupportable in Christian and civilized societies, must far more often prove intolerable and hateful in semi-barbarous and heathen communities, totally unaccustomed to social restraint or to moral influence" (1870, quoted in Risseeuw 1988:38). While the British interpreted this behavior as immoral, many contemporary scholars have reinterpreted these materials to claim that women in precolonial Buddhist Sri Lanka were far more emancipated than their western or Indian sisters (Devaraja 1991:9). The Kandyan law manual *Neethi Nighanduwa* provided necessary provisions for the custody of children and comparable securities for both parties in the form of property rights. According to Risseeuw (1988), the fact that a woman never broke her emotional and economic ties with her natal family to join the husband's family provided Sri Lankan women with greater independence.

Another aspect of Sinhala life that came under colonial criticism was the low regard given to women's chastity and fidelity within marriage.

According to Percival (1803), "The infringement of chastity scarcely subjects a woman either married or unmarried to the slightest reproach" (177). John Davy (1821) and Henri Charles Sirr (1850) both give further evidence as to how Sinhala women did not hold chastity and fidelity in high esteem. According to Sirr, "[in Ceylon] the want of conjugal fidelity (and chastity in the unmarried) is most terrible" (1850:165). Sirr also stated that a husband could lend his wife to a man of higher caste to fulfill an obligation (234). A hundred years later, Ralph Peiris (1956), a Sri Lankan scholar, in his book *Sinhalese Social Organization,* also claimed that in the Kandyan era a man could offer his wife or daughter to a high-caste person or an official traveler who stayed overnight in his house.[5] However, there are also accounts of men committing physical violence against women because of alleged licentious behavior. According to Sirr, a woman could be killed because of a low-caste liaison. But Elizabeth Harris (1994) holds that this latter custom declined long before the British arrived.

Changes in Divorce and Property Laws

Various British authors (including Sirr 1850; Forbes 1841) interpreted polyandry, as practiced in Kandyan provinces, as prostitution, infidelity, and incest. British observers were especially concerned about how to decide the children's male parentage within such marriages. Polyandry was practiced among landed families with many sons to prevent the fragmentation of land. However, these practical arrangements clashed with British ideals of the nuclear family and patrilineal descent. These special arrangements, like loose marriage ties, which gave women a chance to leave an unfulfilling marriage without being socially punished, provided women with a variety of life choices. Women inherited their parents' property equally with their brothers and did not have to relinquish their claims at the time of marriage. If a woman wanted to divorce her husband she was entitled to take back her dowry, a provision that her British counterparts did not enjoy. However, British missionaries and officials interpreted this arrangement as damaging to the stability of marriage; as a result, the British government in 1858 started a process to implement new rules and laws concerning marriage and property rights. These laws had devastating effects on women's property rights and freedom of choice and greatly facilitated the perception that women's main role was to be the creator and protector of domestic space.

Not only did colonial writers critique Sinhala marriage customs, but many also saw women as exploited and degraded (Binning 1857:48). The attacks on the way men treated their wives elicited angry reactions from the western-educated local male elite (Rutnam 1899) and initiated a movement among those elites toward standardizing marriage practices. The elite aided the British government in implementing homogeneous laws for marriage, divorce, and inheritance. In 1859 the British government issued Ordinance No. 13 organizing marriage customs into one cohesive set of rules based on the British understanding of marriage. According to the ordinance, monogamous union was the only legal form of marital relationship. The formal registration of marriages and births was made compulsory. Divorce was abolished, and it was decreed that no marriage could be dissolved without court proceedings. To obtain a divorce, strict criteria had to be followed to establish grounds: adultery, adultery with cruelty to the wife, or desertion for five years.

These changes effectively stopped women from leaving their husbands to return to their parental villages. The district judge of Colombo, Berwick, in special session papers of 1869–70, noted the devastating effects of these changes on women's property rights and on equality within the conjugal family. Giving detailed examples, he asserted that this change of law was a bitter gift to the women of Sri Lanka (quoted in Risseeuw 1988:42–43).

British officers did not grasp the importance that equal family land ownership had had for women's security and equality within the family (Risseeuw 1988:53). They required one distinct owner of land per family and, although not legally limited to males, the chosen owner usually was a male family member. With time, local male elites internalized these British perceptions that were clearly advantageous to male family members.

Educating the Goddess of the Home

British observers emphasize that before Christian women missionaries started schools for women, literacy levels were very low—almost nonexistent among lower-class women (Cordiner 1807; Selkirk 1844). However, missionaries and female educational professionals based their conclusions on British perceptions of formal education at the time and did not take into account the expertise that had been passed on to women for generations in fields such as indigenous medicine, midwifery, astrology, and religious scholarship. The discussions of an appropriate system of education for women were framed around contemporary British ideals of gender roles. One Christian nun, Sister Mary of Moratuwa Convent, had this to say about women's education, "I consider the main object of the education in the higher classes of girl's English school is to fit girls to become suitable companions and help for their parents and husbands, and to enable them to move in the society of people having good morals and good manners" (quoted in Harris 1994:33).

Marie Musaeus Higgins, a theosophist and the founder of Musaeus Girls College, stated her objective in starting a girls school in Colombo as follows: "Happily, in Ceylon, woman has no necessity to enter into the rough and tumble of the world in competition with her male relatives. She has still to be wife and mother, and we have to train the growing girls in all that makes woman the goddess and the light of the home" (quoted in Harris 1994:33).

According to Malathi De Alwis, women's education curriculum is one of the few areas where the nationalists and British educators concurred (1995:140). Many housewifery skills such as needlework, hygiene, and child care came to be taught in school under the heading "home science." While educators sought to teach native girls virtues of femininity and domesticity, nationalists saw this professionalization of domesticity as significant to transforming the Sinhala Buddhist woman into a symbol of national greatness, thereby ensuring the proper regeneration of the nascent nation. After independence, the educational curriculum that emphasized home science for girls was standardized and disseminated throughout public schools. Swarna Jayaweera (1990) contends that even today the "educational material and 'hidden curriculum' reinforce stereotypes and tend to circumscribe the experiences and aspirations of girls" (8).

Producing Docile Bodies and Class Sexualities

Many missionary accounts concentrated on the native woman's obstinacy, carelessness, talkativeness, restlessness, and inattentiveness (De Alwis 1997). Missionary women educators in particular paid much attention to the task of converting native women to Christianity, thereby making them more "civilized"—docile, obedient, and serene. Focusing on the schedule of the Uduvil Girls' College in Jaffna, De Alwis shows the special attention paid and time spent on teaching needlework to local Tamil girls. She comments, "Sewing played a crucial role in the very molding of the Christian women, in the construction of a particular moral demeanor. It was a practice that insisted on neatness, orderliness, concentration, patience, precision, qualities which [missionary educators] found so wanting in the native women" (1997:22). The way native men and women clothed themselves ("barely covering the upper bodies") and their habit of letting the children go without any clothes until they were five or six years old also disturbed many writers (Selkirk 1844). According to De Alwis (1997), the emphasis on needlework at Christian girls schools was also tied to the desire of missionaries to clothe the natives and thereby prevent "impure thoughts" (29).

Orientalist writings also allude to the effeminacy of the Sri Lankan man and also to the nonsexualized nature of the Sri Lankan woman in the early British colonial era. According to Forbes (1841), Sri Lankan women are "comparatively inferior in appearance to men" (298). Knighton (1854) was struck by the "lack of femininity" in their dress styles (37–38). Missionary educational goals for native women addressed this issue by inculcating new manners and habits in young women that were distinct from those for men and thereby initiating gendered spheres. The projected ideal was that "to be civilized" was to be "restrained in all manner and thought," thereby implying that not to be so was to be "uncivilized," "uneducated," "unsophisticated," and "uncultured." This emphasis on discipline and restraint in the school curriculum resulting from colonial discourses on marriage and family went on to produce the appropriate morality and sexuality for the "educated" and "civilized" people within the emerging local middle class.

Orientalist writings also romanticize Sinhala Buddhist villages as self-sufficient centers of harmonious living that should be protected from the corrupt influences of colonialism and consequent individualism (Samaraweera 1978; Moore 1985). According to Vijaya Samaraweera (1978), the writings dealing with how outside influences spoiled the simple village life were influenced by writings on cultural decay in the English countryside at that time. This notion of the pure Sinhala Buddhist village along with the ideals of female domesticity captured the imagination of local elites who were, at the beginning of the twentieth century, grappling with an infant nationalist movement.

Colonial Humiliation: Elites and the Construction of the "New Woman"

I have described how the unfavorable and prejudiced writings of various British agents elicited angry reactions from members of the local male elite. This humiliating colonial experience prompted some members of the emergent nationalist elite to construct a notion of the "new woman," one who would be educated and accomplished at the same time as she upheld all the spiritual qualities for which Asian women are thought to be renowned. This process contributed to the rising Sinhala Buddhist nationalist consciousness in the early part of the last century. The Sinhala Buddhist woman had to be symbolic of the emerging nation seeking self-government: rich in spiritual heritage, yet capable of tackling matters in the public sphere. Nationalist elites adopted classicized Buddhist traditions from ancient texts and reformed those to counteract any future charges of irrationalism or immorality. In the late nineteenth and early twentieth centuries, their efforts incorporated and transformed syncretic and often locally specific cultural ideologies into what became mainstream Sinhala Buddhist ideology. Gananath Obeyesekere (1970) terms this new value system Protestant Buddhism because it was formed as a protest against the decay caused by colonialism and Christianity and some aspects of the new ideology that were modeled on protestant moral codes.

Within this relatively unified religious, cultural formation, the sexual division of labor was constructed by an admixture of local patriarchal values and British Victorian ideals. The nascent middle class, which was not only Buddhist but also Hindu and Christian, started to project an ideal of women as "passive, subordinate and confined to nurturing and servicing roles within and outside the home" (Jayaweera 1990:8). This admixture of Victorian ideals also contributed to new expectations that middle-class women should be protected within the fold of the family, "exhibiting the same aura of passive 'feminine' serenity as women of their class in Britain at the time" (Risseeuw 1988:52). However, this unified ideology quickly began to spread to other sections of society and eventually affected women of all classes. Among the elite who were responsible for these changes, Anagarika Dharmapala's contribution was a singularly important factor in forming an exclusive Sinhalese Buddhist nationalism and recasting woman as protector and reproducer of spirituality, tradition, and culture.

Anagarika Dharmapala

Anagarika Dharmapala was born Don David Hewavitharana, son of a wealthy businessman and Buddhist philanthropist. He was educated in Christian schools and was continually subjected to Christian evangelical pressures. In the early 1880s, he came under the tutelage of the founding members of the American Theosophical Society, Helena Blavatsky, and Colonel Henry Steel Olcott. According to David Little (1994), it was under the theosophist leaders' influence that Dharmapala started studying Pali texts to discover the "pure" Buddhist doctrine. By the late 1890s, he was completely immersed in the Buddhist revival activities of the Theosophist Society even while being increasingly dissatisfied with the society's strong ties to Hinduism.

The newfound knowledge of Pali texts provided Dharmapala with ample grounds to counteract charges of immorality concerning women and family. He wrote in his newspaper, *Sinhala Bauddhaya*, that the ancient high spiritual qualities of the Sinhala Buddhist had been eclipsed by centuries of colonial rule and were now in a shamefully degraded condition. In 1902, he started touring the country with the message "Sinhalese Awake, save Buddhism."[6] His message was clearly influenced by

orientalist and theosophist writings on Buddhism as well as his own research. His method of consciousness raising was based on shaming people who had adopted western styles of dress, food, and manners.
According to his biographer, Dharmapala was well aware that his message should be "so planned that the benefits of western civilization such
as education, science and technology were retained while only 'western
abominations' were eradicated" (Guruge 1965:lxxiii).

Ridiculing both men and women for imitating western fashions,
Dharmapala advocated the Indian sari for women and the cloth and
banian for men. Thirty-two years after his death, his biographer notes
that "in no field of reform had the Anagarika had such quick results as
in giving the womanhood of Ceylon a dress more in keeping with her
natural grace" (1965:lxxvi). According to Obeyesekere (1979), Dharmapala's mother was among the first women to follow his advice, and the
new dress soon caught on. The same happened when Dharmapala advocated name changes. Deciding that people should first be decolonized
within the cultural domain, he wanted Sinhalese to shed their European
names and take up "Aryan" Sinhala names. He himself started this trend
by changing his given name, Don David, to Dharmapala. His close asso-
ciates did the same, and a mass name-changing movement followed in
both urban and rural areas.

Sinhala names chosen for women were to be emblematic of their role
in society. The names denoted softness, comfort, kindness, beauty, and
sacrificial qualities. Male names, however, tended to denote ruler,
guardian, hero of Dharma, victory, clan, and so on. In his writings and
speeches, Dharmapala further extoled the virtue of the woman who
stands beside her husband in all his endeavors and makes his home
happy and comfortable. Citing Buddhist Pali texts, Dharmapala dictated
that a wife's duties were to "1. Order her household aright; 2. Be hos-
pitable to kinsmen and friends; 3. Be chaste; 4. Be a thrifty house
keeper; 5. Show diligence and skill." The husband was to "1. Treat his
wife with respect; 2. Treat his wife with kindness; 3. Be faithful to her; 4.
Cause her to be honored by others; 5. Give her suitable ornaments and
clothes" (Guruge 1965:18). This sexual division of labor, with a mas-
culinized public sphere and feminized private sphere, was further stabi-
lized by the publication of a general manual of conduct and a special
thirty-rule manual of conduct for women. The manual for women contained instructions regarding manners as well as efficient conduct of
household duties. These rules sought to recast women befitting the
emerging nation as religious, moral, educated, and accomplished. All
this played a role in adjusting bourgeois women's life to fit the British
colonial ideal, while at the same time resisting the role of British ideals
by drawing from ancient Pali chronicles and Asian mythology. In doing

so, Dharmapala used the same logic as colonial writers to discredit colonialism by claiming that Buddhist society had upheld these values until the colonial influence destroyed them.

Dharmapala's close associate and fellow nationalist ideologue Piyadasa Sirisena was also instrumental in creating a model of the ideal virtuous woman befitting the emerging nation.

PIYADASA SIRISENA

Like many young Buddhist revivalists of the day, Piyadasa Sirisena took Dharmapala as his model and changed his given name of Pedrick De Silva to an "Aryan" name. He also changed his dress style and took up the new "national dress." In 1903, he started a journal called *Sinhala Jathiya* (Sinhala Nation) and continued the line of propaganda enunciated by Dharmapala. In 1906, Dharmapala made Sirisena the first editor of *Sinhala Bauddhaya*. However, Sirisena's main influence on the nationalist cause came from his novels, which extolled the Sinhala Buddhist virtues for both men and women.

According to Nissan and Stirrat (1990), Sri Lanka has always had a high literacy rate, and print capitalism was of major importance in creating a sense of commonalty and linguistic community (34). In this early period of nation-building, the newspapers *The Buddhist, Sarasavi Sandaresa*, and *Sinhala Bauddhaya*, all of which showed Dharmapala's influence and included Sirisena's provocative writings, together with nationalist novels, became popular throughout the Sinhala-speaking population and played a major part in disseminating urban middle-class elite ideologies to the masses. Sirisena wrote many novels and became a household name on the island, while helping to create a new Sinhala Buddhist community. Besides being nationalist, these novels projected the image of an ideal woman who was chaste, sacrificial, and giving—in short, the goddess of the household. This ideal woman also acted against evil outside influences and protected her husband and children from falling prey to temptations. Any threat to her or to the young, unmarried women of the household was shown as detrimental to the honor of the whole extended family. Male family members taking up arms (most often the only weapon was the rhetoric of dharma) to destroy such villains was valorized as exemplifying masculinity. Throughout Sirisena's novels, good men and women with valorized qualities fought against evil and westernized men and women, at times even putting their lives in danger. However, in the end, the good characters invariably overcome evil while the bad men and women either perish or embrace Buddhist qualities.

These novels reiterate the image of the good woman, and typically the novels' characters give lengthy lectures on their virtues. In one of the most celebrated novels, *Dingiri Menika*, a young, female college student is abducted by an alcohol-drinking, meat-eating group of thieves. Half the novel is dedicated to describing how she succeeds in preserving her chastity by lecturing the drunken thieves on Buddhist values. Because that tedious aspect was intertwined with intensely provocative nationalist rhetoric, Sirisena's novels became immensely popular and the ideals they promoted became embedded in popular imagination.

Sirisena started serializing his novel *Jayatissa and Rosalin: A Happy Marriage* in the newspaper as a reaction to Christian missionary Issac De Silva's novel *Two Families*, which portrayed a happy Christian family and an unhappy Buddhist family (Amunugama 1979). De Silva portrayed the Buddhist home as a disorganized, dirty, ugly place where the devil rules. The condition of the Buddhist home was blamed entirely on the woman's lazy, uneducated, and unrefined nature. This negative image was compared with the clean, industrious Sinhala Christian woman who learned many things from the missionary women at church. Sirisena's story reversed De Silva's images and celebrated the virtues of a Buddhist marriage. At the same time, it provided a popular model for the ideal division of labor within the family and further crystallized the woman's role as creator and protector of the domestic sphere and the reproducer of the nation.[7]

The nationalist elite also noticed orientalist writings dealing with the flawless culture in Sinhala Buddhist villages, which resulted in a deep desire to shield villages and their women from outside influences. Ananda Kumaraswamy's writings were especially focused on protecting the spiritual and moral qualities of the village (Brow 1999:71). These later writings heavily influenced the constructed notion that the villages, in particular the up-country villages, were not strongly influenced by westernization and were therefore the loci of authentic Sinhala Buddhist culture. Together with the constructed qualities of the Sinhala Buddhist woman, this imposed an unfair burden on village women as being more Sinhala Buddhist and, therefore, the bearers or guardians of their nation's authentic cultural traditions.

Disseminating the Ideal

The reformation of Buddhism through an intensely puritanical reading of its texts and traditions gathered massive support from regional, religious, and educated leaders. The dissemination was further aided by the print media—newspapers as well as literary sources such as novels and poems, which promoted nationalist rhetoric. The dominant ideology was clearly designed to serve the interests of the bourgeoisie by showing the British that the Sri Lankan elite could be just as "well mannered" as any British person, while at the same time highlighting the "pure ideological base" of the indigenous culture. Contained within the nationalist movement, this new form of Buddhism along with new ideal gender roles quickly captured the fascination of Sinhala Buddhists at every level.

After independence in 1948, the country's new leaders adopted this unified, protestant Buddhist ideology and its attendant rituals as the basis for state culture.[8] Subsequently, this ideology was officially disseminated through schools and the mass media. This process was significantly intensified after the MEP's (*Mahajana Eksath Peramuna* [Peoples United Front]) 1956 election victory. The MEP campaigned on a platform of making Sinhala the only state language and a theme of "five great forces": monks, indigenous doctors, teachers, farmers, and laborers. The active involvement of village elites and the masses in politics for the first time in 1956 further facilitated the penetration of state culture into rural agrarian society. Coupled with the constant bombardment through news media, films, songs, novels, and textbooks, this further etched ideal images of the village, women, family, and sexuality into the public psyche.

Newspaper articles and creative writing, especially advertisements, in the postindependence era portrayed a virtuous wife and mother who was clean and efficient and who smilingly served the family.[9] Women who sacrificed and suffered with cruel husbands and unkind children were valorized as the ideal women who kept families together. Many movies made during the 1950s and 1960s portrayed the good woman as one who was obedient to parents, a virgin at marriage, and an efficient and religious wife and mother after marriage. Commenting on the Sri Lankan cinema from 1947 to 1979, Laleen Jayamanne (1992) writes that the narrative structure of the generic Sinhala cinema contains a set of binary oppositions such as city/village, bad/good, and westernized/traditional (57). Further extending this analysis, Abeyesekera (1989) writes that the good woman in Sinhala cinema is portrayed as full of "virtues of passivity: patience, self-sacrifice, willing submission to suffering, obedience to patriarchal authority." Visually, too, she dresses in a "simple manner, is unostentatious, full of gentle smiles and down cast eyes, non aggressive" (52). The bad woman, according to Abeyesekera, is portrayed as westernized, trouser wearing, aggressive, loud mouthed, and of loose moral character (1989:53; 1998:39).[10] In many of these movies, the bad woman meets with some kind of punishment, such as public humiliation, great sorrow, illness, or death.

In precolonial times, the Sinhala people did not think being a virgin at marriage was important (Peiris 1956). This notion was also developed as part of protestant Buddhist ethics. Although the current importance was a result of Victorian influence, the ritual of checking a woman's virginity on the wedding day is still touted as an ancient custom (Gombrich and Obeyesekere 1988; Grossholtz 1984). Thus many movies, though centered on romantic love, lectured about the "evilness" of premarital sex and the importance of virginity at marriage. Two movies released in the 1980s focused exclusively on the ritual of checking the bride's virginity on the wedding day. Both depicted how women suffer when they could not prove their virginity. But the overall objective of the movies was to show that there could be reasons other than premarital sex, such as being born without a hymen or having had a sports accident, for not showing signs of virginity on the wedding day. Going to the marriage bed with a shy virgin was projected as an ultimate male fantasy through poems and songs. "A bee taking the fresh fragrance [*nebul suwanda*] of a flower" is a common metaphor used to project a romantic value to the virginity requirement that also framed the couple's subsequent sexual relationship on unequal grounds.

Songs and poems also advised women on ideal behavior and celebrated the "good woman" qualities. Novels and teledramas were central to promoting the image of the morally superior village where an unsullied form of culture exists. According to Tambiah (1992:110), novels and teledramas criticize the evil and immorality in the cities while valorizing the image of the paddy farming villages where simple, peaceful life is presided over by the temple. The Sarvodaya community-development organization, which has branches in almost all villages, has also been a major force in the spread of protestant Buddhist values in villages (Lynch 2000:96). In general, the chauvinist nationalist discourses on ancient Sinhala civilization (which has its roots in Dharmapala's anticolonial, antiminority ideology) was one that also influenced Sinhala Buddhist people's everyday discourses and practices on women, sexuality, and morality.

School textbooks were also an important aspect of this dissemination of newly constructed values and norms. The stories in textbooks for lower grades especially were peppered with advice about ideal norms of behavior and the consequences of breaking these rules (Gunasekera 1994:18). The textbooks for the Buddhist religion class included constructed values and norms of ideal behavior in addition to the material on religious texts. The grade 7 social studies textbook included a short biography of Anagarika Dharmapala under the heading "National Heroes." Many education districts held annual "Dharmapala day" celebrations that included oratorical and essay contests focusing on Dharmapala's life and work. Although it was not compulsory, many Buddhist parents sent their children to Sunday schools to learn Buddhism. There, in addition to religious education, Buddhist children learned rules of proper comportment and attitudes as well as the value of religiosity and social work. It is in schools and Sunday schools that young women were given additional instructions on norms of shame-fear to which they had been introduced in their homes.[11]

The limited social roles prescribed to women under the protestant Buddhist formulations influenced development planners since independence (Jayawardena and Jayaweera 1986). This resulted in women being overlooked as a potential target group for development programs until Middle East migration and FTZs opened up employment avenues exclusively for unskilled women. Even these avenues, especially FTZ work, were planned within the patriarchal understanding of women as "nimble fingered and docile" and the assumption that they will leave employment once they accumulate their dowry in gold and cash. The influence of discursive constructions contributed to the effective marginalization of women from economic and social life. However, this marginalization takes different forms among women of different social groups, and women of all classes differently negotiate these ideals in their everyday lives.

Contemporary Discourses

Research has shown that women negotiate different roles and positions through varied economic, religious, community, and political activities (Obeyesekere 1981; Risseeuw 1988; Schrijvers 1988; Stirrat 1988; Bartholomeusz 1994; Brow 1996; De Alwis 1998; Gamburd 2000). However, it is also apparent that people of all classes subscribe to the ideal gender roles of women as wife, mother, and protector and nurturer of the spiritual and domestic spheres. Contemporary discourses on FTZ employment and workers' lives derive their notions of women and sexuality from those earlier constructions while at the same time contributing new meanings to this already dense discursive field.

When former President Ranasinghe Premadasa initiated the 200 Garment Factory Program (200 GFP) in 1992, it was heralded as a solution to many problems faced by rural youth. This program was the result of a recommendation made by the presidential youth commission, which was appointed after the government brutally suppressed a youth insurrection, to examine the causes of unrest among the vernacular educated rural youth. The 200 GFP aimed to establish a garment factory in each of the 200 Assistant Government Agent (AGA) Divisions in the country and was to create nearly 100,000 jobs. Even though the vast majority who participated in the insurrection were men, more than 80 percent of the jobs created by the 200 GFP, in keeping with the perception of women as "nimble fingered and docile," were filled by women.

Every factory was inaugurated with pomp and pageantry by the president himself. The visual images of neat and clean factories, new machines, and new female employees in neat and clean uniforms were disseminated almost daily to television audiences throughout the country. Weeks after an inauguration ceremony the state television channel, the Rupavahini, showed footage of the president's visit to the factory and different parts of his speech. These news segments usually included images of broadly smiling young women welcoming the president by presenting betel leaves and flower garlands or a group of them singing a welcome song. Then the president, ministers, and entrepreneurs visited the new factory and walked along neatly divided lines of machines occupied by new female employees in their uniforms, usually in a hue of pink or baby blue. As if on cue, each woman would turn and smile at the group of her "benefactors" as they passed by.

This objectification of women as docile, grateful recipients of "welfare" by almost exclusively male benefactors was intensified by the president's long speeches directed at the predominantly Sinhala Buddhist constituency. Through these speeches, Premadasa managed to reconcile the ideal woman image, the capitalist work ethic, and Sinhala Buddhist nationalism. Referring to Sinhala Buddhist cultural values as they applied to working women, he attempted to show that capitalism and cultural values can coexist harmoniously if working women did not forget their role as the bearer of national values and morals. In one speech, Premadasa referred to the depraved and debased activities into which the FTZ workers had been forced and pledged that with the opening of village factories this situation would be avoided (Suresh 1992, as quoted in Lynch 1999:66).

Mainly because of these speeches and various forms of media reinterpretations, people started to see the 200 GFP as a program designed to prevent rural women from migrating to distant cities for employment. Within a short time, village factories became places that saved "innocent" young rural women from coming under immoral influences in the cities. Some of the state television programs showed parents praising the 200 GFP for providing women employment near their parental homes, saying that it prevented their daughters from becoming corrupted in the city and thereby bringing bad influences back to the villages. The meanings generated by the propaganda surrounding the 200 GFP intensified the already-stigmatized image of the FTZ workers and, as a result, even village factory workers projected their "purer" morality compared to that of the Katunayake FTZ worker.

When I was visiting the native village of one of the FTZ workers in Weligama, her father raised concerns about his daughter's insistence on working at a Colombo factory.[12] "We have been telling our girl to come and get a job in the factory located near our house, but she wouldn't listen. She will see her foolishness when [marriage] proposal after proposal will be turned down because people don't know what she has been doing there," he said. According to Lynch (1999), village factory officials and owners prefer rural workers to the workers in the urban FTZs because the village workers are "more obedient, shy, respectful, controlled, disciplined and better mannered than urban women because they are under parental control and still behave according to cultural norms. . . . [They further] contend that urban [migrant] women abuse their freedom and are spoiled and more stubborn because they are away from their parents. And furthermore, cities are rife with people who will lead village girls astray, as evidenced by the reports of the illicit sexual activities of village women in Colombo" (68).

These attitudes illustrate how migrant workers are characterized as sexually degenerate and socially dangerous as a result of their living away from their parents' villages. Similar fears about women's migration to cities for factory employment have been documented by many writers in other geographical areas (Ong 1987; Mills 1998). It is the fear that capitalist modernity will corrupt young women and in turn will harm the traditional values that has made women targets of strict control and discipline.

Politicians from different political parties show that they all agreed on the importance of women's proper behavior for the national moral identity, and their speeches objectified FTZ workers as unwitting destroyers of national morality. In 1994, the Sri Lankan Freedom Party (SLFP), together with many smaller parties, formed a coalition against the seventeen-year-old UNP regime. This coalition, called the People's Alliance (PA), also included many other sections of the population, especially workers' unions and student groups. Leftist parties and major trade unions affiliated with the SLFP actively sought the support of FTZ workers, not only as a worker group but also as canvasing agents in their respective villages. The hardships suffered by the FTZ workers were hot topics at political rallies, especially those held in the Katunayake area. Both parties promised to change the situation for the workers, although it was clear that the majority of workers preferred the PA.

Many workers thus actively engaged in organizing other workers to support the PA and several were key speakers at political rallies. Many speakers, including the FTZ workers, heavily critiqued the way the workers' sweat and blood profited foreigners and talked of how the new government would make plans to channel some profits to improve workers' labor and living conditions. Some speeches, especially by male leftist politicians, intimated that it was a shame that the politicians had let Sri Lanka's young women suffer under foreign hands and claimed it was their duty to save the women from this degradation. They also talked about the way women got into trouble because of relationships with men and how if they come to power they would change the living conditions so that women would not feel pressured to have boyfriends. It should be noted, however, that none of the speakers talked about bringing women back home to the domestic sphere; rather, they proposed improving security and moral protection for the working women. The UNP attempted to benefit from its 200 GFP by extolling the virtues of women who lived with their families in the village. While all party speakers wanted the modernity and development associated with the FTZ and its female workforce, they also mourned the loss of traditional values linked to village women. These speeches demonstrated the intense contradictions faced by politicians within the dense discursive field regarding women, sexuality, development, and modernity.

The FTZ women speakers and the trade-union workers focused on workers' rights and the need for improvements. According to one worker, who was present at several rallies, FTZ workers often broke down crying while talking about their hard lives. The PA won a resounding victory in the parliamentary elections and the presidential election held a few months later. But in 1995 when the workers and I discussed their experiences with electoral politics and the new government, many workers expressed disappointment that nothing had changed. Many of them looked back at that period as a wonderful time when women workers organized themselves into a political force and had a say in spaces that were not open to them before. There were two cynical workers who thought that many of those speeches were choreographed and that the women were asked to cry at least once in their speeches to bring attention to their weak, emotional nature.

Politicians from leftist parties, the vast majority of whom were men, reproduced notions of ideal womanhood by painting a picture of women workers as a group who should be cared for by the country's governing bodies (that is, men). One leftist politician, Vasudeva Nanayakkara, in his capacity as the then deputy minister of labor presented a proposal to establish safe places for young lovers to meet and have fun without being subjected to public humiliation and harassment. This was proposed with the FTZ women's troubles in mind. Nanayakkara supported his view by claiming that such public places would prevent young couples from going to rooming houses even for simple conversations. Critiques of his view held that these places would encourage young people to date and engage in premarital sex. While the idea did not reach fruition in other areas, Katunayake got what is called a "Garden of Love" (*Pem Uyana*), a piece of land adorned with flowering bushes and artistically trimmed hedges. When I visited this garden in 2000, it was a lonely and an unkempt place. According to the workers and NGO officials, nobody used the place and young couples especially avoided it. The fate of the Garden of Love shows the futility of isolated actions that do not fit cultural discourses or lead toward major changes in discursive understanding.[13]

NGO POLITICS

Many NGOs work with and for FTZ workers. They all understood and responded to the contradictory discourses surrounding FTZ employment and female morality in different ways. These agents too reproduced the existing images of FTZ workers while expressing their concern about workers' health, welfare, and safety. Their descriptions of programs about those latter issues were dotted with words and ideas from dominant cultural discourses and they sought to emphasize the need to protect women from bad city influences. Some of these ideas will be analyzed in the section titled "Alternative Print Media." Class and ideological differences existed among the NGOs even while they seemed to consider FTZ workers as a profitable constituency that legitimated their claims on foreign donor funds.[14]

VICTIMS OF OTHERS: MEDIA REPRESENTATIONS

Various media representations derive from the image of the ideal woman and contribute to the ongoing discursive constructions by portraying the contradictory pictures of "innocent village women" who get corrupted in the city and of young women who have little self-control and are, therefore, sexually vulnerable. For example, an article that appeared on the Internet site Third World Net lamented the fate of rural women who came to cities for employment:

Many social workers here have mixed feelings about the increased job creation for women under Sri Lanka's economic liberalization policies since 1977. . . . Most of the women who work in these [FTZs] are young girls who have been protected in their villages and are now on their own in these zones. Miss Balasooriya [executive director of Women in Need] says . . . [that there are] large numbers of girls coming to the center pregnant, crying for help. Recent studies done by the Colombo University have found that the FTZs have been the preying grounds for pimps from brothels in Colombo and the tourist centers on the coast, where they befriend unsuspecting village girls. They are gradually transformed from being girlfriends to sex workers. (quoted in Siriwardena 1996)

This excerpt reiterates several prevailing assumptions about FTZ workers among middle-class women. One assumption is that the women have previously been sheltered in their villages. Many such writings ignore that the sheltered woman is an ideal and the extent to which ideals can be put into practice depends heavily on social class. A second assumption is that the rural migrant women are unsuspecting (ignorant) victims of male and city vices. It denies agency and physical or emotional desire to women by projecting an image of women aligned with the nationalist gender ideal. Articles containing such images about FTZ workers appeared in daily and weekly newspapers as parts of political or religious speeches or in weekly women's magazines as feature articles, short stories, and poems. According to newspaper writings, the "unsullied ideal Sinhala Buddhist womanhood" has come under threat by the very force that threatens the sovereignty of the nation—economic liberalization. In short stories and poems, migrant FTZ workers wrote about heroic efforts to stay away from evil influences that threatened to make them "bad women." Just like Piyadasa Sirisena's heroines, they preferred death over breaking sexual norms. The ones who follow the "wrong path" soon realized their folly and gave moral advice to the "innocent girls from villages" who came to the "evil, inhuman city."

Alternative Print Media

Dabindu, the monthly magazine of the Dabindu Center, publishes articles that also create images of FTZ women for women. Because of *Dabindu's* involvement in labor politics and grass-roots organizing, its articles usually take a more politically oriented stance than mainstream newspapers and call for changes in labor and living conditions. Editorial comments and the major articles written by people associated with *Dabindu* repeatedly call attention to FTZ women's deplorable working and living conditions. *Dabindu* also publishes many reports about problems arising from premarital sex, such as pregnancies, abortions, and infanticide. While the articles in *Dabindu* do not explicitly advocate avoidance of premarital sex, the constant references to stories of cheating and stealing boyfriends demonstrate their stand on this issue. When I interviewed them, many Dabindu workers clearly stated that it would be to the FTZ workers' benefit if they did not get into relationships with men they met in the FTZ. Several of the features that appear regularly in *Dabindu* emphasize different aspects of women's victimization at the factory, boardinghouse, and the FTZ.

Although the Dabindu organization and the magazine consider women's FTZ employment good and are concerned with improving the women's working and living conditions, some feature articles and readers' creative writing suggest that the city is full of evil that corrupted innocent village women and that it is good if they do not come to the FTZ. A monthly feature titled "Letter" is published as a communication from a father to an FTZ daughter and her reply to him. The daughter's letters mostly discuss work and living difficulties and how she manages to stay away from bad influences. They also express her anger toward management and politicians for the workers' suffering. The father's letters are written in simple, rural Sinhala and subtly challenge the patriarchal ideas on women's roles in society. Nevertheless, the father constantly asks the daughter to come back and live with the family even if the family members were to go hungry. These letters are a good example of the everyday contradictions that Dabindu, as a leftist grass-roots organization working in a society rooted in patriarchal understanding of women's morality, is grappling with.

Dabindu does periodically publish reports of women workers' courage in organizing in the factory and showing that they can fight for their rights. The pages set aside for readers' writings, mostly in poem or short-story form, include writings by both workers and people who are not FTZ workers. The workers' writings here seem to follow the lead of the paper's own articles in that the workers write about their harsh work and living conditions and include unrealistic threats to owners and managers. Although some of the workers' writings are on romantic relationships and the pain of separation, they never refer to sexual desire or activity.[15] What the writing does contain is praise for women who manage to live in the city without tarnishing their reputations.

Another recurring theme in the workers' writings in *Dabindu* is the romantic relationships between soldiers of the Sri Lankan army and garment factory workers. Most of these writings show how class interests and nationalist leanings wrestle in workers' consciousness. While they express some sympathy for women and children in war zones, usually the poems end in hopes for a victory that will enable soldiers and garment workers to get together again. One poem, published anonymously (April 1999), displays these contradictions:

When I heard you had gone to Mannar [town in the war zone]
Warm tears filled my eyes
How much *they* love recruits from *our* class
Will only be known when something bad happens [to people from our class]

We hear about the war in the North
And I worry about you so often
I am telling you this with much love
How could one win [the war] without proper training
[Translation and emphasis added]

These two quatrains, taken from a ten-quatrain poem, written as a letter to a soldier from a garment factory worker, display the worker's understanding of the war as a project of the other, the bourgeoisie, and critique the government for sending newly recruited soldiers to the war zone without giving them proper training. Later, the writer resorts to nationalist sentiments in wanting the Tamil militant movement crushed and wishing victory to the government forces. These later quatrains, however, rather than being distinctive, follow a pattern found in many other Sinhala poems on the war published in Sri Lankan national newspapers.

Niveka, another magazine published about and for FTZ workers by an NGO named *Kalape Api* (Us in the Zone), also publishes reports on labor-law violations and other injustices done to workers. (Ni-Ve-Ka are the three Sinhala letters that denote the FTZ.) It covers many stories of worker protests and strikes. The page that this paper allocates for readers' contributions is also filled with poems on love and separation as well as hardship and suffering in the FTZ. However, the paper differs from *Dabindu* in that some of the staff's writings directly question patriarchy. In particular, some of the issues after January 2000 questioned patriarchy in response to the outrage caused by a pocket calendar issued by *Niveka* for the year 2000. The calendar contained a photograph of a man and a woman in an intimate embrace. The two characters were Caucasian, and the photograph was obviously taken from a foreign magazine. This calendar angered some groups who wrote to the paper saying that this imaging would tell the world that FTZ workers are prostitutes who like such base pictures and that such pictures would in turn motivate the workers to engage in debased activities. The paper's responses show an understanding of patriarchal forces at work and how those forces insult women in the guise of protecting their honor. Staff writings also note how the calendar opened a new space for people to understand that FTZ workers have a right to enjoy love and sexuality. The writing also implied that the readers' outrage was more intense because the woman has both her arms and legs around the man while kissing him. This aggressive and desirous woman is, according to *Niveka* writers, what angered both men and women who had been taught that women are passive recipients of men's sexual desire. One usually does not find such debates in mainstream Sinhala media, and it was especially encouraging to read this in a paper that reached the constituency in whose lives these discourses play a central role.[16]

Niveka certainly brings a different analysis to many issues and especially tries to change attitudes about patriarchal understanding of women's work and sexuality. But the magazine reaches only a small group of women and not many men. According to the staff, their goal in publishing images such as those described that were taken from foreign magazines is to open a space to discuss sexual desires. The May 2000 volume included a call for beautiful women, asking them to send color photographs of themselves if they would like to get their faces on the front page of *Niveka*. Many workers and several officials denigrated both these tactics as attempts for wider circulation by catering to people's "base desires." This represents another form of conflict these publications face. While showing that the behavior and sexual norms of the ideal woman are cultural constructions, they go along with another form of patriarchy—objectifying women for male consumption. Both these trends, paradoxically, may be advancing the existing stereotypes of FTZ women.

Moreover, these much-touted empowering spaces, opened to discuss matters that have remained unspoken until now, themselves can reproduce and strengthen existing oppressive cultural expectations. One of *Niveka*'s back-page poems, titled "Tear Drop," talked about virginity and a rich politician. The purpose of this poem seems to be to shock people into thinking and talking about topics that have been shrouded in secrecy in Sinhala Buddhist society. While it may succeed in doing so, the poem also reiterates the importance of being a virgin, an expectation that is at the root of the stigma attached to women living away from their parents' protection. Thus while demonstrating the thin line one has to tread in attempting to change attitudes about women in a society in transition, this poem also shows that media representations may contribute to the ongoing process of shaping FTZ workers' subjectivities in ways they did not intend.

Television Representations

The extent to which the FTZ women's victimization captured the popular imagination is evident through the serialized Sinhala teledramas shown on the state television channel Rupavahini. Shown during prime time between 8:30 and 9:30 P.M., these teledramas have become major sources for producing and reproducing meanings and values for the mostly Sinhala Buddhist viewers. While several programs indirectly referred to FTZ workers and factory-related men's jobs, several teledramas based their plots on the lives and trials of FTZ workers. One titled *Grahanaya* (Stranglehold) is based on the story of a migrant garment factory worker who is drugged and raped by the factory owner. Consequently, she starts to enjoy a luxurious life as his mistress until he finds a more beautiful worker to be his mistress. The story ends when the first woman attempts to kill the factory owner and is taken to prison. Throughout the series, the producer projected an image of the stereotypical "innocent" migrant worker who gets deceived into sexual activity and then, through her own weak will and poor judgment, gets deeply entangled in disastrous affairs. This image was accentuated by including a character from another garment factory who becomes a prostitute to supplement her income. Although the protagonist lived in an area full of boarding-houses (a boardinghouse cluster area) just like the FTZ area, she seemed to work in a factory located outside the FTZ. However, people who talked to me about this teledrama did so in relation to FTZ work-ers' morality and assumed it was about an FTZ worker. Those interviews indicated that the teledrama helped to sharpen the negative image of FTZ workers already etched in the public mind.

The teledrama *Ira, Handa Yata* (Under the Moon and the Sun) fea-tures a migrant garment factory worker who gets pregnant through her boyfriend. After they have sex, the man disappears with her gold neck-lace. An elderly woman I interviewed identified this as symbolic of the "cultural destruction" brought about by the "celluloid culture of the open economy." According to this woman, rural women come to the city looking for gold and lose the most-valuable possession they have (their virginity). Many workers and others I talked to thought the teledrama's ending was unrealistic because the man finally marries the woman and becomes a good husband. According to one boardinghouse owner, that ending provided a bad example to young women by implying that there could be happy endings to "vulgar behavior."

Another teledrama, *Ek Mruganganaviyak* (A Doe), focuses on the cen-tral importance of virginity in a young woman's life. According to this story, a young middle-class woman is driven away from her home by her parents' unsympathetic response to the information that her boyfriend has raped her. Fallen into poverty, she shows much strength of charac-ter by finding a garment factory job and trying to live on her own. How-ever, led by an understanding that her life has no worth as a result of having lost her virginity, she embarks on multiple sexual relationships, showing adeptness at cheating and lying, as well as being insensitive. This behavior, of course, leads to many problems and finally lands her in prison. This portrayal also shows women as uncontrollable and morally dangerous when they are not under patriarchal control, while reiterating the assumption that having sexual relationships was common among FTZ workers. Moreover, it alluded to women's image as "victim-ized [and] ignorant of the consequences" by using the title, *A Doe*, a sym-bol popularly used to create an image of women as innocent and childlike.

In 2000, one of the new private television channels, Sirasa TV, was tele-casting a program titled *Lunch Time TV* every weekday from 12:00 to 1:00 p.m. The producers traveled to different workplaces, mostly to FTZ facto-ries, at lunchtime to record a show consisting of workers' songs, skits, and conversations. This program took a different approach to showcas-ing FTZ women by accentuating their new lifestyles. The program brought to light the workers' dresses, jewelry, and accessories as well as their tastes in songs, dances, and movies. Mostly watched by middle-class housewives, the program provided a glimpse into how the migrant industrial worker lived.

The interviewers sought to emphasize a process of attitude change by asking questions about workers' feelings on love, arranged marriages, and their specific romantic relationships. Interviewers and the respondents carefully avoided questions regarding physical desires or premarital sex. Nevertheless, many middle-class people thought the program showed how corrupt the FTZ workers were. Many viewers seemed more offended by the workers' honesty in discussing their romantic relationships than by the fact that such things were common. One middle-class woman with whom I once watched the program said, "Why can't they lie? Don't they know that this brings shame to their families?"

The program, however, seems to portray the realities of workers' lives without being judgmental. Although they do not use the image of the ideal woman to measure how good or bad the workers are, the producers use elements of that image to measure the changes that were brought by the workers' new situation. The audience, however, interpreted the message differently based on their class and gender. For many, it is another example of how wicked the migrant workers are; for others, it is another example of journalists exploiting "silly women workers." Ironically, none of the FTZ workers I talked to had watched the program because of its inopportune telecast time. Only a few had even heard of the program.[17]

As stated earlier, Sri Lankan generic cinema featured several interconnected binary oppositions such as village versus city and good versus bad (Jayamanne 1992:57). Many films over the short history of Sinhala cinema, such as *Kolomba Sanniya* (Colombo Craze), *Gehenu Lamai* (Girls), *Seilama* (The City), and *Ayoma* featured "good," "innocent" village women coming to the city and getting into moral trouble. A recent feature film, *Kinihiriya Mal* (Flowers under the Anvil), by Sri Lankan movie director H. D. Premaratne focuses on the life of a poor village woman who comes to the city to work in the FTZ. This movie also followed the good-village-girl-becoming-bad (or barely managing to escape from being bad) formula. According to the story, Sanduni, who misses the feeling of belonging and protection she felt in the village, suffers much in the factory and at the boardinghouse. Gradually she is attracted to the consumer culture in the FTZ and becomes an easy victim of city vices. Because of the influence of bad men and the need to maintain her new lifestyle, Sanduni leaves her FTZ job and becomes a masseuse at a luxurious massage parlor. However, retribution for her "wrongdoings" follows Sanduni and her family when her village learns her occupation.

The incensed villagers stone her family home, leading to the deaths of her father and brother. Incidentally, another FTZ worker from the village manages not to be swayed by the new attractions in the city and at first is laughed at for her continuing financial hardships. When Sanduni, who abandoned "good values of the village," ends up bringing destruction to herself and her family, the virtuous woman who chose poverty over "quick money" triumphs. In the end, it is marriage, the most traditional means of honor for women, that promises to save Sanduni from the "debased life" and the dishonor she brought her family. But when she tries to turn her life around, the same urban evil people who "corrupted her" thwart her efforts by destroying her life. Media promotions heralded the movie as "a story of a seamstress of our time." *Kinihiriya Mal* ran for months to packed audiences and received glowing reviews in the mainstream media. However, *Niveka* and *Dabindu* both criticized the movie for the stereotypical image it promoted.[18] According to *Niveka* (June 2000), *Kinihiriya Mal* become the anvil that hammered a disadvantageous image of FTZ women even further into the public psyche. *Niveka*'s July 2000 issue published reactions from several FTZ workers who had seen the movie, and they all agreed that the movie did not depict their lives.

Innocent Women and Powerless Workers: Factory Officials as Parents

Just as the politicians, NGO officials, and factory officials did, neighbors and boardinghouse owners expressed ambivalent opinions about women's migration and FTZ employment. While almost all of them acknowledged the need for development and modernity, they were deeply ambivalent about the effects of rural women migrating to the city for work on the Sinhala Buddhist culture. I had a chance to see such ambivalence when I attended RAC's New Year party.[19] I was talking to an RAC worker, Nalini, when Mr. Dassanayake, the company's managing director, came to talk to me. I introduced Nalini to him and told him how she had taken me to the most interesting dancing groups among the employees and even had taken me to the singers' tent to pose for a photograph with a celebrity.[20] Being a new worker, Nalini did not know that Dassanayake was the big boss. When he inquired about her work, she asked him why their immediate supervisor, who was popular among the workers, was transferred. "Everybody in the section is unhappy. They think Duminda sir was transferred because he is too good to us," Nalini further explained. Mr. Dassanayake answered, "If the boys in the lines tell you to not obey managers this daughter should not follow those ideas. We don't do anything bad for you. What we do, we do with your welfare at heart. Those boys will tell you to do this and that, and then will take you places saying it is to discuss factory matters. And in the end it is these innocent children who get into trouble. Whatever happens, these children [*lamai*][21] should keep in mind your poor parents who have brought you up with good virtues. Never forget your rural values."

Mr. Dassanayake said this last sentence looking at me and then turned to speak to me in English. Translating some of his final advice to Nalini, he went on to explain how it is harder to manage RAC than other factories because of its large number of male employees who are "always misleading the innocent girls into defying the management."

"What these stupid children do not see," Mr. Dassanayake continued, "is that these men do not have their interest at heart. Boys are always looking for cheap pleasures by acting like film heroes. They try to impress the girls by shouting against the management in front of the girls. So these stupid girls get entangled in unnecessary activities." After recounting several incidents of young women getting into trouble, he continued in a slow, sad tone, "We need these girls' labor. The economy needs it. But I really do wish that these girls would not have to leave their homes and come so far to get into trouble. They just don't understand the badness of these city people." While Mr. Dassanayake seemed genuine in his concern for the well-being of his female workers, his belief that rural young women are innocent (sexually ignorant), stupid, and easily led to sexual "misdemeanors" is clearly influenced by the ongoing discursive constructions on women and rural customs and traditions. These conflictual desires of modernity and development and safeguarding traditional values figured into many factory official testimony.

Suishin, the factory where I had worked, held its New Year party rather late, on February 12. It was on a much smaller scale than that of the RAC and was held inside the meal hall, which was cleared of tables and chairs. In the middle of the hall, a stage was raised and when I arrived for the party at 2:00 P.M. a band was playing fast dance music. All lights were switched off except for the swiveling colored lights on the stage. The sound from the band was deafening, and all I could see in the dark was a sea of heads and hands going up and down to the fast rhythm of the songs. It took awhile for my eyes to see that workers were in colorful dresses and that several top-level managers were at the partitioned section in the rear pensively watching the dancing. The party ended at 8:30 P.M. It was one of those days when I had to return to Colombo. Mr. Perera, Suishin's elderly human resources manager who lived close to my parents' house in Borelesgamuwa, and I started back to Colombo in one vehicle. We discussed the success of the party on our way to Colombo and Mr. Perera said,

Do you know how many cases of beer we ordered for today? This factory has 500 girls and not even a hundred male workers. Where did all that beer go? These girls come from villages and learn all the bad habits here. They think it is such a fashionable thing to drink beer. They are not used to it and get drunk soon and boys find it easy to catch them. You must have seen all the couples in the corners. It is such a pity. Both Gamini [deputy managing director] and I wanted to leave, but we couldn't. Who knows what would have happened if we left them alone like that. We have children, too. I have asked the junior executives to keep an eye on the dancers and stop them if too much is happening. If this [partying] continues like this, we will not even know till the Tigers capture the whole country.

Mr. Perera's monologue clearly showed the patriarchal attitude he held toward industrial workers.[22] It was also interesting that he connected youthful hedonism and women's wickedness to the collapse of the nation. Unlike politicians, Mr. Perera's doing so was not politically motivated, and it points to the way discursively constructed layers of meaning converge in people's understanding of everyday events.

Isuru, Suishin's newly recruited work-study officer,[23] hailed from Galle, the capital city of Sri Lanka's southern province. Many times, Isuru shared his thoughts on issues that he believed would be important to my research. The Friday before the Suishin party, he predicted that I would learn many things from the party and asked me to bring a camera and if possible a camcorder. "You will be surprised by [the] behavior [of the workers] and of course by their fashions," he said. During the party, he sat beside me several times and pointed to the embracing and kissing couples in dark corners.

The Monday following the party, Isuru said, "Now you know why many young men do not want to marry garment girls." When I again protested, he reminded me how he had pointed to women workers drinking beer, flirting with men, and kissing and hugging men who were sometimes not even their boyfriends, as well as how they even initiated touching any man who was around. Further demonstrating how much some of the ideal gender characteristics such as docility, serenity, and sexual passivity have been internalized by the Sinhala Buddhist people, Isuru continued, "I agree that some girls were just sitting and watching, but how can one distinguish a good girl from a bad one? If I take one home to my mother saying that this is a good one, how would she know? She will throw both of us out." When I told him how good it is that at least a section of the Sri Lankan female population had become honest with their bodies and desires, Isuru left the room laughingly saying, "My mother has only two sons" (meaning that she could not spare a son to an "immoral" woman).

Many of the senior and junior executives and factory and office staff echoed Isuru's sentiments in different forms and at different times. The workers' boisterous, aggressive, and unrestrained behavior when an industrial conflict occurred especially evoked heavy criticism. *Dabindu* (April 2000) quoted part of a letter sent to striking women workers' parents by the management of the Ishin Lanka Pvt. Ltd. It said, "Due to the provocations by few, our factory workers are engaged in a labor strike. . . . Under current circumstances, your daughters are freely running around with boys and idling about in public places. This is not good for their protection and as neighboring villagers we do not approve of this. For your children's protection and the factory's future, we request that you come and advise your children."

Although the letter claimed to be signed by villagers, the workers and the *Dabindu* activists assumed that the management had mailed it because the letters were addressed to each worker's parents, using the parents' legal names. This shows the way some factories attempt to manipulate cultural values to curtail industrial struggles.[24] This perception perhaps is not surprising, considering that the BOI of Sri Lanka has acknowledged that the logic behind the recruitment of these women is that they have little chance to find other employment and are "nimble fingered and docile." In my interviews with the BOI's assistant director for research and documentation and the chief statistician, incidentally both women, they repeatedly used the term "garment girls" to refer to women workers. According to the assistant director, one additional reason for recruitment is that women are more responsible toward their families and, therefore, could not be led into unionization as easily as men. Because of their upbringing in patriarchal villages, they are seen as the ideal workforce for FTZs. At the same time, they are stigmatized for the very space this work, under industrial patriarchy, provides them for attaining knowledge, sexual and otherwise.

NEIGHBORS AND BOARDINGHOUSE OWNERS

This is how Kusuma, a boardinghouse owner in Amandoluwa, described FTZ workers' lives: "I am not saying that there are no bad men around and these children do not get in trouble because of them. But there is blame on women's hands, too. Remember that teledrama about the FTZ girl, *Grahanaya?* In that, it is the girl's fault that she stayed with the factory owner. In the past, a good woman would commit suicide if anybody defiled her. But this girl stayed in his house. Nowadays where can we find good qualities?" Fifteen women resided in Kusuma's four boarding rooms. Most of them were present when we had this discussion about women getting into trouble. Kusuma continued:

My girls are very good. I won't take each and every girl who comes here asking to stay. I will only take girls who are accompanied by their parents. Girls who come with that elder brother and this elder brother . . . , I won't accept them. There are boardinghouses that are appropriate for such women. I only take girls who come right from the village; uncorrupted, innocent ones. Then I look after them like my own daughters. Ask anyone around here, my girls come home at decent hours. They would even fight with factory managers saying that they can't work overtime because boarding auntie will throw them out if they are late. No unrelated men can visit them here. They live here with me for years, and I have arranged marriages and settled some of them, too.

Agreeing with the boardinghouse owner, several women started telling stories about boardinghouses that have bad reputations as a result of allowing any man who claims to be a brother or cousin to stay. Boardinghouses without an elderly woman to oversee the workers received heavy criticism. One of those, they laughingly told me, was the one where I stayed for the major part of my research in Katunayake. When I was about to leave, Kusuma took me aside and told me in a low tone, "I am saying this for your own good. There are really bad stories about Saman's boardinghouse. It wouldn't be too good if it is known to this daughter's intended gentleman's family that this daughter is staying at a place with a bad reputation." While I appreciated Kusuma and her boarders' kindness toward me, I was struck by the way they drew from the three teledramas and some newspaper reports, including *Dabindu*, in understanding workers' lives. They also used these media representations as a moral measuring tape.

The few times I was at Kusuma's boardinghouse, I did not have the opportunity to talk to the workers without her present. But many workers in other boardinghouses, to whom I talked without the owners present, claimed that they resent the owners, especially landladies, trying to act as their moral supervisors while financially exploiting them. According to one worker, "They are the biggest gossips around the area and tell bad stories about workers to journalists. They exaggerate simple little love stories into the worst jungle stories," she explained. According to the landladies, the women are immoral and crafty. "These women's behavior is a shame not only to their families but to the whole nation. I mean these factory management people; they must be telling their families in America and England that Sri Lankan women are sexually promiscuous," one landlord said spitting betle cud onto the ground. According to many landladies, being a boardinghouse manager is hard because they have to protect both the young women from loiterers and the area's young men from the women. "If I do not keep my third eye open, one of them will catch my own man under my eyes," one landlady commented. An elderly man who traveled to the Katunayake area to oversee a bicycle repair shop said, "If you have spare time, give these young men an education to stay away from those women. There is nothing left to save in those women. The day they left their mother and father they forgot their culture. That's when the [cultural] destruction started."

In formal conversations, these neighbors drew heavily on the popular discourses on women's purity and sexuality in "othering" the FTZ workers. Any outsider (including journalists and researchers) asking questions prompt them to start drawing from popularized forms of nationalist discourses on women and cultural purity. This in its turn contributes to the ongoing discursive constructions on women as deserving censure because they are morally degenerate and deserving sympathy, as they are also the victims of forces outside their control. However, it should be noted that in practice boardinghouse owners and neighbors are quite understanding of women's need for a social life and allow flexibility in boardinghouse rules. In arguments among themselves, neighboring boardinghouse owners swapped insults about whose girls were more promiscuous. In these situations, landladies vehemently defended their boarders' moral character and projected good moral character as an expression of their own selves as women who uphold traditional cultural norms above financial consideration.

The opinions of neighbors, boardinghouse owners, factory officials, and politicians showed how closely related gender and nationalist discourses are. Women's honor and purity still seem to be taken as an indication of the nation's purity and pride. Consequently, the gradual erosion of women's morality is equated with the nation's downfall. My examination of speeches by politicians, factory officials, landlords, and neighbors, as well as writings by NGO officials and media representations, demonstrates the way these agents produce multilayered complex meanings that create and re-create images for FTZ workers using the historical discursive constructions of an ideal woman as a basis. Made mostly by middle-class representatives of capitalist institutions, these speeches target the Sinhala Buddhist middle class, which has long prided itself on being the guardian of nation and national culture. The flow of ideas between official and popular representations contributes to a complex array of discourses that become part of the panopticon surveying women at the intersection of gender, class, and sexuality.

Discourses surely affect the shaping of women's sense of self. However, they also maneuver for agency and negotiate alternative identities in everyday social interactions at different sites. The following chapters will examine the processes of reproducing already-constructed identities as well as the negotiation of alternative identities as expressed and performed in expressive cultural practices and everyday social interactions.

Chapter 3

On the Shop Floor

The Suishin workers were already lined up according to their assembly lines in the space between Floor 2 and the final quality-control (QC) section when I arrived. The factory officers stood right across the aisle facing the workers. An eerie silence ensued and Sanuja, the Floor 1 production coordinator, took two steps forward and uttered about three sentences in Japanese. Then a young woman wearing a red apron stepped out from one line and, in Japanese fashion, bowed from the waist while flaring her skirt as in a European woman's curtsy. She said one sentence in Japanese. Then all the workers bowed the same way; their waists bent, their skirts flared. Some officers responded with slight nods while others just stood watching. A loud score of music was played and the workers hurried across the floor in many directions. The time was exactly 8:30 A.M. and within five seconds everybody was settled at his or her machine or worktable.

"Japanese managers insist on this ritual. We follow it so faithfully. I mean, this is no different from lighting a lamp for Buddha in the morning. Just to start the day with a good heart. Those Japanese words were greetings for good morning and a good day," Sanuja, who accompanied me to the morning ritual on my very first day at work, explained.

"Why was it that the workers' greeting lines were shorter than your own greeting?" I asked while walking toward the stores with Sanuja.

"Well, I don't know Japanese, so I cannot help you with that," Sanuja answered apologetically.

"What is the meaning of a greeting if you don't understand the language?" The question shot out of my mouth before I could catch myself.

"Don't say that. The ritual is good. It makes us always remember that we all are working toward the same goal," a somewhat annoyed Sanuja said.

However, for the seven months that I was a part of this ritual, it represented for me a reiteration of authority and subservience. Because the workers were overwhelmingly women and all except three factory officers were male, the ritual also manifested the gendered dimensions of power relations, and I avoided it whenever I could.

The morning ritual was not the only marker of gendered power relations that was displayed around Suishin or inscribed on women's bodies. Yet, on this very factory floor young migrant women encountered capitalist industrial regimes and learned to respond to these new situations by negotiating contextual identities. Everyday social interactions and expressive practices are spaces where ongoing negotiations of alternative identities take place. In this chapter, I focus on such spaces within the shop floor to show how workers create and negotiate their identities—resisting, appropriating, transforming, and re-creating the images constructed for and about them in dominant discourses.

I seek to show that as rural young women learn to become FTZ assembly-line workers, they develop an overarching work identity and rudimentary forms of proletariat consciousness. But this new understanding as industrial workers coexists with a constantly configuring complex of intertwined strains of conventional perceptions such as age, class, caste, and other aspects of Sinhala Buddhist cultural perceptions. These strains of consciousness enable the workers to negotiate several subject positions within the shop floor as daughter, sister, girlfriend, confidante, and political activist. Their movement among these positions is tactical or at times even strategic and women negotiated and enacted the best possible stance according to the specific relation of power with which they were faced. It is through these negotiations that workers complicated notions of discipline, resistance, consciousness, and identity.

All the Small Parts

I had my first leisurely look at the Suishin shop floor from the North entrance side. I surveyed the scene for a few minutes while waiting by the door for Sanuja to join me. What I saw reminded me of a huge machine with many tiny parts moving in different directions to perform whatever it is that the enormous apparatus was supposed to perform. The individual workers; their machines; and the separate lines, sections and divisions were all rolled into one space called the shop floor. Disoriented by this crowded, constantly moving, noisy environment, I was happy to let Sanuja give me a tour of the production floors before even thinking about working in one assembly line. Until this first visit to the Suishin shop floor, I had considered entering boardinghouses and making friends among residents the hardest part of my fieldwork experience. The seemingly chaotic shop floor generated doubts as to whether I

would ever be able to learn anything about individual machine operators who seemed such a miniscule part of the whole machinery of producing garments. It is to find some form of structure (or to discover how
all the small parts fit into the big picture) that I gleefully agreed to be
taken around and given the formulaic introduction to the production
process.

Production Process and the Factory Layout

"This is where everything starts," Sanuja declared as we entered the
store. It was a long room with rolls of fabric and other materials stacked
to the roof. The heavy jacket material in blue, beige, and cream dominated the room. The store, which was staffed entirely by men, led to a
large room that held the cutting section.[1] When a particular roll of fabric was first brought into the cutting section it was tested by putting it
through a large machine that subjected the fabric to water, steam,
scrunching, and stretching. This function and the fuseling (pasting a
special material onto the cloth that was to be used for collars and buttonholes) were done entirely by women workers. Because the glue used
in fuseling was toxic, these workers were supposed to wear protective
covering over their mouths and noses. However, none of the workers
wore any covering. When I asked them why, workers said the protective
covering made it difficult to breathe.

The next function in the production process was marking. There were
two long tables on which white paper was laid, and two workers, a
woman and a man, drew patterns on the paper using pattern blocks.
These blocks were drawn at the sample room under the watchful eyes of
Japanese pattern maker/designer Kimura san. The sample room was located between the two shop floors where women cut and sewed "sample
garments" for buyers and the assembly lines. After these samples were
perfected and approved by the buyers, the blocks were sent to the markers. The markers' job was to use these blocks to mark the white paper
and not allow even an inch of fabric to go to waste. It required much
thinking, training, and dexterity to use the blocks in the most efficient
way.

When markers finished the layout for the fabric, the white papers
were pinned to the hundreds of layers of fabric laid out on cutting tables. The cutters then used cutting machines to simultaneously cut hundreds of pieces of cloth. Except for one woman, all the cutters were
men. The management justified this imbalance by pointing to the
greater physical strength needed to maneuver the heavy cutting machines. Several cutters wore cloth over their noses and mouths to protect

them from the dust created by bulk cutting. The cutters were also supposed to wear gloves to protect their hands, although no one did.

Women workers, however, engaged in other work associated with cutting, such as layering (laying the rolls of fabric on cutting tables) and moving the cut pieces to labeling tables. Women workers stood around two tables and labeled bundles of cut pieces to ensure that the finished product would be made from a single layer of fabric. This was necessary because the colors started to change once the fabric unfolded for hundreds of yards. Even though the change in color was slight, workers had to ensure that the garment was of uniform quality. The job of labeling appeared particularly tedius, as the workers stood all day and used a small device to continuously paste a little number onto the bundles of cut pieces. The cutting-room quality controllers, who checked the cut pieces for minor mistakes, were mostly women. Three clerks—two women and a man—documented supplies, workers' attendance, and workers' leave. The cutting manager was in charge of all this work and was assisted by three male supervisors.

After labeling, the cut pieces would be fed to the different assembly lines. There were seven assembly lines (A, B, C, E, F, G, H) distributed among two production sections. Floor 1, located in the large area adjacent to the cutting section, housed lines A, B, C, and E. Lines F, G, and H were located on Floor 2 and both sections operated under officers called "floor coordinators." Lines were organized in a "U" shape with the machines arranged one in front of the other. The line work usually started with the collar work and then progressed onward. The first operator sat with her back to the aisle and the machines were arranged in front of her to the back wall of the building. Then the line made a U-turn to proceed the other way with operators now facing the aisle. In addition to sewing machines, each line contained one or two overlock machines. I later came to know that overlock machines needed to be operated by skilled and experienced workers. Each line had an issue girl, a worker responsible for bringing the numbered bundles of cut pieces to the lines.

Each line also had a production assistant who was in charge of the line, a supervisor, an assistant supervisor, and a line leader. The former three were directly responsible for achieving the set targets and, therefore, prodded the workers to work harder and faster. A plastic box, called "wild box," stood by each machine and the cut pieces were kept in this box. When an operator finished her part of the sewing, she would give it to the worker in front of her to complete the next step. Operators usually waited until there were about five sewn garments before passing them to the next worker. The ironing tables were arranged next to the U-shaped lines and women workers ironed out wrinkles on the newly sewn seams and pockets. The machine operators sat at their machines all day; the ironers had to stand all day. The relentless work pace allowed the workers only a little time to engage in other activities, and the women stitched or ironed with their heads bent over the garments.

After the last sewing machine, three or four trimmers stood around a table and took the labels out and trimmed the thread ends. The QC desk was located after the trimmers' table, and the line's quality controller checked the lengths and sewing quality of the garments. A board on the QC desk provided information about the garment type and pattern, the expected hourly target, and the actual hourly production, which was noted each hour by a factory clerk. When the checked garments piled up near the QC table, they were wheeled to the *matome* section,[2] where the buttonholes were sewn and buttons attached. This section was smaller and a supervisor and an assistant supervisor oversaw the work. *Matome* workers operated in a somewhat more-relaxed environment than their assembly-line colleagues did. Unlike the assembly-line workers, the *matome* workers enjoyed a variety of physical movements. The next stop for the garments was the Final Quality Control section, and there the QC manager, an auditor, and several other women QCs checked the garments one final time. They often found mistakes that had escaped the line QC inspection and sent the garments back to the respective lines. Line supervisors considered these returned garments a disruption because by this time the line was reorganized to produce a different style of garment. This resulted in heavy criticism, and the workers responsible for these mistakes (called damages) were often verbally abused.

From the final QC section, the garments were sent to the ironing section. This section contained nine big ironing machines, and all but one of the ironers were men. These machines were different from the ones used by the line ironers and required greater strength to operate. Because the ironing was performed at a fast pace, a high level of efficiency was required, and these ironers got paid more than machine operators or line ironers. Once ironed, the garments were ready to be packed and shipped. The next section, located on the other corner of the long, one-story factory building, was called the packing section. Women in this section, working under the supervision of men, packed garments into plastic bags, labeled the bags, and prepared them to be loaded into containers for shipping. Mr. Douglas, the finish manager, was in charge of both the ironing and packing sections.

The building also had a medical center located in a long, narrow room between Floors 1 and 2, which employed two nurses who examined workers who came to the center complaining of different ailments. The meal hall was located in an extension to the main factory building and sometimes served as a gathering place for the rare educational events and the company-sponsored New Year party. This annex also consisted of workers' restrooms and their lockers. Although the factory was supposedly fully air-conditioned, the temperature at particular places depended on what kind of machines were in use at the time. While certain areas, especially the cutting and ironing sections, were warm, some workers complained about extreme cold because the air conditioners were located near their machines.

After the factory tour, Sanuja took me to the cubicles reserved for time-study officers and further explained workday rituals and other matters. All of these became familiar to me as my work at Suishin progressed. The beginning and end of the workday were signaled by blaring music at 8:00 A.M. and 5:00 P.M. There was a tea break at 3:00 P.M. Those working overtime were given another tea break at 6:00 P.M. Following the afternoon tea break, the music played[3] and a production assistant announced "off time" and "overtime" information for each line. The cutting and *matome* sections generally finished work at 5:00 P.M., while the assembly lines went on until either 7:00 P.M. or 9:00 P.M. Sometimes several lines had to work until 9:00 P.M., while the other lines finished at either 5:00 P.M. or 7:00 P.M. Workers signing off at 9:00 P.M. were given dinner packets to take home with them. They were also given transport to the closest lane or avenue to their boardinghouse.

The starting salary for workers was Rs. 3,000 ($30) per month. Overtime work paid one-and-a-half times the hourly rate. The workers had fourteen days of leave per year. Several no-pay leave days were also allowed before absenteeism was countered through warning letters. In addition to an attendance incentive (Rs. 200 for a month of attendance without leave), there were also several production-target incentives (for example, Rs. 200 for all workers of the line that achieved the highest efficiency rate for the month, as well as other informal treats, such as ice cream or chocolate). Several times, I was able to observe the salary distribution and noticed that the women's monthly salaries ranged between Rs. 2,800 and Rs. 5,300.

Dress Codes and Gendered Discipline

"This is the reason, miss," Niluka started to explain when I asked why workers are wearing various colored aprons over their dresses with matching head scarves. "This is how you can say whether a worker is a trainee, a supervisor, or an assistant supervisor. Now, I am wearing this blue apron with the yellow stripe on the chest. That shows that I am a lowly worker and I have no power here." Laughing, Niluka pointed to another worker and said, "Now that *nangi* (little sister) is wearing a blue apron without a yellow stripe. That means she is even more lowly than we are. She is a trainee."

Niluka stood up and looked around her before turning back to tell me, "Now Kamali—there she is standing by the target board over there—has a yellow apron because she is an assistant supervisor. But Pushla is supervisor Grade 3, so she wears a purple one. Each line has a yellow apron and a purple apron and of course the purple can yell at the yellow." The workers around Niluka, who could hear her description, were laughing while still bent over their machines sewing.

"But I saw somewhere an avocado green apron," I said, prompting her for more information. "Oh, yes, they are the special ones. There are only two for the whole floor. They are supervisor Grade 2. And then there is one bright orange apron. She is the one who says the greeting at the morning ritual. She is supervisor Grade 1. She is the highest ranked among the workers." I then asked why men in similar positions did not wear aprons or head scarves as women did. "Ahh! They are very special around here. It is one man for about fifty women," Niluka countered, but I knew that she just noticed that this was the case. Several lines had one or two men machine operators and the majority of QC inspectors were men. However, none of these men wore aprons. This extended to cutters and the male supervisors in the cutting section. The only woman final ironer wore a blue apron, while the men did not. The same was the case with men and women workers in the final QC and finish sections.

Instead, all the men workers, including machine operators, wore neat long-sleeved shirts tucked into well-tailored pants accompanied by leather shoes and belts. The cutting supervisors and the production assistants especially seemed to follow all the latest fashions in Colombo and were very well dressed. In contrast, women workers almost dressed down. Although one or two young women on the shop floor might be over-dressed on any given day, most wore simple home-sewn dresses made of cheap material with rubber slippers on their feet. Usually when workers went to the fair or on any other outing, they wore beautiful dresses and fancy sandals or shoes. "There is no point in wearing good dresses to work, miss. As soon as we come here we need to cover the nice dress with the apron. What I hate the most is that we have to put the hair up in a knot and then put the scarf on. It is impossible to keep a good "bump" with scarves,"[4] Mangala explained.

Because the rule on aprons and head scarves did not apply to male workers, one could rule out prevention of industrial accidents as the reason for requiring them to be worn. Writing about factory discipline in Bangladesh, Dina Siddiqi (1996) notes that the apron and scarf requirement was instituted more to establish order and uniformity than for safety. She also notes how loose and unruly hair was discouraged and the restrictions focused on a connection between loose hair and female malevolent spirits as well as prostitution (151). In Sri Lanka, too, the female seductress spirit, Mohini, appeared in untidy, loose hair to seduce unsuspecting male victims. Supervisors sometimes used the term "Mohini" to insult a worker who wore her hair loose. Two possible assumptions could have resulted in this gendered dress code: first, the FTZ working women (rural, lower class) are more frivolous in their clothing and hairstyles and, therefore, needed to be kept under more control; second, the "unruly, undisciplined native/rural women" would be more easily made into industrial workers through such forced and gendered uniformity.[5] The dress codes marked a gendered category of workers for stricter body control and resulted in an unspoken understanding that the men workers of the same status had more power than women workers.

Workers learned how to subvert the apron and head-scarf requirement in a way that would not earn them a serious reprimand. "When I want to show off a new dress, I wear it and jewelry, high heels, and everything but without the apron. When [the managers] ask about the apron, I tell them that I took the apron home to wash it and forgot to bring it back. If you don't use this excuse too often, you can work without the apron for that day. This does not happen often. Many of us try to work without wearing the scarf at least once a week. I mean, we are young girls, we like to show off our long beautiful hair, so we wear it loose or in a bump. Managers hate loose hair and they inquire when they see us wearing our hair loose. But if I say that I washed my hair today and that I will get sinus problems if I wear it in a knot before it gets dry, they go away murmuring to themselves," explained Rena, while taking a playful, secretive look in the direction of Pushla. During my time there, I noticed that this culturally meaningful reason for wearing one's hair loose was almost always accepted, albeit grudgingly.

Food and Power

Dress was not the only space that was marked with gender and class codes. The lunch packet the factory gave its workers, staff, and managers was also a stage where the factory hierarchy was reenacted everyday. The type of food provided in a lunch packet, where lunch was served, what table a worker sat at, how a worker ate, and whether a worker had to wait in line until a seat at a table opened up displayed the factory's power hierarchy akin to an organizational chart.

The office building consisted of two main areas: one with glass cubicles for different office sections and the other a large room that was the executive parlor. One corner of the large room held a small kitchen. It was in this executive parlor that I had my lunch during the first few days at Suishin. Although I expressed my desire to eat at the workers' meal hall, Shanil, the finance manager who helped me get into the factory, suggested firmly that I have lunch with the managers to cultivate the goodwill that was needed to pursue my research at the factory. I sat at a table with Gamini, the deputy managing director; Perera, the human resources manager; Kasun, the shipping manager; Jayantha, the production manager; and Shanil. Younger factory officers like Sanuja, Ashen, Indika, and Isuru, whose designated title was junior executive, sat at the next table. The seating arrangement concerned me because I felt alienated not only from the workers but also from the junior executives whose support seemed just as important as that of the workers and top management.[6] Interestingly, the Japanese managing director, Ando san, did not join the Sri Lankan executives for breakfast or lunch. He and the Japanese designer, Kimura san, ate at the Airport Garden Hotel, a five-star tourist hotel located near the FTZ. Everybody who ate at the factory consumed lunch packets provided by the company, but while the people who ate in the executive parlor used forks and knives to eat their pricier lunches, the clerks ate cheaper lunches inside the kitchen using their fingers. Some of the junior executives struggled with the cutlery and many of them later confided that they would rather use their fingers, although no one dared do that. The workers also got the cheaper lunch packets, with a choice of fish or chicken.

After I got to know several Line C workers better, I asked them whether I could eat with them at the workers' meal hall. I was alarmed by the left/right power symbolism in place, whereby the smaller, well-dressed group walked down the same aisle but turned right to go to the office building while the others turned left for the meal hall. Kamali agreed to take me but was concerned about the seating arrangement. Only when we were there did I realize the reason: The meal hall was hierarchically organized as well and there was a separate long table by the distribution counter that was reserved for the middle- and lower-level factory staff—production assistants, supervisors, and factory clerks. Then there were rows of tables and chairs for workers. Because I wanted to sit with the workers, the supervisor directed me to a chair in the workers' section. I instantly regretted sitting there when the supervisor asked a young woman, who usually sat there, to wait until I was done. In fact, there was a shortage of ten to fifteen seats in the meal hall and some of the new workers, mostly trainees, had to wait until others finished their meals.

For this reason, I decided that it was best to eat at the junior executives' table where I did not delay a worker from enjoying her well-earned lunch. I ate at the meal hall two more times when invited by supervisors, who shooed away a worker to find a place for me. Even though I made very close friends with some workers, they never invited me to come and eat with them or encouraged me when I said I would rather eat with them. At the tea break, however, I usually went to the meal hall with the workers and talked to them while they drank tea. Because many workers sat outside on the lawn during the fifteen-minute tea break, rather than fighting to get a cup of tea, a seat was not hard to find.

On the days they worked overtime until 9:00 P.M., the workers were given tea and biscuits at 6:00 P.M. Workers pushed and pulled at each other to get at the biscuit boxes and expressed their unhappiness with the way the biscuits were distributed. Showing their displeasure, they sometimes used the biscuits to poke fun at the officers. Always concerned about finding "interesting facts" for my book, Niluka once summoned me to where she was sitting and showed two biscuits, one a vanilla creme and one chocolate. She then put the chocolate biscuit on the table and said, "This is Sanuja sir." Then, moving the vanilla biscuit toward the other, she said, "Here comes Indika miss." By this time, the crowd around us was roaring with laughter. Then she opened another vanilla creme biscuit and showed everyone the white creme on the underside of one biscuit. "Here comes our Priyanka." Niluka moved it tantalizingly close to the chocolate biscuit, swaying it a bit to imitate Priyanka's walk. Then she pushed the first vanilla biscuit with one finger and announced, "There goes Indika miss down the *pallan* [precipice]." Realizing suddenly what she was alluding to, I let out a surprised, "Ohh-hhhh!" which seemed to satisfy everyone around, and they enthusiastically provided me more information on how the arrival of Priyanka, a Line C worker, had dashed any hopes Indika, a junior executive, had for starting a romantic relationship with Sanuja.

Oppositional Consciousness and Negotiation of Identities: Everyday Social Interactions

Line C

During my first few days at the factory, I walked from line to line talking with any worker who had earned some spare time by working faster. After a few days, I realized that it was more useful to spend time with one line getting to know its workers and supervisors. I chose Line C as my primary observation site for several reasons. First, Sanuja offered his table located beside Line C to me if I needed it; second, the Line C workers had already won me over with their particularly warm smiles and greetings. Line C's production assistant, Sanka, also captured my attention because he closely resembled the supervisors described in the

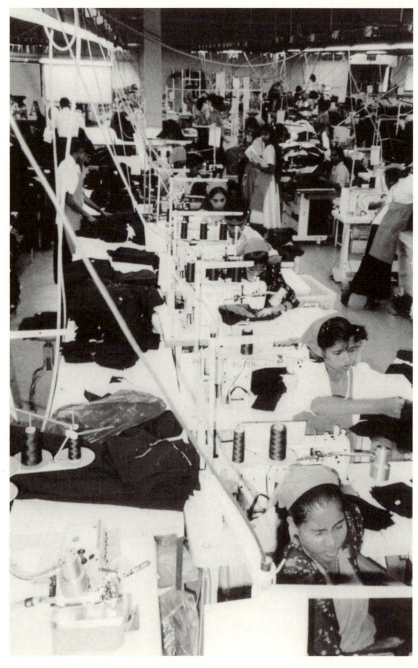

Figure 1. Line C. Photograph by the author.

media. Line C supervisor Pushla encouraged me with her friendly attitude. Because the supervisor had more time to talk to me, she became the person through whom I first contacted Line C. Fortunately, this did not hamper my relations with the machine operators and, in fact, made it easier for them to engage in conversation with me when they were not supposed to. However, as my relationships with Line C workers advanced, my relationship with Pushla deteriorated significantly.

I was first able to become friends with the few workers whose machines were located closest to the table. I gradually started to walk down the two rows of assembly-line machines and the line of irons and talk with whomever dared respond or had earned a little spare time. The few outspoken workers seemed always to be a minute or two ahead of the others and actively sought out my association, and we became good friends. While all forty-five workers belonging to Line C became my friends and were proud and boastful about my association with them, about twenty workers became close friends. Some women from other lines and sections actively sought my friendship and eventually became close friends as well. I will trace the relationships I developed with the workers in Line C through the accounts of subaltern cultures and political activities. Notes of my observations at Line C present an unfolding drama of everyday work and power relations. They show how workers carved little spaces for themselves within strict rules by manipulating industrial work ethics and cultural ideals for Sinhala Buddhist rural women. Most of the everyday struggles of the women occurred as confrontations with the male production assistant and the female supervisor and did not extend to higher officials. Yet these struggles amply highlighted the way women workers configure their work identities within power-laden discourses.

Subaltern Work Cultures

"This is how it happened, miss," Vasanthi started after silencing several others who also wanted to relate the story. When I was finishing my lunch at the executive meal hall that day, Samanthie, an office clerk, called me to the kitchen and asked whether I had had time yet to talk to the workers about why they stopped eating with forks and knives as the Japanese factory owners wanted them to. This intrigued me because Sri Lankans usually eat with their fingers, but Samanthie refused to provide more details and told me, "Ask the workers. They are the ones who know. And tell us what their story is."

When I broached the subject that afternoon, the workers became quite animated. "The Japanese didn't like it that we ate with our fingers," Vasanthi continued with obvious delight. "They thought the food smell would get into the fabric. It is like these stupid Japanese had never heard of soap. No, it is just to make our lives miserable. I hated eating with forks and knives. *Ane* miss, we come from villages. What forks and knives for us? At 12:00 noon we are hungry and God has given us two hands and ten fingers. Why go to war with forks and knives? Many of us hated this. I did not know who started this. But we started throwing cutlery down the drain or dropping them in wastebaskets after eating. In the beginning, we didn't think anything will come of it. We were just angry having to use the cutlery because nobody can enjoy food with cutlery and we were half hungry everyday," said Vasanthi making a face that indicated her unhappiness with the situation.

I interrupted and asked Vasanthi who first asked her to throw the cutlery in the trash. "Nobody asked me. I heard that others were doing it. So I did it, too. I did it about once a week for about two years, but I haven't seen anyone else doing it. Not that I would tell anyone even if I had seen it. But every month supervisors and factory managers pleaded with us not to do that since it is costing so much money to keep buying new cutlery. Then about two years ago, they stopped replacing forks and knives and provided us with more soapdishes. Now, thanks to all that thrown cutlery, we can enjoy what we are eating," Vasanthi concluded on a jubilant note.

The workers sometimes used collective resistance to turn situations in their favor. But collective action was rare and involved much risk. More frequent were the everyday acts of resistance and displays of oppositional consciousness in workers' daily interactions with the factory staff. The popular perception of garment factory supervisors is of mean, abusive men and women wielding absolute power over the workers who just take all the abuse. Accounts of transnational factory staff being controlling, oppressive, and sexually exploitative have been published throughout the world, especially with regard to Mexico (Pena 1997; Prieto 1997). Suishin workers, however, participated daily in demonstrating how they were participants in a constantly fluctuating series of power relations and not just meek victims of despotic power. As they engaged in the politics of shaping the work culture, the workers also resisted structures of domination and discursive constructions in a mutually constitutive process of gender- and work-identity formation.

Learning to Subvert

"Where did you go? Who gave you permission to go? Do you think this is your daddy's factory to come and go as you please? Go to your seat and do not even think about getting up until the tea break," Pushla

screamed at Bindu who had just returned from an apparently unautho-
rized visit to the restroom.

Embarrassed and close to tears, Bindu, a relatively new worker, countered, "But I have seen others doing that. Why, about half an hour ago
this Sujatha *akka* went to the restroom and she didn't tell anyone." Di-
recting Bindu toward her seat with a finger pointed high in the air, an
even more enraged Pushla yelled, "You cannot have 'such powers' as
soon as you start work." Then in an apparent jibe at the experienced
workers, she continued, "Only people who have grown old here (*at-
takuna vechcha*) could do that."

The jibe hit the mark as several experienced workers who were mostly
placed within the middle of the left and right lines of the U-shaped Line
C became agitated. While Pushla strategically moved to the front of the
line, I moved closer to the workers to hear their reactions. "This Pushla
can't stand us. You may have already noticed how Perera san, Kasun sensei, and everybody likes us. She hates us for that. Why? Because she cannot then rule this line like a queen. Because if she shouts at me I go
directly to Perera san and he shouts at her for making me unhappy," Vasanthi informed me with a smug smile on her face.

"If you do not sew 'damages' [make mistakes that damage the gar-
ment] and do your job right, then nobody can control you. Those
managers want us. It is not easy to find good workers like us and that
makes these supervisors so jealous," Mangala joined in from two machines away. "Now this Batti, she does the overlock machine. If she
leaves tomorrow, can they get anyone else and ask them to sew like
her? Will not happen. It takes time to learn how to sew right, find mistakes, and even help the supervisors find how a damage starts," continued Mangala, pointing to Batti who worked at the more difficult
overlock machine.

"This is the situation, miss. Workers come and go. They don't stay, so
it is difficult for factories to find experienced, good workers. You were
commenting just yesterday about notices in front of factories asking for
machine operators. So even managers have to work hard to keep us
here," Vasanthi explained, putting a bundle of finished waistbands on
my hands. By then I had also noticed that management was treading a
fine line when applying rules and punishing workers, especially skilled
workers. Thus, experienced and skilled workers in specialized positions
gained some agency and power.

As a result, the application of disciplinary measures regarding breaks,
dress codes, and other movements varied considerably according to
workers' seniority and level of work efficiency. It took some time for new
workers to realize these double standards, and part of being socialized
into a full-fledged Suishin worker involved learning when and how to

subvert rules without trespassing the informal limits for workers with different experience and skills. New workers learned by observing and socializing with senior workers. This process included learning to subvert rules, which was a major factor in forming work identities in relation to the immediate supervisory staff and everyday work relations.

Line C had about ten experienced, valued workers who were well aware of their worth and thus enjoyed unspoken privileges. While many workers did not let a remark from the supervisory staff go without an acid retort, the experienced workers at times outrightly defied the supervisors and often engaged in verbal battles with the staff about the latter's treatment of other workers. Because of their experience, they worked faster and had more time to talk among themselves and with me. However, they were vigilant about the production pace and helped around the line as work piled up around other workers. They solved simple production problems within the line without the supervisors' involvement and actively helped the supervisors troubleshoot problems. Although several less accomplished workers also talked and joked with executive officers and me, they did so by risking the displeasure of the line supervisors. Experienced workers, however, were able to talk to several junior officers and develop a close friendship with me without getting into such trouble. These alliances brought workers a certain power and, consequently, aroused insecurities among line supervisors.

Each new worker learned to create a delicate balance between subversion and conformity through socializing at the factory.[7] By learning to subvert the factory rules, new workers learned to subscribe to a general worker identity that situated them against the factory rules and supervisors. However, workers manipulated differently the skill to subvert, thereby negotiating specific, contextual identities for themselves. During the seven months of research, I closely watched four new workers going through this process on a trial-and-error basis. They learned how to properly address personnel as well as which other workers to consult for advice about Suishin factory life. Soon all four workers joined "lunch groups"[8] and learned how to subvert disciplinary measures, interact with the staff and other workers, and adopt popular language and dress styles. Even those who had previously worked in other FTZ factories had to resocialize themselves into the specific Suishin shop-floor culture.

A major part of the informal education the experienced workers provided focused on becoming aware of the exploitative working conditions, learning the value of being united against the supervisors, and fighting for worker rights on a daily basis. Usually workers supported experienced workers in their struggles with the supervisors, but whether they totally bought into the specific worker identity that the experienced group espoused depended on many factors, such as the duration of

Figure 2. Line C: Close-up. Photograph by the author.

their employment (the shorter the time the more they felt bound by cultural teachings of obedience), the lunch group they joined, and the individual's capacity to develop into a skilled worker. Rather, many workers drew from all those cultural and social discourses and identified with different stances as best suited the situation.

Tyrant of the Line, Father of the Children

> Sanka went rushing down the line to Mangala's machine. He folded the damaged garment and hit her with it and stood staring down with his hands on his hips. Mangala slowly bent down and picked up the garment. Then she folded it back and hit Sanka's face with tremendous force. Red faced, Sanka hurried down the line yelling at another worker.

My research notes on Line C were replete with entries like this one, which showed that the women were not meek victims of supervisors' aggression but responded to dehumanizing working conditions with actions and words. They did not let Sanka's accusations go unanswered and at times got into heated verbal duels with him. When new workers chose to be silent, others urged them to speak up or they themselves took up the fight with Sanka or Pushla. Sanka's voice usually boomed over the general din of the factory as he yelled commands to his workers. The other production assistants did not shout like Sanka, who seemed to be constantly berating his workers. The very process of industrial production situated the supervisors and workers in two camps as the supervisors' efficiency depended on achieving the target production. This required the supervisors to urge workers to work fast and prohibit them from focusing on anything other than their work. Because Sanka was especially obnoxious, I felt sad that Line C workers had him as their production assistant.

I was surprised, therefore, to be informed that the workers cried and begged the managers not to transfer Sanka to another line. But after a few weeks at the line, I realized the contradictory feelings they held toward Sanka and also many other officers. While they resented him for the way he treated them, they also had developed affectionate feelings toward him based on culturally meaningful reason such as class and caste and beauty ideals.

"*Ane*, to tell you, miss, when I first came to work here I almost fell in love with Sanka and Sanuja sir. I mean they are beautiful and they sounded so nice in the beginning. Not only me, many girls felt the same way toward them in the beginning. It takes time for one to realize that their only goal is to work us to death [*marawala hari*]," Rena once said. In fact, many workers' everyday interactions with Sanka and other supervisors were characterized by these opposing emotions and became the site where they acquired consciousness as exploited industrial workers. This class consciousness, however, existed alongside other strains of consciousness such as religion, gender, and caste. These intertwined strains of consciousness figured into their everyday lives on the shop floor and influenced the way they negotiated identities.

"Sanka is a handsome and beautiful 'boy.' He must have scores of girls after him," Vasanthi once speculated. This prompted many workers to join the conversation and affirm that they also thought him fair and beautiful. Fairness of skin is valued in Sri Lanka and over the past century it had become an essential part of what constitutes beauty among the Sinhala Buddhist.[9] Sanka's skin was fair and he was a good-looking young man. While criticizing him mercilessly for his obnoxious behavior, the workers could not help but be attracted to him. Although a major part of the workers' critique was to construct a difference and a social gap between themselves and Sanka, part of their attraction stemmed from this very social gap. They talked endlessly about his family and how his parents were professionals and how Sanka drove the family car and how his mother protected him from girls because "he is a fair, beautiful boy."

"With all his nastiness, one good thing I like about Sanka is that he eats whatever we give him without showing off his highness [*lokukama*; class pride] and refusing to eat. We all belong to the Govigama caste, that is true. But most of us are from poor, rural families. Other people will worry about whether these foods are clean or washed. Sanka doesn't think twice but eats anything we offer," Vasanthi once told me while looking to see where Sanka was to offer some fruits she had brought to work. Although not strictly followed, an important aspect of the Sri Lankan caste system is the taboos on sharing food with lower castes. There also were more latent reservations about eating from lower-class households because of prejudices dealing with cleanliness, and workers appreciated whenever the officers blurred the caste or class boundaries.

"He loves to eat home-cooked food. He is boarded near here and eats from restaurants everyday. So he begs me to bring a rice-and-curry parcel for him when I come back after visiting my village. He especially likes what my mother cooks. The other day I brought a rice parcel for Kumudu in the other line because she is pregnant. And this guy [Sanka] snatched it before I could give it to her," said Vasanthi with an indulgent smile. Both Kamali and Chandani then joined the conversation to tell me that he loves the rice parcels that they brought also.

In Sinhala households, girl children are socialized into caring for their menfolk from a young age. In these discussions, the women showed a motherly concern and kindness for the supervisor who constantly pushed them beyond limits in his demand for more production. Once when Sanka injured his finger while trying to repair a machine, the workers surrounded him and attended to his wound. Several shed tears when he came back from the medical center with a dressing on his finger.[10]

Although at times they appeared to be mothering him, at other times the workers accorded Sanka undisputed leadership over them and called him father of the children (*lamayinge thaththa*), though he was only a few years older than they.[11] "*Aiyo*, how could we go on a line trip without you? You are the father of this line," said Amitha, who was at least five years older than Sanka, when trying to persuade him to join a trip. "This is one *good* father of the children. We had to protect him from other girls the last time we went on a line trip," Chandani, who was standing near Sanka, said while giving a half indulgent, half flirtatious tug at his sleeve. Sanka blushed and stole a glance toward me while warning, "Be careful, girls. Sandya will write everything."

Once the management decided to temporarily break up Line C to solve a production backlog on Floor 2. Line C was in the usually slow-paced transitional state from one garment to the other and was in a position to spare workers. Soon after the angry and reluctant sixteen workers were sent to Floor 2, one of them, Amila, came back complaining that she did not even have a stool to sit on. While taking her own stool from Line C, she shouted to Sanka that if he had given his workers away he should have also provided what they needed to work with dignity. While I was thinking how similar that was to a statement a daughter would make about the father's choice of a marital home for her and the lack of dowry, Sanka seemed truly perturbed by the new events. When a few minutes later the Floor 2 coordinator came to ask for machines and supplies, Sanka, showing his own possessiveness toward the line, shouted, "Not being satisfied with taking *my children*, now they are asking for *my machines*." After the machines were taken, Line C looked like an abandoned warehouse with empty spaces and boxes strewn around. I asked Sanka whether he felt sad that his line was broken up. He said he was sad and then added, "When we ask them to go, they go while scolding us." This statement specifically aligned him with the managers and demonstrated how he skillfully manipulated connections with both managers and workers in a way that made it easier for him to move between the two spheres.

Niluka's comment made it clear that at least some workers understood this play: "We like him because he is straightforward. He does not keep anything in his heart. These other production assistants keep anger in their hearts and silently strike you, and you don't even know why they do so. When Sanka is angry, he yells and we yell back and then it ends there. It almost feels like it is between friends. But then nobody should forget that the supervisor is a biggie [*lokka*]. They don't feel our pain," Niluka said as she thrashed a sewn cut piece into the wild box by Vasanthi's machine as if to warn others who spoke of Sanka's virtues.

Father Figures and Flirtations

"*Ane* miss, some of our girls have no shame. They like to flirt [*ukulu mukulu*] with the managers, especially those "fair, slim, long haired ones. Biggies gravitate toward them like bees to the honey," Rena complained, and then added in a low voice, "Now take Nishan sir,[12] he just loves to talk to Vasanthi. If he takes photographs of the lines then he zooms in on Vasanthi and she gets in ten more pictures than any one of us. Whenever he visits the lines, he spends much time talking to her." I was intrigued by this information especially since Vasanthi was one of those experienced workers who constantly espoused the need for workers to unite. "But does she like that when Nishan sir pays special attention to her?" I asked, lowering my voice to match hers. "I don't know, but they talk a lot," Rena replied without looking at my face, her cue that I needed to talk to Vasanthi herself about this.

When I asked whether it is true that Nishan sir paid special attention to her, Vasanthi replied, "Yes, he talks too, but Perera san is the one I like the most. He is like a father to me. Even just seeing his kind face in the morning makes me happy. Reminds me of my father. I mean, I know he is one of the managers. But he is different. Kind and gentle." Despite being consciously combative with their immediate supervisors, even the experienced workers could not escape the "charm and wisdom" exuded by Perera san, the elderly human resources manager. He was calm and soothing whenever he talked to workers and many treated him as a father figure. He actively promoted this image by his words and his concern for protecting workers. The affection many workers had for him effectively prevented their criticism targeting managers and directors. Describing gentle exploitation (violence), Bourdieu (1977) writes that exercise of gentle exploitation/violence demands a personal price from its users. Authority, charisma, or grace can inspire confidence, which gives the person who exercises such qualities a protective authority over those who entrust themselves to him (193). Perera's charm, grace, and kindness gave him such authority, which he manipulated in different situations in ways that benefited the managers and the factory.

"Why do you call your supervisors *akka* [elder sister]?" I once asked.

"We are rural people. It is hard for us to address people who are older than us by even a single day by their names," Renu promptly answered, and then added, "We call them *akka, akka*. Then when they try to get us to do more work by calling us *nangi, nangi* (little sister) it is hard to say no."

It was obvious that the workers constantly struggled with their new perspective as exploited workers and their already internalized cultural perceptions as young, unmarried, and rural women. Young Sri Lankan men and women belonging to different age groups, irrespective of their class affiliations, addressed each other using sibling kinship terms in schools and certain workplaces. According to this tradition, Suishin workers usually called female supervisors *akka*. This brought with it a certain closeness and expectation that the workers would obey and respect supervisors as they would their elder sisters. Workers usually found it hard to disobey and disrespect anybody who was older than they and this discomfort was more pronounced regarding older men in authority positions.

"This is the case, miss. When these factory bosses flirt with them, these girls think, 'Oh, he is interested in me and now we will love each other, get married, and be happy.' So they work hard to make the factory boss happy and say 'You good girl, I will marry you.' But they know this love stuff is only dreams. So they have boyfriends elsewhere, too. Still they like to dream about big branches [*loku athu*; rich people]," said Mangala, whose outward image did not in any way conform to the ideal beauty image of the fair, slim factory girl.

Many Sri Lankan women are socialized into thinking that marriage is a means to upward social mobility and they therefore desire relationships and marriages to people from higher social classes even as they dread some of the consequences. If Perera san was able to work his elderly charm on the workers to make them comply with factory rules, younger managers and male factory staff used flirtation to win over women workers. It struck me when I first encountered them how exceptionally handsome and well dressed the men factory staff were. While the officers paid more attention to the "fair, long-haired, and slim" workers, they flirted with everyone they wished to manipulate. Flirtation also helped cultivate general good will among workers and staff. When workers got angry with an officer, a higher-ranked officer would use his charm to soothe the worker, thereby preventing the incident from developing into a problem. While I was at the factory, six workers received special attention from factory officers, ranging from serious flirting to romantic relationships. Five of these six workers chose not to participate in the labor strike that took place in April 2000 and most remained loyal to the factory and the supervisors throughout. Two married managers used charm that bordered on flirtation, but unlike flirtations by unmarried officers these managers did not give workers hopes about serious relationships. Many workers who received such attention, though, expressed pride in their association with the managers. Flirting thus worked as a controlling device on the shop floor.

Buddhist Workers, Sharing Cultures, and Industrial Control

The day the factory reopened after the long New Year vacation in April 2000, I watched the morning ritual (standing alone a few paces behind the line of officers and partially hidden behind some broken machines stacked by the door) and came to Line C holding hands with Rena and Mangala. The workers were busy removing the coverings they had put on their machines before the vacation started. The evening before the vacation started, the workers in every line had carefully cleaned their machines and covered them with plastic bags. Then they covered the racks by their machines and the clothes on them with plastic bags. Finally, they swept the line area before leaving for the vacation. As I started wiping cobwebs from the table where I kept my backpack and sometimes wrote in my notebook, I heard Chamila talking to her machine while carefully taking off the coverings: "Ooohh, were you lonely without me? Did you think of me, too?" she said, as if addressing a baby or puppy even as she lovingly stroked the machine that she sometimes claimed was trying to make her a machine, too. Noticing the half-smile on my face she claimed, "Like seeing a relative after a long time."

Sri Lankans share a general understanding that workers should love and respect their workplace and tools. While subsistence agriculture is fast being replaced by industrial and service jobs, people bring their established cultural understandings to these new spheres. Garment factory workers had only a small opportunity to personalize their spaces. Still, they became attached to their machines, wild boxes, and sewing supplies (bobbins, correcting tools, and pencils). They decorated the machines, wrote their names on wild boxes, carved their names on pencils, and fought hard when they were transferred to other machines or when supplies were given to other workers. They sometimes fought over the tools supplied by the company even though they could obtain new items freely.

Once Menike accused Mangala of borrowing her bobbin and not returning it. Mangala protested, saying that the bobbin belonged to her and that she had carved her name on it in tiny letters. Menike stomped to Mangala's machine, demanding to see it as she also had carved her name on the bobbin. Geethi turned around and admonished both of them, saying, "That bobbin does not belong to either one of you. It is Suishin's property and you have to return it when you leave one day." Menike managed to get the bobbin back and came back, saying, "Mangala must be thinking of taking this bobbin as part of her dowry."

This attachment to factory-owned property inhibited intermittent sabotage of the kind that some factory studies have evidenced (Pena 1997). In an interview I conducted, a BOI officer said that women, unlike men, were naturally responsible about their families and homes and as such would not be led to destructive behavior. The women's nurturing and affectionate relationship with their tools showed that their responses to the industrial working environment could not be fully divorced from Sinhala Buddhist culture.[13]

Workers' happiness in bringing food for male supervisors as well as for pregnant female supervisors also relates to notions of giving and *karma* that pervade the Buddhist worldview. Factory workers, just like other Sri Lankans, loved to offer and share food and normally associated these acts with happiness. They were also concerned about the good *karma* they acquired through giving. The notion of *karma* also sometimes figured into their decisions not to extend their criticism over some acts beyond the line supervisors' level. Once, workers complained consistently for about a week that the new caterer was including spoiled curries in their lunch packets. Mangala complained, "*Ane* miss, we have such a weakling as a production assistant. We told Sanka about a hundred times to go and complain to the human resources office about what this new caterer is doing. He is too scared. He does not want to complain about food, so the managers think he is the one who wants better fare. But if he cannot do that, what good is he?" A number of workers joined this conversation and the many others that ensued later. While criticizing Sanka for his inactivity, they talked endlessly about how they themselves should talk to the human resources office.

Finally, I asked Vasanthi why she would not talk to Perera san since he obviously listened to what she had to say.

"*Apoi* miss, I don't want to be branded as someone who complains about food. Didn't our Lord Buddha say that we should be happy and not complain about what is given free? Didn't he eat anything that was given as alms, and he a member of royalty? Now before you ask, let me tell you, I know that the lunch packet is part of our salary package and not alms. But didn't Buddha show us we should be simple and modest?" Vasanthi asked in an attempt to tap into my own sentiments. However much she used this Buddhist logic to understand the situation, I gathered from other comments that she and the others also feared that complaining would cause the superiors to think they lacked food at home. In fact, when I later presented their grievances at the office, several managers expressed similar thoughts about workers' home meals and about the need to be happy with whatever is given free.

Rather than complain to the relevant authorities and lose face, the workers resorted to wishes of cultural punishments. Reminding themselves that a person who would steal another's meal would go hungry in the next birth, they shared folk stories about kings who owned every good food in the world but could not enjoy their food because of sins committed in previous births. "My little cousin cannot eat rice and curry. My aunt went from temple to temple and made vows at a local shrine for seven days. The eighth day *malli* [little brother] ate some rice. But that was the last time. Now he only eats crisp bread and runs away if he sees rice and curry," Vasanthi explained. These stories satisfied workers with the belief that the caterer would receive his just punishments in his next birth.

The assembly-line work was conducive for creating animosities between the workers and supervisors. Workers constantly fought with the supervisors and regularly expressed the need to fight for their rights as a united front. Supervisors, especially Pushla, resented workers gossiping and harshly scolded them for not working faster. At times, however, the workers' shared beliefs brought them together to undermine the production demands. Kamali, the assistant supervisor, sent a woman away from the line, explaining that the worker had a cyst in the corner of her eye and that she went outside to rub the juice from the *thuththiri* plant on her eye. Then she shouted after the worker saying that she should not talk while applying the juice. According to Pushla, who then joined us, it was no use performing this ritual at noon because the best result could be acquired only by applying it at dawn. Joining the conversation, Amitha said, "I have this skin rash. And I always feel sick. There is no doubt that all this is due to evil eye. I went from doctor to doctor and did test after test, yet they could not find any problem. The only thing now is to do a good lime-cutting ritual." Hearing this, Pushla stopped what she was doing and moving toward Amitha asked, "Have you heard about Suma *Gurunnanse* [ritual specialist]? He is the best for lime cutting on this side of Gampaha." This prompted the workers around Amitha and the two supervisors to engage in a discussion of "evil eye" incidents, healing rituals, and healers.[14]

Once Sanka, Pushla, and several other workers informed me about a ghost that haunted Suishin and about different scary incidents that happened around the factory. Everybody tried to tell their version of the story, giving way to raised voices and abandoned work. This went on until Sanuja came and urged everyone to get back to work. At different times, top managers as well as junior executives took up the same matter. According to one manager, he stopped working alone in the office at nights after both doors to the office building closed on their own. Workers told me that there was an all night *pirith* chanting ceremony[15] to drive away the ghost. When I asked whether this is true, the deputy managing director, Gamini, said that the *pirith* chanting ceremony was held because at one time three Suishin workers died one after the other from different causes. The ceremony was organized to bless the workplace and workers and not specifically to drive away ghosts. This ceremony was reminiscent of Ong's (1987) account of a ritual held in a Malaysian garment factory to drive away the spirits that were attacking its female workforce. The Suishin ceremony was also an example of the way workers and managers both drew from a similar cultural repertoire in responding to the contradictions they faced within industrial capitalist production.

Negotiating Individual Identities

Assembly-line work has been characterized as boring, repetitive, uncreative, and dehumanizing (Pena 1997:3). Contrary to these perceptions, Suishin garment factory workers planned and strategized their work independently. They stitched not only garments but individual working identities and consciousness as a group of marginalized women workers. They did this in response to immediate supervisors and in relation to other workers. Their emerging work identities were expressed not in conventional terms and in conventional situations, such as marches and political rallies, but through performances in social and work interactions at the factory. Moreover, the class consciousness and work identities were not single, unitary fixed wholes but were based on gender, age, class, and caste hierarchical understandings and other Sinhala Buddhist cultural perceptions. It was within these power-laden discourses that the workers negotiated contextual identities through narratives and performances.

INDISPENSABLE REBELS

As stated earlier, each line had a few experienced and skilled workers who had more space to maneuver within the disciplinary measures. In Line C, Niluka, Rena, Vasanthi, Batti, Sujatha, Geethi, Chamila, and Menike were known among other lines and managers for their quality of work as well as for their combative nature. They occupied adjacent machines located in the first row and possessed the skills and the aptitude for problem solving, which earned them grudging respect from their immediate supervisors and admiration from higher officers. There were three other such workers in the second row (Amila, Mangala, and Chandani) but because the former group of workers were located close to each other, they, as a group, had more influence in the socialization process for new workers as well as in defying the supervisors. Nevertheless, their words and actions expressed an intense desire to excel in their work and thereby achieve a powerful and irreproachable status. They advised others that doing so was a prerequisite for defiance and subversion.

Except for Chamila, they all belonged to the same lunch group and they sharpened their work identities at these social meetings. In our discussions at the lunch group, at least five of them clearly expressed a proletarian class consciousness using conventional Marxist terms. However, in everyday conversation, they used the weaker terms "our unity [*ape samagiya*]," "little people" versus "big people" in a sense similar to proletarian consciousness, and worked vigorously within the line to achieve worker unity against the supervisors. As noted earlier, they fought for workers' rights and did not hesitate to take their grievances to officers above the line supervisors. On different occasions, Sujatha, Batti, and Vasanthi directly approached the human resources manager to complain about the supervisors and working conditions. Each time, they were able to turn the situation to their advantage. This bold attitude caused the line supervisors and Sanuja to deal with them carefully. Their expertise and devotion to work distinguished them from the usual rebellious workers. It was through their narratives of excellence and work ethics juxtaposed with rebellious attitudes that they negotiated a unique work identity for themselves as "indispensable rebels," whose work was beyond reproach but whose dignity would not allow them to let any slight to them or "their kind" go unanswered.

VASANTHI: INDISPENSABLE REBEL AND LOVING DAUGHTER

"Miss, I am boarded at my brother-in-law's parents' house. So life is not as hard for me as for workers who are boarded at nonrelatives' houses. I am happy I found this job. This factory is clean. And I like my work. You must have noticed that I am a good worker. I don't make damages. I am one of the most senior workers in this line. It is my idea that we need to learn our craft and excel at it if we want to make demands. That is what I do. I cannot stand injustice. I fight for justice. But nobody can touch me because I am such a good worker. I tell all new workers to become a good worker and then work with your head held high. I don't think work is that hard in this factory," Vasanthi smiled as she said this during a taped interview.

"What I cannot stand is these supervisors treating workers like toys that they can push around. I also hate the music they blast in the morning at 8:30 A.M., at lunch and tea, and at the end of the workday. The music reminds me that I am a lowly worker. However good I am at what I do, the music makes me a slave to the clock. We need to be in our seats within seconds of the music. Then I feel as if the music controls us and we are not thinking, feeling human beings. Of course, we have our own ways of beating the music. We would just hang around until the music came on to end the break, come back to work, and then one by one we go to the restroom. So we beat the clock by about five minutes that way," Vasanthi smiled as she said this, obviously happy with what I was taping. It was almost at the end of my seven months that I asked for an in-depth interview with her. Well aware, by this time, of my interest in their lives, she talked without much prompting and from time to time checked the tape recorder to see whether the tape was still running.

"I get about Rs. 5,000 [$50] a month. Not a lot, considering how good a worker I am. But since I will be soon finishing my five years in this factory, I am not thinking about moving. Besides, I like my lunch group and most of my friends. The big managers here have been nothing but kind to me. Even if I try to leave now, these people won't let me leave. In fact, about six months before you came I wanted to leave because my parents wanted me to get married. But Perera san and Sanuja sir and everybody begged me to stay for six more months. Then you came when I was again thinking of leaving. I like you and you also said you like to hang out with me, so I am staying until you leave. Then I hope they will sign my papers [to release her Employment Provident Fund (EPF) payments] and let me go. But I am not sure. They just want me here," Vasanthi said, throwing her arms in the air and laughing.

Although the "indispensable workers" were active in creating worker awareness and unity in the line, they too at times had to deal with intense contradictions presented on the shop floor by choosing existing class, caste, and cultural perceptions. As did many workers, they too sometimes negotiated subject positions as daughters of senior managers. Vasanthi especially drew heavily from existing cultural understandings to deal with the contradictions when compared to some other members of this group. Unlike other members, she was presented with such difficult contradictions almost daily.

Recognized as one of those "fair, long-haired, beautiful girls" and chosen as Miss Suishin at an annual factory celebration, Vasanthi received much attention from top managers and factory officers. She was torn between her awareness of exploitation and the appreciation she felt for the kindness shown to her individually. She responded to this conflict by tapping into a familiar cultural idiom in which people understood those who were elderly and educated as worthy of love and honor. While resisting supervisors and factory officers on a daily basis, she constructed her uncritical attitude toward Perera san as a relationship between a parent and a child. It was important that she talked only about her daughterly relationship to elderly Perera san and never acknowledged her friendly relations with the younger manager, Nishan. An attempt to do so through the same idiom certainly would have failed, unlike in the case of her relationship with Perera san. In the next chapter, I will examine the way Vasanthi negotiated these contradictory relationships and reconciled her expressed class consciousness with these attachments during crisis situations.

Madhu: Line Clown and Little Sister

"Freedom is not given, we have to find it," said Madhu in response to Vijee's complaint that there is no freedom in assembly-line work. True to her words, Madhu found a certain space to express herself and fashion her image in a way that was unique to her. "I am a good worker. You can see that, right? I do my work. I help others. I sometimes find damages. I like my line. When we do the same garment as another line, I am the one who prompts everyone to work hard and beat the other line. You saw that the last time with that pink pajama top, right?" she challenged me to contradict her. I did not tell her that the supervisors and experienced workers considered her a mediocre worker. All workers crafted their individual identities differently within fluctuating, everyday power relations. In contrast to the group of experienced, skilled workers, Madhu attempted to create an identity for herself as the line clown.

While working, she might run to the restroom or walk around the line without permission, singing songs and constantly starting conversations with officers—actions that would have been chastised if committed by other mediocre workers. Madhu surpassed that hurdle by developing a nonchalant, clownish attitude toward the supervisors' controlling actions. She walked around the line silently challenging the supervisors to shout at her, thereby providing her the opportunity to respond with gimmicks that would make other workers laugh. By the time I came to Line C, the supervisors had more or less learned to ignore these provocations. Sometimes Sanka took up the challenge and got caught up in exchanges that distracted everybody from the task at hand. Madhu drew from a wide cultural repertoire (parts of popular songs, metaphors, proverbs, analogies) and used a petulant, babyish voice that typically made other workers laugh. These humorous exchanges almost always ended with Madhu on top, even though she retreated back toward her machine while talking. On more than one occasion, I heard Sanka as well as one male QC supervisor call her the "nut case" or "crazy Madhu."

"I never get angry or bitter, especially with the supervisors. My philosophy is 'Let's be jolly during the short time until we die.' Indika miss and Isuru sir are my good friends. You must have noticed how they always stop by my machine to hear my jokes. Laughter is good for everyone. Now you will also write in your book about my jokes and I will become world famous," Madhu declared, laughing loudly.

"I like Pushla *akka*. I belong to her lunch group. She is like a sister to me," Madhu added. In fact, it was obvious that Madhu had an affectionate, sisterly relationship with Pushla. Madhu rebelled the way a younger sister would try to annoy an elder sister. Pushla, for her part, administered gentle slaps, squeezes, and spankings as she would to a younger sister. After committing a transgression, Madhu typically stood or knelt expecting Pushla to punish her and this action usually deterred Pushla from doing that. Many times Pushla would start to berate Madhu and then with an exasperated look on her face ignore Madhu's antics.

Madhu also displayed a strategic balance between transgressions and compliance that allowed her some extra maneuvering space. Once when Sanka yelled at a worker down the line, Madhu pushed all the "cut pieces" aside, saying, "I'll go see what is wrong with her" and walked down the aisle to Sanka. Pushla started shouting at her and then stopped with a look on her face that seemed to say, "There is no use telling her." Madhu passed Sanka to go to the other row and brought a heavy pile of "cut pieces" that they needed for later work. The action began as a transgression but ended in compliance, perhaps demonstrating the intricate ways that power and resistance work.

Over time, I noticed that Madhu was also a major actor in spatial politics within Line C.[16] Once when the experienced workers and I arranged a pleasure trip, Madhu almost sabotaged it by acting along the lines of these spatial factions. Her belief that she was being left out of the decision-making process and her possessive attitude that sought to monopolize my attention influenced this. In fact, Madhu displayed a penchant for associating with people who had more power than she and crafted her identity through the strength of her relationships with those people.[17] Madhu's close association with supervisors or her constant play with the supervisors' wrath did not amuse experienced workers. Although they too joined in the laughter provoked by these incidents, they did not think it was fun to get scolded. They said that it reflected badly on all workers and might encourage people to conclude that they were a bunch of clowns who would take any treatment with a smile.

At times, though Madhu showed that she desired solidarity with the other workers over and above factional politics. "I had a boyfriend in the village. To get me away from him my father brought me to Katunayake. But the day I started working at Suishin a boy in the iron section asked whether he could be my boyfriend. I said 'Yes, fine,' so he walked with me to the bus stop. Sujatha *akka* had seen us and she advised me the next day to stop the relationship right away. This man was a notorious womanizer, she said. But I said, 'No, I already agreed to be his girlfriend.' Then Sujatha *akka* threatened that nobody in Line C would ever talk to me if I did not stop this. That made me stop seeing this guy. Whatever is the case, the girls in this line are more important to me than anybody else." But her daily actions belied this statement until the factory experienced a labor strike. In the next chapter, I will analyze this labor strike and the subsequent changes that it initiated for certain workers, including Madhu.

AMITHA: THE RESPECTED IMBECILE

"I am thirty years old and I have two children. My house is about two miles away from the FTZ and I travel by bus to come here everyday. I like this factory and my work. I want to achieve our target and I want us to not make damages. It makes me feel good when Sanuja sir and other managers come and say good things about our line. But if they come and criticize my line, I get mad and I tell them to look at our side of the story too. And they listen. . . . I think we need to love and appreciate our workplace. Sandya miss must have seen that article in *Niveka* magazine criticizing the factory. A worker wrote that, right? I think it is disgusting the way workers talk bad of the place that puts food in their mouths. I worked here for five years. *Ane,* I have never seen such strict disciplinary measures or bad conditions as the ones described in the paper," Amitha said during the formal in-depth interview I conducted with her.

Amitha, whose machine was located at the beginning of the first row of Line C, looked much older than her thirty years and, in fact, dressed and behaved as an older woman would. She also gave the impression of being a fool by the way she spoke (slowly and haltingly) and by the awkward way she held her head and hands. These characteristics could have made her an unimportant actor in Line C except for the fact that she manipulated several other advantages to negotiate a unique and strong position within the factory. She had worked at the factory for just over five years and was regarded as a fine worker, though not skilled enough for problem solving. Being a "hem sewer," she could finish her work fast and help others. Amitha was loyal to the line and the factory and defended both when it was necessary.

This attitude was a result of her special situation in the factory. Because of her relatively mature age, motherhood, and show of loyalty, she managed to earn the supervisors' respect, especially Sanka's, and did not exactly share others' working conditions. During my seven months of research, Amitha was the only worker who did not get scolded or yelled at. This respect certainly did not result from Amitha's faultlessness. Amitha managed to earn some free time by working faster than the average pace. She used this time to walk around the floor, visiting her old friends in other lines. As soon as Amitha finished a batch of garments, she stood up and went on her errands. She did not ask anyone or tell anyone before she left her machine. It was only after a while that her neighboring workers noticed her absence. Nobody knew where she went and it was a common joke among the workers to realize suddenly that Amitha had "disappeared." Amitha somehow managed to time her absences carefully and usually was back at her machine just as the next batch of "cut pieces" reached her.

While all the other workers had to fight, beg, and cry for leave, it was expected that Amitha would take two days off a month because she had to stay home on *poya* day (monthly Buddhist holy day) and the day after as her mother, who usually looked after her children, went to the temple on those days. Sanka and Pushla made provisions in advance for Amitha's absence on these days by asking Sanuja to send a temporary worker. Amitha also took unexpected leave when she or her children were sick. Rather than being berated, she received sympathetic inquiries from Sanka and sometimes even from Sanuja. Some days Amitha worked while complaining about many ailments, and her neighbor workers as well as Sanka offered sympathy and help.

For her part, Amitha addressed all the male supervisors as "sir" and when she talked to them repeated it every few minutes. She was especially fond of Sanka, and, knowing that I was concerned about his constant yelling, frequently defended him, saying that he did not mean harm. "He is like a soda bottle, exploding one minute, and settling down the next minute," she explained. She also was loyal to her neighbors, including Madhu, and the trimmers. Many times, she urged trimmers to speak up against unfair treatment and sometimes spoke on their behalf. Because of her location at the front of the third row, she belonged to the spatial faction that consisted of younger, more-compliant workers. However, there was a difference. While the younger workers had a hierarchical relationship with Pushla at the top, Amitha did not even talk to Pushla and the latter kept her distance.

When I asked about this, Amitha replied, "I am more senior than Pushla. And the management wanted to make me the supervisor first. But since I have my children I knew I could not take on added responsibility. So I said no. The management then promoted Pushla to the vacant supervisor position. Pushla did not like it that someone who is senior to her is in the line. So she asked the management to transfer me to another line. But I said, 'No, I won't leave my line and my friends,' and the management said, 'If she wants to stay, she will stay.' Pushla did not like this at all. She knows she should stay away from me. I only deal with Sanka if I need a supervisor. Pushla is scared of me and will never try to discipline me." Amitha declared this with a smug smile clearly acknowledging her privileged existence in the factory.

Three factors contributed to Amitha's special situation. First, she was a loyal and useful worker. Second, she was older and senior to both the supervisors. Finally, she was a mother. Her special working conditions, influenced by these factors, ensured that she developed a work identity that was different from that of other workers. Her situation demonstrated how discipline and resistance as well as the subsequent work identities themselves were shaped by the cultural and political contexts in which they were being enacted.

As could be expected, she did not participate in the labor strike. She, however, once used the threat of resignation to influence another worker's reinstatement at the factory and many times used her voice, body, dress, and skills to save fellow workers from difficult situations. One day, two workers near Amitha's machine asked Sanka for leave but were refused without any reason being provided. The two workers got into a screaming match with Sanka. He seemed especially rude, and Amitha, in an exasperated and angry tone, loudly declared that she needed leave on Monday, too. Thus attracting Sanka's attention, she pulled the top buttons off her blouse and said, "Look, I have a wound on my chest. I need to see a doctor on Monday." Sanka stopped screaming, blushed, and turned away. Amitha pulled the blouse open a bit more and, standing up, said, "Look here, sir, it is on my chest." Sanka rushed toward Floor 2 while the workers congratulated Amitha. Although in this instance she acted unlike an older, motherly woman, it was precisely her unkempt, desexualized appearance that allowed her to get away with such acts. Being a middle-class young man who obviously subscribed to notions of shame-fear, Sanka was expected to act the way he did and Amitha and her friends sometimes manipulated these cultural conditions to their advantage.

Priyanka: Innocent Rural Girl and Manipulator

"My village is in Pollonnaruwa district in the dry zone. A very remote village. Both my older sisters worked in this factory and only went to back to get married. They married men from Pollonnaruwa. I have lots of friends in this factory. I don't like cliquishness in the line, so I try to be friends with all the groups within the line and also workers from other lines. I am good friends with the workers around my machine, of course. But I am good friends with Amila who is stationed in the right row of machines, and I like all her neighbors too. And I often visit Vasanthi and the crowd in the middle to listen to their jokes. I seem to be the only one who is even trying to do that," Priyanka declared proudly, while taking a surreptitious look at the tape recorder to see whether it was properly recording this bit of valuable information about her.

Priyanka was well liked as a "pretty, shy, and innocent girl." However, she did not excel in sewing, she made mistakes, and she fought back whenever mistakes were pointed out. She resisted rules on a daily basis, albeit in a subdued way, using her downcast eyes, shy smile, and ready tears to undermine the severity of her transgressions. She, in fact, attempted to be friends with all the spatial factions within the line. She often visited Vasanthi's group in the middle and did not hesitate to support them verbally when they got into fights with Sanka. Usually critical and selective, the latter group, however, did not criticize Priyanka as they did some others who had close relations with the supervisors. Priyanka did not participate in the labor strike and, according to Priyanka and several eyewitnesses, Amila dragged Priyanka back to work and the experienced workers accepted this as a valid excuse.

Many thought that Priyanka, who was slim and fair, was among the factory's most beautiful workers. She promoted the image of the "innocent, pretty, rural lass [*ahinsaka, gami kella*]" by giving a rural twist to her "FTZ fashions" and by manipulating a series of gestures such as downcast eyes, smiling without showing teeth, blushing, and wiggling. Sanuja, the floor coordinator, was from a rich, urban family and had a fiancé from a similar background. Priyanka was attracted to Sanuja and expressed her interest in different ways. On Valentine's Day 2000, she wrote a verse from a popular song on a piece of paper, drew flowers around it, and was hoping to give it to Sanuja as a gift. Before she could do so privately Sanka grabbed the paper and read it aloud for everybody to hear and promptly turned it over to Sanuja. The song went, most appropriately, "It is because I could not pick you [as a flower] that you are so beautiful. . . ."

Considering the wide socioeconomic gap between the two, I did not think that her endeavors would result in more than brief encounters at the factory. But by May there was a buzz around the line that there definitely was something between the two. Once I discussed the rumors with Amila and she confirmed that Sanuja loved Priyanka a great deal. However, their relationship was based on brotherly love and they called each other *aiya* (elder brother) and *nangi*.

Several days later, almost all members of Line C traveled to Ganemulla in a rented van to attend Vijee's wedding reception. Priyanka arrived in Sanuja's car around 1:30 P.M. and sat close to Sanuja, who left after a few minutes. The day after the wedding reception, the lunch-group members filled me in with more details on how they had seen Sanuja and Priyanka together since 9:00 A.M. the previous day. Within one week of this incident, Priyanka was appointed to the vacant line-leader position. Given her propensity to subvert rules and to frequently "produce damages," it was surprising that she was chosen for this position over other diligent workers. Many blamed her for using her relationship with Sanuja to gain this promotion. Her behavior prior to the appointment, however, convinced me that her interest in Sanuja was based more on emotional, physical desire than on material gain. Priyanka never confided in me about the relationship and, after becoming the line leader, stopped having clandestine conversations with me. It appeared to me that Priyanka's developing proletarian consciousness was hampered by her emotional attachment to an executive officer. But it did not entirely prevent her from engaging in everyday resistance until a fringe benefit from the relationship came her way.

Amila: Officers' Favorite Friend and Confidante

"I come to work from my house which is right across the Colombo-Negombo road. My parents do not like it that I work at the FTZ, but I am bored at home and want to work until I get married. It is fun to be working here. Workers who say factory work is bad are the ones from remote villages who stay in boardinghouses. It is hard to live away from your family, and they understand that problem as a work problem. We also have boarding rooms in our compound. We treat our boarders well. You should come and visit our boardinghouse before you leave for America. I really don't need to work. It is not like my parents need my help. Whatever salary I get goes for my clothes and make-up. I don't have to pay rent like other girls. So I have more money to spend and I usually go to Colombo shopping malls to buy my clothes. I don't like all this glitzy FTZ clothing. I want to wear what other Colombo people wear. These other girls don't understand that when they wear these FTZ styles, they get branded as "garment girls." That is why I don't shop here in the bazaar or in Katunayake. I go to Liberty Plaza or Majestic City in Colombo to buy my clothes. Because my fiancé has a vehicle, he takes me there often. I mean, really, you must know by now I am different from the girls who travel so far away from their families to work in the Zone. They come here because they have no other choice. I am here so that I could have fun before getting married." Amila thus reiterated during my formal in-depth interview with her what she had been telling me almost every day and had displayed through her clothing and demeanor throughout my time at the factory.

Amila willfully refused to acknowledge the subject position as a "garment worker," and the clothing and cosmetics she acquired in Colombo were similar to those that were popular among middle-class young women in Colombo. This set her apart from the other workers who followed "FTZ styles" by choice and by necessity. Through her clothing and declarations that she worked for fun, Amila attempted to create a difference between the "migrant garment factory workers" and "workers from the neighborhood," and sought to dissociate herself from the stigma of FTZ work.

Consequently, Amila had a different attitude toward work and supervisors. She vigorously attempted to show the supervisors how diligent she was and volunteered to help when a crisis occurred. She always kept her machine neatly pasted with white paper and in many ways tried to create an image as the ultimate factory-friendly, loyal worker. She worked well and followed the rules and regulations. Although she unfailingly addressed all male supervisors and officers with honorifics, she also actively sought friendships with them and offered help with their professional and social lives. Both Sanka and Pushla used Amila's parents' address for confidential correspondence. For Sanka, it was to apply for other jobs; for Pushla, it was to communicate with a paramour. When Amila's father found out about this, he beat Amila and told her to stop helping a woman who was cheating on her husband. Showing uncharacteristic disobedience, Amila continued helping Pushla and continued to receive special privileges on the line.

Sanka also accorded Amila special treatment. It was common knowledge at the factory that Amila had a crush on Sanka, but at times their conversations and actions demonstrated that Sanka was more than willing to reciprocate the sentiments. Indika, Isuru, and I sometimes joked about this relationship, and Amila enjoyed such jokes enormously, yet blushingly denied any special relationship in a way that told onlookers there indeed had to be something special between the two. Although perfectly understanding the social differences that set them apart, Amila still pined after Sanka. However, she acted realistically by starting another relationship that offered her a secure future and manipulated the interest Sanka showed her for material benefits at the factory. Once I heard Sanka suggesting that Amila be made the new line leader because she had the ability to yell at the whole line.[18] The officers agreed, but the proposal did not go through because of the news about Amila's impending departure from the factory.

Amila actively negotiated a position as the supervisors' friend and confidante and was proud of her knowledge about their private lives. She constantly talked to factory officers and offered support in their romantic relationships. Within a few days of getting to know me, she directly asked my age and whether I had a boyfriend. At first I replied vaguely to the latter question just as she did about her relationship with Sanka, but Amila managed to get a direct answer just by speculating on which junior executive officer could be my boyfriend. Although I was much closer to several other workers, it was Amila who gleaned the most information about my private life. She also advised me on new fashions, offered to receive letters from my boyfriend at her parents' house, and constantly offered to take me shopping. She voluntarily took me to visit her father's boardinghouse and helped many times by delivering my phone messages to other workers whose boardinghouses did not have telephones. Judging by how strongly she sought my friendship, I was not surprised that she was a friend and confidante to several male and female factory officers.

Priding herself as Indika's confidante at the factory, Amila, however, used Indika's problems to make other workers feel better. Whenever she talked to me about Priyanka's relationship with Sanuja she ridiculed Indika for desiring Sanuja and failing to win him. If Indika were around, she teased her about Sanuja, all the while hinting to others that she was ridiculing her.

Once when I was talking to Indika several machines away from her, Amila said in a loud voice, "I wonder why Sanuja sir is getting fairer everyday. . . . mmmhh! He must be rubbing himself against a fair person." This enthralled Indika who had an obvious crush on Sanuja and attempted to dupe both the workers and me by making up stories about Sanuja's interest in her. As soon as Indika left the line, Amila laughed again and said, "I was talking about Priyanka rubbing against Sanuja sir and Indika miss thought I was referring to her. I mean, really, Indika miss is not beautiful enough for a handsome boy like Sanuja sir." Gesturing toward Priyanka, Amila said, "He likes fair-skinned, long-haired, slim girls."[19] The experienced, rebellious workers who resented Amila for her supervisor-friendly actions used somewhat similar methods to get back at Amila. By telling me that Amila would never win Sanka's heart, they also brought up gossip about Amila's current and former boyfriends to show that she did not achieve the ideal in romantic relationships either.

The labor strike occurred exactly one month before Amila left the factory to get married. "I did not want to spoil the good name I earned with the supervisors and the managers just before I am about to leave," Amila later told me when explaining why she did not join the strike. One month after the strike, she left on the same day as did Kamali. Known as a catalyst for worker solidarity and support, Kamali's departure inspired much sadness and tears. Even the supervisors were paying more attention to Kamali, and a disappointed Amila told me that several women in the locker room paid obeisance at her feet, wailing that she was the only one who looked after them when they first joined the factory.[20]

When I asked about this at the lunch group, they said that nobody worshiped Amila and whatever affection she received had resulted from workers not wanting to hurt her feelings because she stood together with Kamali. Many later laughed, saying that Amila stood with Kamali and told people that it was she who was worshiped. Workers in general wanted to be mourned and worshiped in the way that only a few workers, such as Kamali, Batti, and Vasanthi were. It was strange that Amila, who refused to be recognized as a worker, seemed to value the same farewell reserved for workers who were considered organizers, educators, and political activists. This was perhaps because of the disappointment she felt about the carelessness with which the factory officers she attempted to identify with greeted her departure. Ironically, in a reversal of Amila's own betrayal of the workers, the officials were more concerned with Kamali's departure that day.

Six weeks later, Amila again tasted similar betrayal when only Sanuja made an appearance at her wedding ceremony for about fifteen minutes. Two days after the wedding, there was a reception for all the Line C workers and factory officers. Amila was reduced to tears when only eight workers attended the party, and only Sanka and I represented her favorite kind.

Kishali: Elder and Organizer

When I asked whether I could interview her, Kishali readily agreed and then requested that we sit inside the training center for the interview, as opposed to under the temple flower tree where I had interviewed the others. "What I have to say to you cannot be said outside," she said with a wink. When we sat down at the training center on a late June afternoon, she poured out her heart to me and the tape recorder which sat on a third chair by us.

"This part you already know. I am thirty-six years old. I am not yet married. I have worked here for about two years. I followed a course at the National Apprentice Board and they [the institution] sent me to South Korea for a training program in garment merchandising. I was working in merchandising for a long time at another factory, but I resigned from that job to go to Italy. Then my parents said, "Don't go. You are unmarried. If you go now, nobody will marry you. So get married and go." So I did not leave. I know that you are wondering why I am working as a machine operator with such experience and education. But Perera san will give me a better job when a vacancy opens up. I am also planning to go to Italy or Canada soon. I mean, your lunch-group friends do not believe me much. But this is the truth and you must believe me." Even if I had doubts about this first part of her narrative, it was easy to feel her sincerity when she related the latter part of her story.

"I have had several love affairs and nothing worked out. After a few months of seeing someone, I fall in love with these good-for-nothing bastards and I spend all my salary buying them clothes and jewelry. And then they leave me for younger, better-looking women. The last boyfriend I had was a bus driver. After about one year, another driver told me that he was having relationships with two other women. I once went looking for him and, lo and behold, here he comes hand in hand with one of those whores. I had the umbrella in my hand and I beat them both with it until it broke into pieces. Afterward, I went from temple to temple, *kovil* to *kovil*, asking gods to bring him back to me. I mean what else can I do? At this age, all the men I meet are either younger than I or already married. They befriend me only for temporary pleasure [*thavakalika sapaya*]. So magic is the best way to keep a man with me." She looked directly at me and signed that I ought to turn off the tape recorder. As soon as the recorder was switched off, she started giggling and said, "This tape recorder is so small, so funny." These interviews almost at the very end of my stay at the factory in fact ensured much giggling mostly because the women found it hilarious to tell a tape recorder what they knew that I already knew thanks to my seven months among them.

But the giggling was also because of the insecurity Kishali felt about her age. On several earlier occasions she expressed concern that she might be alone for the rest of her life. She was obese and had an imposing demeanor. This made her stand out in a factory full of young and slim women. Kishali was also known for producing damages and had to defend herself often against supervisors and fellow workers. She caught my attention, however, with her attempts to carve out a particular space for herself within Line C that was in keeping with her age and demeanor.

"I am the fund-raiser and organizer for almost all Line C functions and obligations," she said with a smile. "Remember when that pregnant worker was laid off because she couldn't work fast? I am the one who started the list to collect cash donations. I said to others, 'That Sandya miss is here too. She might make a large donation. Let's start a collection list.' The others in these lines don't know how to get things done. When Kamali and Amila left the factory I again collected money to buy them farewell gifts. Both of them were happy to receive the plastic flowers I bought.[21] I am the one who usually hires the buses when we go on trips or visit workers' houses for funerals and weddings. I collect the money, arrange for the bus, and deal with the drivers. Miss must remember that I came in the van to pick all of you up from the junction to go to Vijee's wedding. You sounded surprised that day to realize that I went early in the morning to Negombo town, bought the plastic kitchen table and the set of four chairs, packed it into the van myself, and then came in the same van to Katunayake by 9:00 A.M. These other girls don't know how to get these bus drivers and cleaners to work. I am good at this. I collected the money for Amila's wedding gift, too. I had to bring the two heavy gift boxes in public buses to her house. But I am happy to help," she said in an obviously happy tone.

I was fascinated by the way Kishali insisted on sitting in the single seat near the driver and then talked with the driver and the helper when we all went on trips. Although her leadership in these matters and all the work she did were accepted without resistance, she was unfortunately unable to make friends or cultivate followers. While nobody avoided her, she did not belong to any one group. At times I saw workers laughing about the way she looked or behaved. While she acquired leadership, perhaps because of the absence of competition, she was never fully accepted.[22] Her age, looks, and demeanor set her apart from the other workers. If she had told the other workers about her foreign training, she would have exacerbated the gulf between them because the others would have expected her to become a supervisor soon.

LALITHA: HOLDING THE BEST "WORKER POSITION"

"Working in the cutting section is more satisfying. As you can see, it is not assembly-line work. We don't need supervisors. There is only one supervisor for the whole section, and he is almost like a worker. Markers are even better off. We work almost independently. We have to think and come up with the best marking plan. There are two markers, me and Sarath *aiya* [a male marker]. But I usually attend the 'cutting meetings.' These meetings are held before a pattern is first introduced to the cutting section. Several top managers, factory staff, line supervisors, and cutting-section members attend these meetings. In fact, markers are the only nonsupervisory-level members who attend these meetings. One day you mentioned that I was a very active participant in these meetings. I know my craft, so I am not afraid to give my opinion. Even if Gamini sensei says something impractical, I correct him and they admire me for that. In fact, I am the only person that Kimura san gets along with. Everybody knows how tense her relationship with junior factory staff is," Lalitha proudly declared.

"In fact, I wondered how you communicate with Kimura san, given that you don't speak Japanese and she does not speak Sinhala," I asked Lalitha. "This is the case, miss. Because Kimura san is the designer, she must talk to markers. So we kind of found a new language, you know, a mixture of Japanese, English, Sinhalese and also hands and legs talk," said Lalitha, erupting into loud laughter, remembering perhaps the many times she and Kimura giggled by the marker tables trying to understand each other. Her participation in the meetings and this unequal association with Kimura elevated Lalitha's status among the cutting-section workers. Lalitha understood this and valued the friendship and opportunity to participate in such meetings.

"Miss, this marker position is the most valued position among workers in any garment factory. I mean, the success of a garment order depends on us. If we make even a slight mistake, it could ruin batches of good fabric. We need to be perfect or the whole factory is doomed," Lalitha continued making sure that I understood the importance of her position by throwing her arms up and raising her eyebrows. "This is also the most convenient job in a garment factory. Some women have to sit all day. Some women have to stand all day. Markers can walk around the table for measurements and then we can sit at the table to draw models. This is much better for the body," she said pointing toward the stool that markers sit on to draw models of the layout. Across the stool was written, "This belongs to markers, do not take away" in bold, black letters. I had meant to ask Lalitha about this, but she seemed to read my mind and said, "I wrote that, so nobody will take my stool away."

Although she displayed and expressed a strong attachment to her job, Lalitha did not hesitate to voice her anger and disappointment over rules and conditions she considered unjust. One day I heard the top executives talking about a change in leave policies. There was an individual incentive scheme regarding leave, according to which workers who did not obtain any leave during the month would get an "attendance payment." But with the new policy, a whole section would receive an incentive if the section workers took no more than two days of leave per month. When I went to the cutting section, all the workers were gathered around the cutting manager and arguing loudly about the new policy. Lalitha's voice was audible above the general noise, and it became obvious that they were all unhappy about the new leave policy. When Lalitha came back to the marker table, she explained their stand on the new incentive scheme in an agitated voice. According to her, this was a conspiracy to cut the attendance payments that diligent workers like herself had been earning every month. While talking to me, she again urged Mahinda, the cutting manager, to talk to the office right away.

Given Lalitha's involvement in this issue, I was not surprised to find that she was a front-line activist at the labor strike. But the fallout from the strike affected her in a different way than it did the others. I will follow these consequences in the next chapter.

Chapter 4
Loving Daughters and Politically Active Workers

July 2005

The three-wheeler taxi we were huddled in sped along the Kimbulapi-tiya road that bordered the FTZ on the left. Vasanthi, her sister Nilani, and I were squeezed into the backseat and were holding tightly to the metal bar erected behind the driver's seat. With the dust and wind in our eyes and the monotonous noise of the old three-wheeler in our ears, we ceased talking and gazed at the passing landscape, deep in our own thoughts. We had just left Preethi's house where we were treated to Mal-iban biscuits and tea. Over tea, we talked about how Pushla had had to leave her job as the supervisor of Line C after her husband discovered her sexual liaison with a junior executive. "It was just like her. She has to go find a 'sir' [an executive officer] to even have a dalliance," Vasanthi said, her voice shaking the way it usually did when she got angry. I couldn't help the little smirk that played around my mouth each time I thought of Pushla's predicament. "I wonder whether I could go visit Pushla," I blurted out just as the taxi passed the Averiwatthe junction. "*Ane* Sandya Miss, that is not a road you can find on your own. It is such a roundabout way and I felt disgusted trying to find her house when I went to give my wedding invitation," Vasanthi replied.

Suddenly I lost all interest in finding out what happened to Pushla after she left Suishin. "You invited her to your wedding! Why in the world did you do that?" Karunadasa's uncle who had been driving me around in this old three-wheeler taxi for a few weeks turned to look at me. Nilani also seemed to have suddenly become alert. No wonder! It was rare that I got agitated. "Well, I mean, you guys were fighting all the time at the factory." I was happy with the calmness with which I delivered that statement.

"It is true, miss. All she did to us was wicked [*hathurukan*]. But at least for one day I worked under her and I had to show my gratefulness [*gune*]."

I was still fuming when I got down near the record bar (where audiocassettes and compact discs are sold). Why was it so hard to shake off the feeling of betrayal? Hadn't Vasanthi said that she would never forget the way Pushla treated them like dogs and cats? Hadn't she also said, "Thankfully, she did not come to my wedding"? Hasn't this always been the story of our lives?

Sri Lankan women's migration from patriarchal villages enabled their gradual transformation into dissenting, politically conscious workers. But the struggles of women workers in transnational factories have been labeled as "struggles over cultural meaning" that were not based on class interests or class solidarity (Ong 1991:281). I found it difficult to label these women's struggles as either exclusively cultural or exclusively class. It is even more difficult to discount these struggles as not based on class interest or solidarity. As E. P. Thompson (1963) theorized, class is an outcome of experience and class happens when, as a result of shared common experiences, a group of people feel and articulate an identity based on their interests against others whose interests are different and opposed to theirs (9). Most Suishin workers' shop-floor activities were characterized by an awareness of class identity and opposition to others with different interests. As many studies on working-class politics have shown, class consciousness is always ambivalent and exists together with several other contradictory loyalties (Blackburn and Mann 1975; Nash 1979; Marshall 1983; Hall 1986; Fantasia 1988). Suishin workers' class consciousness also existed in conjunction with other interests and was produced as a result of specific economic and political practices. Analysis of such practices shows that class interests and solidarity are an integral part of cultural struggles at Sri Lanka's FTZ factories.

Work identity is based on feeling and articulating shared work experiences. The migrant women workers articulated other learned and felt experiences together with their consciousness as industrial workers, resulting in contradictions and ambiguity. They manipulated these contradictory strains of consciousness to contextually negotiate different identities. While at times class understanding propelled their actions, at other times it was loyalty to particular ethnic, religious, regional, and other social groups or internalized cultural understandings that informed their political activities. I analyze this complexity to show how the workers negotiated their identities by manipulating these different loyalties.

Rick Fantasia (1988:17) defines "cultures of solidarity" as cultural expressions that emerge in industrial collective action that embody oppositional practices and meaning. I focus on the way workers constructed solidarity around specific needs and demands of industrial crises. I also examine the way the struggles and crises affected new awareness and the subsequent negotiation of new identities.

In Chapter 3, I analyzed everyday cultural politics on the shop floor as women workers negotiated contextual identities within power-laden discourses as they created, learned, and differently participated in a shop-floor culture characterized by resistance to supervisors. In this chapter, I analyze the workers' political activities (collective and otherwise) that created conditions of possibility for transformational politics.[1] While everyday acts of resistance discussed in the previous chapter created an oppositional culture on the shop floor, the activities analyzed in this chapter built solidarity and alliances around specific situations or a sequence of events.[2]

Linguistic Strategies

Sanka bumped hard onto Amila's wild box and then, in anger, began dragging the box down the aisle. "There, there, Sanka is carrying Amila's box," Chandani started shouting. Her use of the Sinhala term for box, *pettiya*, which was also a vulgar term for vagina, ensured that everyone paid attention to the drama. Amila ran after Sanka and brought the box back to her stool. Niluka poked Amila from behind and said, "Ask him whether he is relieved now." Niluka used the Sinhala term *sanasunada*, which when used in the right context with the right intonation denotes sexual satisfaction. The way she used it, loud enough for Sanka to hear but distant enough because she was talking to Amila, effectively prevented Sanka from complaining to anyone about the incident. This exchange not only brought laughter to those who had engaged in a hard day of work but also let the workers express the resentment and jealousy they felt about the special treatment Amila received from Sanka.

Forming work identity goes hand in hand with learning to subvert rules and supervisors through a socialization process. A major aspect of this socializing process was training in a language form that allowed workers to resist, ridicule, and undermine factory officers' authority in a way that did not allow the latter to complain to higher authorities.[3] This included mobilizing a range of regional accents; regionally specific words, phrases, and proverbs, as well as the skillful use of masculine forms of address (*machan, malli, ado*); and jokes with much sexual innuendo. After each such exchange, workers talked about its relative merit and congratulated each other on its successful usage. Every new worker brought with her a wealth of regional linguistic skills and she soon imparted them to others. Each worker developed a repertoire of such linguistic tools, which each one used differently.

The correct use of words and phrases that bordered on the obnoxious required a certain individual savvyness. Rhythms and intonations accompanied certain words and phrases, which, if not used correctly, conveyed a very different message, often one that could get the user into trouble. Certain gestures and hand and eye movements (smiles, a friendly touch, or a wink) usually accompanied these expressions. The workers who frequently used these linguistic tools to express anger and unhappiness and to justify their transgressions seemed to possess more self-confidence and a propensity toward being funny. Interestingly, however, the group of experienced, skilled workers did not use this form much, given their ability to confront supervisors and higher officials directly. It was workers who were not considered skilled but who were also not new workers who often used these linguistic tools in their interactions with the officers.

Madhu, Amitha, Priyanka, Amila, Mangala, and Chandani were among the workers who excelled in these forms. The others used them less frequently, but together with the experienced workers cheered on and participated in follow-up conversations figuring out other such words and phrases. Although Amila had ways of conveying her ideas to line supervisors without resorting to these measures, she seemed to take pride in her ability to manipulate them and get away with it. She received approval from other workers every time she did so; therefore, this could be a way she sought solidarity with the others. A particular tactic both Chandani and Mangala used was to address Sanka and Pushla by using the masculine address forms *machan, malli,* or *ado.* Although in masculine youth groups these words generate closeness and belonging, when women used them for men or powerful women it indicated disrespect. When workers uttered, "*yanawa do yanda* [get lost]," "*ba machan* [I won't, buddy]," or "*malli valiyatada* [younger brother, in for a fight?]" with a nice smile and a wink, supervisors, especially Sanka, became agitated but were left with no recourse. The situation worsened when the workers used mildly ridiculing and clearly insubordinate phrases that had sexual innuendos. While responding to these in kind was beneath the average supervisor's dignity, complaining about such behavior was even more embarrassing and demeaning. On many occasions, workers left a supervisor or a factory officer fuming and speechless while at the same time getting away with a transgression.

Sharing and using phrases and jokes with sexual innuendos as well as explicit sexual content slowly chipped away at the shame-fear their village upbringing had instilled in the women workers. Even the women who held a pacifist stance toward supervisors and officers enjoyed sharing sexual jokes. Workers creatively rearranged words in proverbs and old sayings to give them different meanings. Once I was given a piece of paper they had been passing down the line. The paper contained two lines from a poem and one proverb, both derived from popular folklore. The poem read, "Even though the Niyagala flower is very beautiful, eating the Niyagala tuber will kill you." The proverb read, "Love is a mammoty that digs one's grave." The words in the original work were only slightly changed, but the comments written on the paper showed that the readers understood and appreciated the suggestive use of the words "tuber" and "mammoty" as puns for the penis. When I did not show any emotion after reading the paper, Madhu put her face very close to mine and in her babyish voice asked, "You know what 'tuber' means, right? And the mammoty is like that, too." When I blushed, she turned to the line and announced, "She knows, she knows."

Sexual puns aside, the writings further concurred with the contradictory distrust the workers expressed about love and marriage even while urgently desiring the same. The dangers of love and sex were common themes in the media and among creative writers and they instilled fear and shame concerning premarital sex. The eroticized language used among female friends seemed a particular way of transgressing these bonds of shame and fear. After two to three years in the factory, workers would have learned how to eroticize any factory situation and embarrass any middle-class officer, male or female, who was subscribing to shame-fear.

However, workers were careful not to use these sexualized linguistic skills with top managers, thereby saving space for them to act as daughters with shame and fear at the appropriate time. In one incident in which both Pushla and Sanka had to complain about Mangala, who, according to several other workers, had gone beyond the limit, Mr. Perera found it hard to believe that "an innocent girl like Mangala would say such a thing." At the brief informal inquiry Mangala did not speak but stood with her head bent. When Perera asked her to tell her story, she looked at him and broke out sobbing loudly. Perera quickly sent her back to the line, advising both Sanka and Pushla to be patient and understanding.

While walking back to the line disappointed, Pushla said, "I am fed up with this job. One day I am going to go home, leaving Perera san to handle his fine children on his own."

Working Tears and Farewell Tears

The grief felt tangible on that Friday in May 2000. It fell like a thick, gloomy cloud over Line C and seemed to almost spill over to the neighboring lines. The constant chatter had ceased and the workers were bent over their machines with extra vigor as if to cover their wet eyes. Even

Pushla and Sanka seemed to tiptoe around the line. Kamali, who had refused a supervisor position because she could not stand to shout at fellow workers; Kamali, the most loved and respected member of Line C and my lunch group, was leaving the factory. About 10:00 a.m., the first wave of sobbing went through the line. Kamali, the dear, sensitive, skilled worker, started the first sob and it quickly spread down the line almost like a house of cards falling. This crying must have persisted for a minute, but it felt like an hour. There were two other waves of sobbing before the lunch break.

The gathering of the lunch group started early that day. Because no one could eat, we all held hands and listened to the suppressed sobs. Not a word was spoken. No farewell speeches were made. No formal farewells here. Just the warmth of our bodies as we sat on the concrete steps in front of the training center. At the tea break, everybody gathered in the locker area. It was hard for me to go near Kamali because hundreds of women from all lines milled around her. They were hugging and kissing her and sobbing loudly. Many workers were falling down at her feet paying obeisance. She brought sweets for everybody, but nobody was eating. Sobbing turned into a collective wailing that went up and subsided only to be picked up the next moment. Yet, when the music score signaled the end of the break, women wiped their faces with their aprons and ran back to their machines.

Women workers frequently used tears to deal with the problems and contradictions they faced on the shop floor. Although crying reproduced patriarchal notions of women being less in control of their emotions, it also worked as a form of protest and as a way of inciting protest. In her analysis of maternalistic politics in Sri Lanka, Malathi De Alwis (1998) asserts that tears proved to be "one of the most powerful forms of body speech that was mobilized" by the Mother's Front to engender a crucial political space (233). When used by young, unmarried factory workers, tears helped negotiate a daughter position in relation to top managers and thereby bypass their immediate supervisors. On a daily basis, tears worked as a protest against the treatment by supervisors and to incite protest from others who were more capable of making a strong case (experienced workers). Emotional responses are discursive public forms and whenever a worker resorted to the embodied reaction of crying, it managed to appeal to a "community of sentiment" (Appadurai 1990:108) composed of those who shared the same discursive forms. The others took up the crying worker's cause and started protesting or shaming the supervisors for inhuman and un-Buddhist actions. While protesting focused on the injustice of the supervisor's action, shaming reminded him of his inhuman action, disregard for bad *karma*, the suffering of others, and the transience of material wealth. Supervisors were thus drawn to this contextually constructed community of sentiment, and they almost always dropped the matter of contention following the shedding of tears and subsequent protests.

Some workers used tears to obtain assurances from supervisors of their position and value to the line.[4] Amila used tears several times to obtain statements of trust and value of her negotiated position as friend and confidante from Sanka, Sanuja, and Indika. In keeping with her younger-sister image, Madhu also broke down whenever things did not go her way. Tears called attention to an internalized quality in young women as "fragile, sentimental beings" who needed to be protected and forgiven. These also reproduced the same discursive constructions on FTZ workers as rural young women who were brought up like flowers in rural households with shame and fear and, therefore, became confused by the difficult situations within the factory. Tears not only protested the injustices in a culturally familiar practice but also begged for forgiveness for actions "for which they should not be held responsible." While some workers showed a tendency to break down in tears easily, others reserved them for crisis situations. Especially after a failed labor strike, many workers, including Vasanthi and Sujatha, used tears to renegotiate their positions as valued and privileged workers.

Apart from their function as "weapons of the weak" (Scott 1985), tears influenced shop-floor political activity in an unintended way. As in the case of Kamali, much crying marked the departure of certain workers from the factory. These honors were accorded only to a few workers, and they were always the ones who fought for workers' rights within the line as well as within the factory. Almost every worker desired such farewells and constantly talked about how they valued such shows of love, affection, and sorrow more than any material benefit they could accrue by being among the supervisors' favorite workers. The day Kamali left the factory, Chandani found me bending over the locker-room door trying to hide my own tears. She bent over the door just like me and together we sobbed to our hearts' content. At the end of the tea break, we wiped our tears and walked back to the line hand in hand. As I was about to leave her at Line C, Chandani said, "If you can achieve such tears [from others] that is worth more than gold, gems, or pearls [*ran, mini, muthu*]."

Although these farewell spectacles of weeping and worshiping epitomized several extant ideas on gender—after all, these experienced and class-conscious workers were leaving the factory to get married—they influenced many workers to avoid siding with supervisors and instead show solidarity with fellow workers. Interestingly, the workers who vigorously negotiated positions in alliance with the supervisors also wanted tears to be shed for them on the day of their departure. As noted in Chapter 3,

Amila was disappointed that nobody really cared that she was leaving the factory. Even though she invited all of the workers in Line C to her wedding reception, only a few attended. Looking at Amila complaining about food going to waste because of the low attendance at the reception, Sujatha murmured, "This should be a good lesson to everyone." Maybe Amila should have paid attention when Madhu kept singing a verse from a song on the days workers like Batti and Kamali left the factory. The verse said, "To protect or to lose, I have only one thing in this world and that is your love,"

Many researchers assert that discourses on emotion and emotional discourses serve as means of resistance and rebellion for relatively powerless people (Kaplan 1987; Abu-Lughod and Lutz 1990; Appadurai 1990). Tears and their aftermath provided a political tool that workers manipulated to create solidarity and gain minimal political advantage in a context where the use of other political tools was severely constrained.

Curses and Sorcery Threats

Moved by Bosses' rough voices
And crying with broken hearts,
Spend the day cursing
The brutes who exploit their souls

Thus wrote Nirosha Priyani Perera about her experiences of being a "girl of the zone" in the *Dabindu* magazine's June 1995 issue. Such curses and sorcery threats usually occurred as a result of the same painful situations that produced tears. While protesting through tears, the workers and others who took up their cause eventually resorted to cursing. Obeyesekere (1975) has pointed to the psychological and emotional satisfaction gained from cursing, noting "the sheer sadism and the vindictiveness of the curses" (20). At Suishin, however, workers did not resort to extremely violent curses such as wishing that the wrongdoers should be punished by "making them ashes and dust" or that "their heads should be cracked into seven pieces." Rather, the workers used less-potent curses such as imploring the gods to look at the injustice (then give out just punishment) or to ensure that the wrongdoer be born again as a factory worker to learn about the workers' suffering. The most serious curse I heard was wishing "that lightning should strike," and both times it was uttered not against one person but against the factory as a whole. The second time they cursed the factory was because of the workers' reluctance to curse the wrongdoer, Pushla, who was about five months pregnant at the time.

These watered-down curses and the absence of sorcery threats at Suishin was partly a result of the particular stigma attached to both these
actions as unrespectable, lower-class practices. But as shown in Chapter
3, and as the following chapters indicate, the workers enthusiastically engaged in other things that were considered unrespectable. Although
they consulted palm readers and sorcerers to try to improve their situation at the factory, they did not issue sorcery threats while they were at
the factory. However, at their boardinghouses, workers used these
watered-down curses together with sorcery threats against supervisors,
managers, and owners. Uttering such curses within the boardinghouses
was a safer way of expressing their anger through symbolic violence because it would not be reported to the higher factory authorities. None
of the occasions in which I witnessed these sorcery threats involved Suishin factory workers. Workers who issued these threats belonged to bigger factories where discipline was tight and no direct contact with higher
authorities was possible.[5] Both Obeyesekere (1975) and Selvadurai
(1976) note that, in societies where formal institutions of mediation and
justice do not exist or are rare, symbolic actions such as sorcery flourish
as a regulatory mechanism. As stated earlier, Suishin had several formal
and informal methods of mediation and several workers even had the
capacity to contact management directly. As a result of this structure,
workers were deterred from using extremely violent curses or sorcery
threats because that would render any negotiation of an innocent-
daughter position untenable.

Threats of Resignation as a Bargaining Chip

One day in March I found Nimali waiting by Mr. Perera's door. As soon
as she saw me, she announced that she was going to resign because
Pushla had scolded her for requesting leave for her sister's wedding.

"I am resigning because of Pushla. She shouts at children and does
not respect them. I have worked here for five years. If she treats me like
that, how must it be for newcomers?" Nimali blurted, as she continued
to tell me about Pushla and other factory staff until the human resources
office summoned her in. We hugged each other and said good-bye.

When I saw her working on Line E that evening, she explained, "Perera san promised he would not allow anybody to insult me again and requested that I not resign again and again." She said this loudly, trying to
attract the attention of Pushla who was standing near Line C, and then
she secretively told me, "It was like pricking her eyes with a thorn. She
couldn't look at my face."

As noted in Chapter 3, there was an acute shortage of women appli-
cants for the jobs available and turnover rates were high. This situation

affected all the FTZ factories, and notices in front of factories and around the town announced vacancies for machine operators. Workers who left or got fired easily found jobs in other factories at the same pay rates. As a result, management had to be careful when punishing workers. The ability of Suishin's highly skilled and experienced workers to resist and rebel as well as to think and work independently was a result of the existing labor-market dynamics. This acquired status enabled the skilled workers to protest unfair treatment. The resulting tensions that constantly flared between supervisors and skilled workers created solidarity among all the workers.

During my research, Suishin held many interviews to recruit workers. There was tension among top managers over recruiting sufficient, skilled workers; retaining these workers; and maintaining discipline on the shop floor. I usually did my office observations in the early morning. One interesting and inevitable occurrence was the exchange between the human resources staff and workers who arrived late or took unapproved leave. Workers had a time card that they signed when entering and leaving the factory. These cards were kept at the guardroom, and at 8:30 A.M. the unsigned cards were returned to the human resources office so that those who arrived late could be identified. Clerks reprimanded the workers before giving them their cards. If a worker was absent for three days without letting the office know, she would be sent a letter of final warning. Workers who returned after such absences usually did so with a medical certificate. Most of the time, the clerical staff questioned the validity of the certificate and sometimes even referred them to the manager, Mr. Perera. Perera told me that many Ayurvedic doctors in Katunayake issued bogus medical certificates for a fee. Once he detected a forged certificate and told the woman, "Child, if you want to cheat us, do it right." And then he gave back her card and sent her to the line to work. The whole time I was at Suishin no one was fired for a forged medical certificate, and the workers just had to endure a mild berating for their action.

Disciplinary measures at the assembly lines also had to be applied with caution because of the fear of losing skilled workers. Even though there was verbal abuse for slow work and damages, production assistants and supervisors had to be careful not to push a worker too far because when a worker decided to leave, higher officials usually tried to pacify her, resulting in the loss of face for the production assistant or supervisor. I saw Sanuja soothing workers who were scolded by the supervisors or production assistants. Sometimes the factory manager, and occasionally even the shipping manager and the deputy managing director comforted workers.

The fact that the top managers comforted workers who were rebuked by supervisors made them feel powerful even as it generated a false impression that the former were not at fault and were kinder. Workers celebrated whenever their indispensability to the factory was expressed. They also enjoyed getting back at immediate supervisors for the everyday indignities the workers experienced. Although this provided an opportunity to feel and articulate class consciousness and identity, these dynamics also hampered the development of workers' alienation beyond a certain limit. Because the threat of resignation worked only for highly skilled workers, it encouraged others to become skilled and indispensable workers as well, thus benefiting the factory.[6]

Solidarity, Strategy, and Contradictions: Strains of Consciousness among Lunch-Group Members

"Do you know why these women run like some wild bulls stampeding to get their lunch packets?" Isuru asked, looking at workers running toward the meal hall the moment the music signaling the lunch break started. "They will get their lunch packets, eat in ten minutes, and then run to their *sangame* [association] to gossip. They have formed these little groups and they each have their own designated space to meet. Then they just chit-chat until the lunch break is over. For these people *sangame* is more important than a leisurely lunch," Isuru said, answering his own question. In fact, within two to three days, I noticed that groups of four to eight people sat at different places in the space between the office building and the factory. I later learned that some groups stayed behind in the meal hall while other groups sat at various shady places in front of the building to socialize with friends.

I analyze workers' lunch-group activities as a viable space for creating worker solidarity and articulating class and feminist sentiments. This analysis brings forth the ambivalences and contradictions in the workers' responses to different situations. Yet, as Fantasia (1988) writes, "whether or not a future society is consciously envisioned, whether or not a 'correct' image of the class structure is maintained, the building of solidarity in the form, and in the process, of mutual association can represent a practical attempt to restructure, or reorder, human relations" (11).

The first such group I encountered was headed by Pushla, the Line C supervisor, and included several Line C workers. The day I interviewed Pushla, I stayed behind after lunch with the workers in the meal hall. They sat around one table and joked and gossiped. A few days later Kamali, the popular assistant supervisor of Line C, took me to where her lunch group gathered. Her group included several experienced workers from Line C and met daily by the three long steps leading to the

Figure 3. Lunch group (author second row, first from left). Photograph by Nimali.

training-center door. There were nine members in the group: Kamali, Niluka, Vasanthi, Rena, Batti, Nimali, Sujatha, Menike, and Kumari. All except Kumari belonged to Line C. The reason for Kumari's inclusion in the group was that she was from Kamali's village and, as a new worker, did not have many friends.

Everybody brought fruits and sweets that they shared. While eating, they usually talked about things that happened on the line or about their personal lives. There was much gossiping about factory officers and workers. Group members were happy about and proud of my close association with them and it became an extension of my association with Line C. Group members gradually became my closest friends at Suishin, and they became interested and enthusiastic participants in and supporters of my research. The lunch group was a forum for these experienced and valued workers to vent their anger against supervisors, the factory, and in rare cases management. It was during this seemingly short period of time that they most profoundly expressed their developing work and gender identities, rudimentary forms of proletariat and feminist consciousness, and the intense contradictions they grappled with in dealing with new situations they faced at the FTZ.

The discussions ranged from critiquing and ridiculing their immediate oppressors, Pushla and Sanka, to criticizing the factory for not better organizing and managing the work process. They also talked about everyday injustices and collectively strategized the best way to respond to a situation.

One morning I saw Nimali sewing in Line A and inquired why this was so when I met her at the lunchtime group. "Punishment," she said, using the English word. "I did not come to work because of sickness and Sanka transferred me to Line A as a punishment," she further explained.

Niluka angrily said, "Now Sanka shamelessly goes looking for her. Because the skirt order is coming and then Nimali's work is needed. You, Nimali, don't come back."

"Yes, don't come back again. This is such a bother. To go when he does not want you and come back when he wants you," Rena concurred.

"Like toys. No, I am not coming back," Nimali said.

Just as she promised, she did not return for the skirt order and the new pocket sewers were having many problems. Every time Sanka yelled at a pocket sewer, one of the lunch-group members laughingly reminded him that if Nimali were on the line he would not have these problems.

CLASS CONSCIOUSNESS

"Ah, Sandya miss, come, come," Niluka welcomed me when I approached the lunch-group gathering on a mid-February day, and she continued, "The hot news for today is that we are prohibited from eating anything on the lines from tomorrow onward."

This led to a discussion of Sanka and his rules, and Menike said, "What is it to them? About 10:30 he runs and gets some biscuits from the locker. We don't have those privileges. We have to wait with dry mouths and empty stomachs."

Rena concurred, saying, "Yes, he eats at 10:30 and comes back with crumbs all over his mouth. All the rules are only for 'little us [*podi apita*].'"

Group members' conversations were usually peppered with "us/them" divisions. In fact, the discussions usually were geared toward clearly delineating who "us" were and who "they" were. While alliances with higher officials were strategically made on the shop floor, workers at the lunch group constantly reminded each other why they should think and act as a separate group. Although these ideas were not expressed in conventional ways, they were clearly coming to terms with a worker identity and a basic understanding of proletarian class consciousness.

Whenever I started a discussion with certain buzzwords, such as "labor rights," "exploitation," "capitalists," "proletariat," and so on, many group members gamely picked up the threads of Marxist knowledge they had received in high school and from the leftist party leaflets within the FTZ area. However, in their daily discussions, class consciousness was expressed in weaker and more-familiar terms, in combination with other knowledge and understanding that made sense to them in the local context. Although the lunch group certainly provided a fertile ground for developing class consciousness and political activism, the daily meetings and activities showed that the consciousness and activism they developed existed with other strains of perceptions that resulted in deeply ambivalent and complex responses.[7]

The lunch-group members not only identified their immediate supervisors as the "other" but also developed a critique of some of them. Pushla and Sanuja were the usual targets of these critiques, which came to a head after Kamali left Suishin and Priyanka was made the new line leader.

"I knew Sanuja sir would make Priyanka the assistant supervisor of our line," said Niluka. "*Ane*, yes. Then he wouldn't have to be ashamed about this affair. He can be happy that his girlfriend is not a lowly worker anymore," Menike further explained in a tone that left no doubt as to what she thought of the situation.

"Why wouldn't they promote you to the assistant supervisor position now that Kamali has left?" I asked Vasanthi.

"Perera san asked me whether I wanted to be the assistant supervisor even before he made Kamali one, but it is no use. If you want promotions then you have to forget the other workers and take offerings [in the form of information] for the rulers [*palakayanta kath adinna*]. If you take the workers' side, there is no progress. Didn't we see what happened to Kamali? She talked on behalf of us. That is disgusting to them. That is why Kamali was never promoted to supervisor grade. But you saw how the workers cried when she left." Continuing her angry outburst, Vasanthi further explained how Pushla came to her present position by reporting workers' activities to management.

"Pushla only gives good reports to workers who tell on others. She just hates our group. You know why? Just because we fight against injustices. *Ane* Sandya miss, I would rather beg from door to door than eat what I earn by betraying [*pava deela*] my own people [*thamange evun*]. The day I leave this factory I am going to write a good letter to Perera san letting him know all that is happening in the factory."

Such complicated and contradictory strains of consciousness were common in the women's narratives. Vasanthi once became incensed with Sanka for reporting workers' leave in a way that resulted in two workers losing salary for two days. Although these workers were not even members of her lunch group, Vasanthi, along with the two victims, started voicing dissent.

"What is this? Can he get more when he cuts our salary? I'll tell you, Sandya miss, it is their deeds that are being reported in the papers [*Dabindu* and *Niveka*]. Is there any paper that scolded Perera san or Gamini sensei? No, right? Everybody scolds these factory bosses. Because of them, those big people have to hide in shame," Vasanthi said.

Her resentment, brought on by everyday indignities suffered at the hands of various controlling agents, seemed to miss the elusive target that cloaked itself with kindness and concern. The constantly unfolding FTZ script certainly provided its actors with contrasting scenes that further complicated the process of uncovering the deeper plot and strategizing a suitable response.

The day Batti left Suishin, several workers belonging to the lunch group demonstrated the anger they felt about their helpless situation and the way their immediate supervisors treated them. When she saw Batti sobbing at the line, Vasanthi angrily admonished her, saying, "Why are you crying? The day I leave I am not going to shed even a single tear. Batti, don't be crazy, and stop crying. I am very happy at least one is getting out of this hell [*nara wala*]. If anybody can escape, that is all I want."

Menike seconded this by saying, "What is the point in remaining when we have to take this kind of verbal abuse? They scold us as if we are dogs. They even say we are cows. I am very happy that Batti is escaping. We will all be here only a little bit more."

Vasanthi picked up again, saying, "We came here because we are poor and we have no place else to go. Still, our parents do not like it that we came here. But these officers treat us like we are cats and dogs. I won't cry at all."

However, at the end of the day, when Batti came to say good-bye, Vasanthi could look away dry-eyed only for ten seconds. As soon as she looked at Batti, they both broke down in loud sobs and hugged each other, crying for what seemed like a long time. Niluka later wrote to me that the day Vasanthi left, at the end of August, Vasanthi cried just as hard. During my research, two members of the group left Suishin: Batti and Kamali. On both these occasions, the lunchtime meeting became a sad venue for bidding farewell. These scenes demonstrated the space these groups created for forging and maintaining strong friendships as well as how, despite all the hardships and exploitation, the FTZ interlude provided some positive experiences for young Sri Lankan women.

Although their everyday lives showed many contradictions, Suishin workers in general, and this lunch group in particular, took the stance that they are politically conscious women as opposed to being simply village garment factory workers. When I asked them why they wanted to come to the FTZ when there were factories close to their villages, workers first responded with facial and hand gestures of disgust. According to many workers, village factory workers were much more oppressed, but they did not know that they had the right to protest such treatment.

"Those girls are so grateful for their jobs. Some girls even worship their managers before leaving work," Nimali said.

According to Menike, she saw far more worth in their difficult city living than in secure but restricted and ignorant village life and village employment. "Here, we suffer. But we know that and we fight for better conditions. We don't fight to become 'managers' favorite girl' like village factory workers. Our objective is to become the managers' most hated children," she finished, laughing, while pointing to the other members of the group.

They also referred to more organized activities within the FTZ area, such as labor strikes, NGO activities, and leftist rallies and marches that provided the opportunity to participate and demand their rights. "Village girls have none of these opportunities to learn. They have no idea of worker rights or even human rights. Because they go back to their separate homes every evening, they don't have any time to discuss all the bad things that happen to them," Niluka once explained.

Nimali concurred, saying, "There is no unity among the workers because all the inequalities in the village are brought to the factory. I heard that in one factory the govigama [caste] workers asked for a separate lunchroom."

Vasanthi responded to this by proudly declaring, "Look at us, we don't even know each other's caste. We don't care. We have bigger problems to solve."

Almost all discussions about village garment factories were characterized by this superiority that the workers expressed about their class consciousness and political activism compared to village factory workers. Caitrin Lynch (2000) writes that village garment factory workers negotiated an identity as "newly traditional good girls" by emphasizing their moral superiority compared to FTZ factory workers. Interestingly, FTZ workers used the opposite of what the village workers used (their residence in the village) to measure their own superiority over the village workers (as ones who live in the modern city). According to lunch-group discussions, the village workers were not free. Their families closely controlled their desires, movements, and money.

"Living away from your family makes you strong and capable to face anything on your own. I learned many things by living in the city. I decide what is best for me and my family. True, it is difficult living alone. But I also found the meaning of my life [*haraya*] by living here with my friends," Nimali said.

"All those women would love to come to the city and to work in the FTZ. The only reason that they work in the village is that they are scared to explore the world on their own," Niluka responded.

Through these discussions, workers attempted to construct themselves as class-conscious, feminist political activists. These narratives, however, were spaces where the contradictions and ambivalences they were grappling with came to light. Four of the lunch-group members (Kamali, Vasanthi, Batti, and Kumari) intermittently used the dominant cultural images to express their difference. According to them, migrant workers were morally superior because they were able to ward off evil influences without family or community directly controlling their movements. They also said that working in the village did not necessarily mean that the women did not engage in activities that city workers were accused of.

FEMINISM OF THEIR OWN

These conflict-ridden responses typified the workers' contextually articulated feminist consciousness. Although Suishin workers' everyday responses to situations did not usually elicit evidence of a budding feminist consciousness, lunch groups again proved more fertile grounds for expression and the display of a rudimentary feminist consciousness. Although they did not use associated technical terms such as *sthrivadhaya* (feminism), *purushadhipathya* (patriarchy), or *sthrivadhi aragalaya* (feminist struggle) in their discussions, the group members constantly talked about how women should be united not only against the factory owners and officials but against all men who did not respect them for who they were. In crises regarding relationships and violence against women, they almost always expressed their solidarity and sympathy with the other women workers. Demonstrating the fragility of a notion of universal feminist solidarity, the workers expressed a somewhat hesitant satisfaction when middle-class women were insulted or got into trouble with men from marginalized groups.

The group members fought almost daily with supervisors and officers who were mostly men. Outside the factory, in their private lives, they resisted the influence of middle-class women in many aspects of life, especially when it came to fashion. These oppositional cultural and political processes that they engaged in as women certainly instilled a rudimentary feminist consciousness, which existed in constant competition with other, much older and more established social and cultural perceptions. Their lunchtime conversations, interactions, and resistance showcased these multiple strands of consciousness and the tensions they initiated.

As stated earlier, the group members did not criticize elderly top managers much and at times even treated them as fathers. Women in general also liked to give and share food and appreciated officers who partook of their food. This indicated an egalitarian tendency, because the action was considered an effort to transcend class and caste boundaries. Several officers frequented the lunch group to eat their fruit and candy. Mock fights and much laughter ensued, but women almost always willingly shared their food with officers. It was clear that the value attached to giving in Buddhist culture and the internalized perception that women should nurture men influenced this contradictory action by the workers. It also showed how cultural values influenced people in gendered ways, as the men—both the officers and the workers—who shared women's food did not reciprocate in kind.

Although general solidarity existed among the workers as exploited women, there were also jealousies and tensions regarding relationships and marriage prospects. There was much gossiping, there were many rumors, and there were even arguments about such issues at the assembly line. Although lunch-group members were more aware of class and feminist issues than the others, they were not immune to such tensions either. But the concerns and tensions they expressed were colored by class antagonism. While they generally supported any woman having boyfriends and criticized men who cheated on women, the group members always found fault with women who attempted to forge romantic relationships across class boundaries. Amila especially was criticized because she told me what she thought was lacking in several group members' relationships.

"A woman should always marry up. There is no point in marrying someone if he cannot provide the financial security to [allow a woman to] stay home and be a full-time wife. Now look, Kamali is getting married to Kumara. He only gets about Rs. 3,000 a month. What can they do with that? Kamali must start a grocery store or something like that to make ends meet," said Amila, dexterously sewing a pocket onto a garment. "My fiancé has a two-story house and he owns a van. I can be comfortable as a housewife. His house even has a telephone, so I can call you even after leaving the factory," she further explained, cutting the thread ends with her little scissors.

Seven of the group members had boyfriends at the time, and all of the boyfriends came from similarly poor, marginalized backgrounds. Hearing (from another worker) that Amila looked down on their choices, an angry lunch group informed me that Amila turned her back on her religion to marry up.

"That man is a Buddhist, and you know how devout a Catholic Amila is. Rasika told us that Amila cried for days when she got to know she would not be able to have a church wedding," Niluka informed me.

"After the marriage, he is taking her to Rathnapura, and there is no Catholic church around that area. So Amila cannot even go to church on Sundays anymore," Vasanthi said with obvious satisfaction.

"He has told her that the children would be brought up Buddhist. Think about how many things she will be losing to get a rich man. *Ane*, we don't need such people," Manike declared.

It was during this angry outburst that group members expressed feminist ideas most strongly, asserting that they would not marry a man who did not allow them equal partnership. They also expressed the value and need for women to learn to be financially independent rather than hope to be a housewife to a rich man. On other occasions, however, they indicated that the reason they chose men from their own backgrounds was their sense of reality.

Once, talking about the romantic relationship between Priyanka and Sanuja, Niluka said, "The only reason that Priyanka 'captured [*allagaththa*]' Sanuja was that our Vasanthi [another one of those "fair, slim, long-haired girls"] did not want big people [*loku athu*]." "Why didn't you want him?" I asked Vasanthi. "I did not want to be a toy that they discard when tired of," Vasanthi replied, indicating that perhaps if he had proposed marriage she would not have been reluctant to accept. They all asked me not to worry about Priyanka's fate because she chose this dangerous relationship over advances from several men of her own class.

Niluka, the most rebellious of the lunch-group members and the one who expressed the strongest class and feminist consciousness among the workers at Suishin, was in a romantic relationship with a sailor in the navy and had two brothers in the armed forces. Her emotional attachment to these men saw her taking up virulent nationalistic rhetoric in our discussions of the civil war and its effects on people. Together with other group members, she criticized the government for prolonging the war and being unconcerned about its human cost. While others rarely took up serious discussions on the ways and means of solving the conflict, Niluka thought the best and the only solution was to "destroy the terrorists." When I reminded her about the innocent women and children who suffer just as she was suffering, she somewhat hesitantly said, "Men and women, they are all the same." These conversations showed how these women's developing consciousness encompassed only a limited space surrounding the FTZ women workers and perhaps other marginalized women within their ethnic group.[8]

Almost every worker had a brother or a close relative in the Sri Lankan armed forces, and many workers' boyfriends were also members of the armed forces. These emotional attachments elicited different reactions to the ongoing ethnic conflict. While many workers simply wanted the war to end and their loved ones to come home safely, others adopted popular rhetoric about winning the war and sacrificing for the motherland. On the government-stipulated War Heroes' Day (June 6, 2000), there was going to be a nationwide two-minute silence at 9:00 A.M. to honor those serving in the armed forces. For a few days workers, led by Niluka, kept asking Sanuja's permission to be able to observe the silence but to no avail. At 9:00 A.M. on June 6, following Niluka's lead, many women stopped work and stood up. In a bid to save face, Sanuja suddenly announced that the factory was observing the silence and asked everybody to stand. The tearful workers spent about five minutes paying respect to the soldiers and more time afterward sharing the excitement of their victory. It was, in fact, direct defiance of factory discipline and a semiorganized political activity. However, this intense loyalty to their army soldier menfolk made them blind to military violence on civilians and distanced them further from potential feminist alliances across ethnic boundaries.

INTENTIONALITY

I conducted in-depth interviews with eight lunch-group members, and when I reminded them of situations in which they drew on a common cultural repertoire and dominant constructions of gender, five confirmed that they consciously manipulated some of the expected behavioral traits for short-term advantage. As Rena put it, "These men are so stupid. If you act like stupid, weak women, they love to teach you and feel like big men. How do you think Amila gets Sanka to baby her all the time?"

However, they all seemed to be in agreement (even Rena, who was a Catholic) about the pleasures of giving and good *karma* even if it concerned supervisors. They did not think it might hinder their solidarity and struggles to share their snacks with supervisors. "How could that hinder our unity? I think it hinders their unity as supervisors. They will have to think 'This woman put at least a morsel of food in my mouth' before doing wrong to me. Who knows, one day our meritorious deeds might come in handy," Niluka said.

When I reminded her that it did not happen at the time of the labor strike, Niluka agreed and said in a sad voice, "It is only little people [*podi minissu*] who have such qualities. A little man's heart is made of gold. There is nothing to say about big people's [*loku minissu*] hearts."

Speaking on the same topic, Sujatha said, "Haven't you heard about the saying, 'Kings become poor and the poor become kings'? We will see."

Lunch groups, especially this particular one, were a good ground for articulating a form of class and feminist consciousness that was fraught with a simultaneous attachment to certain traditional cultural values. Within their narratives, workers moved back and forth along intersecting continuums of class and feminist consciousness. Although the chance of these group activities leading to transformational politics was remote, it provided space for imagination and strategizing, which formed part of the women's political lives as industrial workers.

Specific Crisis Situations

The first power failure at the factory during my stint at Suishin was on a day that the production target was increased by 20 pieces to satisfy an impatient buyer. When Gamini asked whether it was possible to increase the target, Sanka readily agreed, angering the already-overburdened workers. Despite the workers' loud protests, Sanka and Pushla started planning for how to meet the new target. Overtime work until 9:00 P.M. would be required that day, and the next day the work would start one hour early. Sanuja and Jayantha joined the line supervisors to plan strategies while the workers continued to protest, vowing that they would not sew one piece more than the normal target. Both executives listened patiently before telling them that they would be given an incentive if they finished the order on time. But the workers kept saying that the new target was unrealistic. At that moment the lights went off, instantly evoking joyous exclamation from several workers. And Amitha proclaimed, "The gods have looked at the workers and sent the lights away."

After a few minutes of anxious discussion, the production manager left and Sanuja, Indika, and several production assistants sat around the table located at the other end of the hall. Workers started standing up and going to their friends' stations. Soon Line C became divided into four or five groups of women, as did the other lines. I joined the group of workers who huddled around Vijee's machine. Workers in different groups remarked about the way Sanka and Pushla sat in a corner crestfallen and angry. In contrast, the worker groups were engaging in fun activities, including reminding Sanka of how his plot to make them work to death did not succeed. The conversation in our group was dominated by Madhu's jokes and antics. She turned her machine light up and started singing into it as if it were a microphone. She sang, "It is only because you are out of my reach [like a flower] that you are so beautiful."

This was obviously sung to provoke Priyanka who had earlier written those lines in a letter intended for Sanuja. Priyanka stood up and walked to another group. Madhu sang behind her retreating figure, "Love is a beautiful mistake. There is no excuse for that." Everybody laughed.

After a few minutes, I joined Vasanthi and the lunch-group members who had gathered around Menike's machine. In contrast to the former group, the latter was engaged in a serious discussion about the way Sanka showed them no regard in his agreement to increase the target.

"Disgusting man of two tongues, he and his bosses will one day kill us to earn a few pennies," Nimali said.

"We suffer because we have no unity. We should unite and refuse to sew a single piece more than the normal target per hour. Let's write a note informing the line of this," suggested Rena.

They asked my suggestions for the letter and were writing the second draft when power was restored. The power failure had lasted twenty-five minutes and both the officers and the workers scuttled back and assumed their familiar positions. Sanka and Pushla started yelling at workers to hurry so that at least eighty pieces an hour could be produced. Although workers did work overtime until 9:00 P.M., the target of ninety pieces was not mentioned again. I excitedly looked forward to observing the other workers' reactions to the drafted note, but unfortunately it was not passed down the line.

In extraordinary situations of crisis, women workers poignantly portrayed a labor force that resented their work and the new work ethic forced on them. They gave voice to the developing subaltern culture. These situations baffled the existing and familiar power structures and allowed women an easier space to give voice to their resentment and their desire for different human and labor relations on the shop floor. Blackouts stemming from the loss of electricity represented a special crisis that initiated power crises within the factory. FTZ factories were built on the ideal of superfast, superefficient productivity, and power failures brought not only financial losses to factories but also harmed the ethic of hard work and maximum productivity. Therefore, whenever a power failure occurred, it stressed and angered the officers while providing the relaxed and jubilant workers a chance to ridicule the officers' distress. Because of their attempts to become highly skilled workers, it sometimes appeared as if the workers and managers strove toward the same goal of maximum productivity. But a power crisis gave them a chance to register that they were in fact marginalized workers who wished and dreamed of different goals than the supervisors, factory officers, or managers.

The second time the lights went off was on a Saturday, and the staff and workers alike were dressed in casual clothing. The blackout started around 8:45 A.M. and workers again gathered in little groups to socialize. Several officers circulated from time to time among worker groups much to the delight of the workers who took this chance to make fun of their earlier commands. This time I did manage to circulate among the groups and discovered how much it meant for the workers to have the free time as well as the chance to abort the supervisors' plans for their time and productivity. The power failure that day was one hour and fifteen minutes long and workers took turns telling jokes and wishing that the power failure would go on for hours. They realized that it meant they had to work harder and longer the next day to make up for lost time, but they still coveted these rare occasions in which they were afforded a chance to criticize the officers and to express their opposition to being considered "producing machines."[9]

The third time the lights went off was for twenty minutes and it was at a time when relations between the workers and Line C supervisors were severely strained because of a popular worker's departure. The power failure was said to be the gods' way of punishing the supervisors for the injustices they had committed against workers. Workers wanted the power failure to continue the whole day and, in contrast to the previous power failure, all Line C workers sat close together and quietly discussed the events leading to Sujatha's departure from the factory. Sanuja and Isuru tried to talk to the workers about the same incident, but the workers seemed unusually noncommittal. I sat near the lunch-group members and they, along with other workers, spent the twenty minutes blaming and cursing Pushla for their friend's resignation. When the power returned, too soon according to the workers, it put a smile on Pushla's face as she watched workers scamper back to their machines.

Factory staff, however, was also controlled by the factory demands on time, body, and space even while they were the agents imposing those demands on workers. They were annoyed and stressed about power failures, which forced them to lay down their weapons of control. They either sat glumly in corners or gathered in small groups to enjoy these rare occasions. I also treasured these moments because it provided the opportunity for me to have the workers' undivided attention. The foreign factory owners' concerns over power failures were different from those among the Sri Lankan senior and junior officers. One of the FTZ investment conditions was that the BOI would provide uninterrupted power to the factories. It was stipulated precisely to prevent this kind of power failure, which could result in huge profit losses. The BOI's failure to keep its promise angered the usually calm and soft-spoken Ando san who berated not only the BOI but the Sri Lankan government and the "always incompetent Sri Lankans."

Later Jayantha, the factory manager, told me that Ando san made a remark about his reading the newspaper, and that he replied, "What are we supposed to do? When the power is gone, the power is gone."

Power of Medicine

"Chandrika, child, now go back to the line," Hemamali, the head nurse at the factory medical center, called out in a sugary sweet voice addressing a woman lying down on a bed at the far corner of the center. The young woman looked tired and, in a barely audible voice, complained of new pains in her abdomen and continued to lie down. While talking to me about her home and family, Hemamali asked the sick woman to leave the bed twice more before she suddenly stood up and stomped toward the bed.

"You have been lying here for more than twenty minutes now. Either you go back to the line or I am going to take you to the hospital. What do you want? Would you leave on your own or should I make you do that?" Hemamali shouted, with her hands on her hips and bending down close to the patient's ear. The woman stood up and complained of more pain while walking toward the door, tears running down her cheeks. This threat to take workers to the hospital was almost always effective, as workers feared going to the hospital for two reasons: first, it meant that they would lose their salary for half a day and, second, most of the time all they needed was a little rest.

The factory medical center had two beds and offered painkillers, lotions, and other basic services to workers who became ill at the factory. Two nurses worked on shifts maintaining the center and making simple diagnoses. Apart from these services, the medical center and the nurses worked as disciplining agents who controlled "unnecessary" disruptions to the assembly-line work. Many workers came complaining about headaches, back aches, and stomach pains on the days I visited the medical center. Nurses administered lotions and painkillers and sent the workers back to the lines within two to three minutes.[10]

For workers, the medical center offered hope of a refuge that they more often than not found difficult to realize. Many times a worker came to the medical center hoping that the nurse would decide that the worker needed a fifteen-minute break. However, a break was only granted to workers who presented with severe symptoms such as dizziness or diarrhea. Usually after ten or fifteen minutes, nurses would ask the workers to leave. I saw workers resisting this by either complaining of new pains or just continuing to lie down. It was then that the two nurses, especially Hemamali, became rude.

Many workers left with protesting grunts or tears in their eyes, mostly in response to the nurse's harsh words. Complaints of headaches, body aches, cold, fever, and menstrual pain received only minimal attention. I saw many Line C workers laughingly get away from the line saying that they were going to the medical center to get some lotion or painkillers. Most of the time Sanka and Pushla yelled after them, but the workers playfully ignored them to enjoy a two- to three-minute break from the assembly line. However, if the nurse refused a break when a worker was actually ill, the worker would return to the line crying and cursing the nurse. Usually almost everybody in the line offered a comforting word by criticizing the nurse and relating their own bad experiences. Sometimes several workers in the line shed tears along with the sick worker. In one such incident, Madhu came back crying and said, "I could kill that nurse woman. She is a devil."

According to the nurse, she had to be careful to determine who was really sick when granting breaks. Because the work was physically arduous, complaints of aches and pains were unavoidable. But in assembly-line work it was important that all stations function properly to ensure the hourly target. If the nurse was too kind, then half the workers would take breaks and the production process would crumble. Therefore, the nurse believed that she had dual responsibilities: one to the medical profession and the other to the factory in filtering requests to determine who really needed care. She said that she too was sorry to deny rest to workers but felt that many were just trying to avoid work, and she thought it was her duty to prevent such misuse of the medical center. This nurse's attitude demonstrates how in a capitalist industrial environment the medical profession can be used to monitor and discourage claims on factory production time and, consequently, how workers can identify medical professionals as agents of control.

Power of Disease

One category of illness brought instant relief to those suffering from it. The workers who developed symptoms of contagious diseases were immediately taken to the FTZ hospital and, if diagnosed, were sent home with 14 days of paid leave. The fear of a minor epidemic within the factory was very real, especially because of its closed, poorly ventilated, and crowded atmosphere. If such a disease were contracted by 25 percent of the workers, all the production lines would have to be closed, bringing heavy financial losses to the factory. Fear of contagion, therefore, provided paid leave, a rare luxury for workers who sometimes felt well enough to return to work in about one week. Sri Lankans call these diseases "gods' diseases [*deyiyange leda*]" and usually talk about them in hushed tones for fear that they would be spread by the mere utterance of their names. In the factory, however, if a worker contracted one of these gods' diseases (measles, mumps, chicken pox, for example), the others considered her lucky. It was common for workers to pray half jokingly that they would contract a gods' disease so that they could get two weeks of paid leave for an upcoming family ceremony. But because these diseases, once contracted, usually provided lifetime immunity, it was rare that these wishes came true.

The lunch-group members informed me, though, that the workers sometimes manipulated the fear of these diseases to get paid leave. They themselves had done this to get Devika, a good friend of the group members, paid leave to go to her village and attend her younger sister's puberty ceremony. When Devika asked for six days' leave, she was granted only one day of unpaid leave. Devika decided to take six days off without approval and risk losing her job. Because Devika was a good worker who did not ask for leave without cause, the whole group was convinced that she was entitled to paid leave. Therefore, the day Devika took her approved leave three of her friends started dropping comments about Devika's cousin who had contracted measles. Both Pushla and Sanka heard these comments and therefore, three days later, when Devika sent a telegram saying that she was suffering from measles no one was surprised. When she came back after seven days with a medical certificate written by an Ayurvedic doctor, who incidentally was one of her cousins, she was sent back home with seven more days of paid leave. After some discussion, the group members said it was fine for me to include this story in my "book."

"Nobody will be able to trace the story back to Devika, what with all this commotion about chicken pox these days," Niluka said confidently.

This confidence was the result of a minor chicken pox epidemic that was spreading in the country and in the factory at the time.[11] The epidemic temporarily reconfigured some of the power relations in interesting ways. One day when I went to the medical center the nurse told me of three workers who had contracted chicken pox and developed symptoms while at the factory. She had to accompany them to the hospital in a factory vehicle. Two or three days later, I started seeing panic in many quarters. One Friday morning at breakfast Mr. Perera told other top managers how the workers were inconsiderate of others' safety and came to the factory even when they felt sick. Workers had been advised not to come to the factory if they felt feverish and were developing rashes, the early symptoms of chicken pox; this absence from the factory would be paid leave. This contradicted the factory's typical reluctance to grant sick leave and its insistence that the workers should not take a day off for "simple aches and pains."

There was general skepticism about the medical certificates that the workers usually brought after unapproved leave. Therefore, it was not surprising that they came to the factory to be legally and ceremoniously diagnosed with the dreaded disease. Knowing how workers wished for "gods' diseases" to obtain paid leave, I also felt that there might be more than the need for approved diagnosis in some workers' insistence on coming to work. According to lunch-group members, the sick workers wanted the other workers to contract the disease as well and qualify for paid leave. The ones who stayed home obeying factory requests, they said, were selfish and did not know the meaning of sharing.

Although I saw several workers lying on beds waiting for the vehicle to take them to the hospital, I did not dare approach them for fear that I would contract the disease. This scare started at the end of May and continued throughout June. I completely stopped resting on medical center beds, as did all the officers. Several times I visited the nurses for short periods of time because it would not look right to abandon them completely at a place now marked with danger and fear. On both occasions, Hemamali, the especially rude nurse, bitterly complained about management pushing the weight of the whole disease onto her shoulders. A young woman, and one who like me had not previously contracted the disease, she feared and resented the long periods of time she spent with workers who had chicken pox while waiting for a vehicle to take them to the hospital. According to Hemamali, the managers had no concern for her welfare and used the vehicles to go to the market, airport, or lunch without sending a vehicle for her to take the workers out.

Managers, however, were very concerned for their own safety. Ando san was especially concerned because Suishin's drivers were assigned to all vehicles and, therefore, the drivers who drove the sick people to the hospital would drive the managers' vehicles, including his own. He had directed Perera to set up a van and a driver who would be on call every day of the month just for the hospital trip. Perera was frustrated in his efforts to find a driver for the "hospital van" and complained that Ando san's unrealistic expectations were borne out of his ridiculous paranoia about contracting the disease from company drivers.

At this time of crisis, when familiar alliances and loyalties were somewhat topsy-turvy, the workers seemed to find the situation empowering. They were now allowed to rest as soon as they complained of headache, fever, or dizziness, even if they indicated no visible symptoms. Unlike many others, workers had no fear of visiting the medical center or resting on the beds. They liked the paid leave that resulted from contracting the disease and also found it hard to resist the temptation to take breaks. At Line C, workers laughingly talked about how "the nurse woman seemed to have suddenly gone dumb." According to them, she did not come to the curtained-off section to shout at the workers. In fear of sending workers who might have chicken pox back to the lines, nurses allowed workers with complaints to remain for one to two hours at the center. Workers who visited the center to obtain painkillers found they could stay a few minutes longer talking with the sick ones lying on beds. The few times I visited the center during this crisis I saw several healthy workers sitting on beds socializing with the sick ones and laughing.

One day toward the end of June I found Hemamali showing some photographs to several workers and describing a ritual ceremony held at her house. Hemamali seemed to have shifted alliances in a moment of vulnerability. However, Line C workers' comments expressing satisfaction with her subdued demeanor also showed that the workers were not ready to forgive past injuries. It was a moment during which Hemamali, the agent of factory control, found herself alienated from both the managers and the workers.

Daily lunch-group conversations also demonstrated how much the workers understood and relished the shift in the balance of power.

"Those days when we came late to work, the staff people made us stand in front of their cubicles like beggars" to get back their time cards, Nimali said.

"Now, when we are just coming inside the door they extend the cards: no more lectures, no more 'next time we will fire you' crap," chimed Vasanthi, beaming.

"But, you know what? I really feel like staying there a bit more just to scare those biggies," said Niluka.

On another day when we were discussing the fear of the epidemic, Rena and Niluka folded their hands and, looking at the sky, intoned, "*Ane* God, please spread the epidemic so that Suishin will be closed for at least a week." During the height of the epidemic, workers were aware of their power, however limited, over the production process and factory profits.

For better or for worse, the epidemic was contained within a few weeks. As the monsoon rains hit the island, the fears of epidemics and tensions of strange power configurations gradually subsided along with the pre-monsoon heat. From the end of June until the time of my departure in mid-July no new cases of chicken pox were diagnosed. For workers, their days of socializing at the medical center were over. Hemamali, however, had not overcome the new demeanor she was forced to adopt by that time. Seven months later, in February 2001, Mangala wrote to me that "the nurse woman is as mean as ever."

Labor Strike

"*Aiyo,* you should have come yesterday to see your friends' little works. *They got their bonus and even went to the fair,*" Janaka, the Line H production assistant, said as I entered the factory.

By that time I had gathered from Mr. Perera the reason for Janaka's smug smile and sarcastic tone. There was a labor strike and the workers had refused to work after the tea break the day before (on April 6, 2000). The workers' grievance was that April 10 was too late a date to distribute the bonus because many workers had to leave the next day to go to their villages to celebrate the Sinhala and Tamil New Year on April 13. This would not leave time for them to shop for traditional New Year gifts (mostly clothes) for parents and family members. Therefore, the Joint Council of Workers (JOC) demanded that either the bonus or half the April salary be given by April 8.

When I arrived at the office that morning, Mr. Perera informed me of the labor strike and shared with me some details of the negotiation process. According to Perera, management proposed to give the salary and bonus on April 8 and close the factory for the long vacation the same day. The JOC objected to this, saying that workers needed two more working days to earn enough money to buy gifts. But when the JOC informed the workers, they protested. Rather than accepting responsibility for the decision, JOC members blamed it on management. Then they forced the workers to stay behind in the meal hall after tea and demanded that Perera talk to the workers. He would have done that, but there was a BOI stipulation that if a manager wanted to talk to his workers directly, he had to obtain prior approval from the BOI. When Perera talked to the workers after obtaining BOI approval, the workers accepted that they had been misled and went back to work. Throughout the discussion, Perera was careful to put the blame on the JOC members and expressed sympathy for the women workers who were misled to commit this "misdeed." In a way, it was not surprising because the major strike activists included some of Perera's favorite "children."

When I went to the meal hall for breakfast, the junior officers told me about the strike. Many junior officers adopted a sarcastic tone in informing me about the strike. According to Nayani, the workers must be feeling ashamed today because yesterday they acted like kings and then got to know that their own people had deceived them. She told me that the workers did not know how to organize something in a way that would benefit them. Isuru's reasoning was that "girls usually go with the wave, shouting and jumping." Both Indika and Nayani said that they felt ashamed to even look at Ando san's face because of the workers' misbehavior.

At Line C, Chandani and Vijee were the first to volunteer their perspectives and cautioned, "Don't tell Pushla anything that we tell you. It is prohibited to talk about the strike on the lines."

At this time Ranjan came to where I was standing and said, "Yesterday these people went on strike. It was the girls in this line that stood out." This comment made Chandani blush and say, "We did not want the bonus so soon because we are from [Katunayake]. We could shop even on the 11th. It is a shame about the people who have to go to villages. That is why we stayed behind and showed support."

I visited the *matome* section to see how they had perceived the situation, and Bhagya expressed the same perspective of disinterested solidarity when she said, "I am from Katunayake. I don't want the bonus. I don't care whether they give it or not. But I felt sad for girls who are boarded here. They have no time to buy clothes for their parents because the salary and bonus will be given only on Monday (April 10). At the weekend when they have time to shop they have no money to buy things. Most *matome* people stayed behind in the canteen though Nayomi *akka* and Anula *akka* [supervisor and assistant supervisor] came back to work. That *nangi* over there is not even entitled to a bonus because she is new. But she stayed with us to show solidarity. Nayomi *akka* scolded her and that *nangi* is still crying because of that." That particular worker heard us talking about her and started to cry again, making everybody teary.

It was interesting to note the way Chandani and Bhagya tried to reinterpret the failed strike as a charitable deed on behalf of others rather than as a struggle for their own rights. Chandani actually was from a remote village in the Southern Province and stayed at a nearby boardinghouse to attend work. Bhagya traveled from her home located in a distant village in the Western Province, but she belonged to an impoverished family. Both of them needed the money and their portrayal of themselves as disinterested parties showed how they used Buddhist perceptions about the virtue of being disinterested in money and helping others to understand the failed strike. It is also interesting to speculate about whether they would have understood a successful strike the same way.

Workers gave different meaning to the strike and its aftermath. When I came back to Line C, Madhu and Vijee, who both looked excited, signaled me to come and talk to them. Both were trying to talk at the same time and especially Madhu seemed very happy and proud talking with much emphasis.

"We stayed in the meal hall until Perera san came. We sat on tables and sang songs. When the production assistants came to take us back we hooted at them. Sanuja sir, Ajith, and Janaka came saying, "Children go, go, go back to work." We hooted. Then Siri *aiya* (a JOC member) said, "If you want to talk to children, you need to come to them." At this last line, Madhu looked up at me with much pride and rebelliousness in her eyes and continued while gesturing toward different workers. "But in this line seven to eight people came back. Pushla (the supervisor), Kamali (the assistant supervisor), Amila, Priyanka, Chuti . . . ah, this Nimmi also worked." Hearing this, Nimmi said, "After tea we just came back and did not know about a strike." Madhu accused her again, saying, "But we came to take the people who did not know. Why didn't you come?" "We tried to go out. But Pushla *akka* did not allow us," said Nimmi, trying to defend herself.

Madhu continued her account of the traitors: "Amila dragged Priyanka back to work. We came from that door and checked to see who was working. Bitches. . . . Even if lightning strikes them, we won't care for them. . . . If the bonus was given, they will shove it too." She seemed very angry and was grinding her teeth and vigorously curving her mouth.

Priyanka then interjected, saying, "I tried to stay back, but Amila dragged me to the line. You saw how Amila dragged me, right, Madhu?"

Madhu ignored her and together with Vijee went on to explain in detail what the strike meant for them. Further along the line, Rena explained the indignities they suffered when they came back defeated. "When we came to the line, Pushla applauded and kept asking whether we went shopping with the bonus money. Sanka put Rs.1, 2, and 5 coins and small bills on our machines, ridiculing us for not getting the bonus." Chamila explained that they had struck because a bonus was good only if it was given at the right time. "It is wrong to ridicule us for that. It is our right to strike. We did what we wanted. It is wrong to attack us again and again."

While I was going around Line C listening to workers' reactions to the strike I saw Madhu crying and went to inquire. "That stinking bitch [*panduru balli*] scolded me. If it was a different time, I would give her some of mine too. [Madhu used *oki*, an abusive term, instead of *eya*, for Pushla.] Her condition these days is not good. [She was referring to Pushla's pregnancy.] I tolerated it by grinding my teeth. She ridiculed us by saying, 'We went like dogs and came back like dogs.'"

The other women expressed their anger over Pushla's outburst and agreed that even though she scolded one person, Pushla targeted everybody who participated in the strike. In fact, there were more than the usual number of verbal duels between the workers and the supervisors, and the workers expressed their unhappiness at what they considered persecuting attacks (*panna, panna gahanawa*). While this time was characterized by a heightened sense of class consciousness, it was also fraught with the embarrassment of defeat and regret at the knowledge that all managers and factory officers were angry with the Line C workers for being the most outspoken group.[12]

At the lunch group everybody was talking at the same time, trying to give their perspective on the strike. They were obviously emotionally involved in the crisis. They were ashamed, sad, and regretful; at the same time, they were aroused by an intense feeling of empowerment and solidarity. Their pride about the power they exercised for three hours was marred by their knowledge that the JOC had misled them. Several expressed regret that they had used an excellent tactic like a strike for a misconceived and petty adventure rather than for something worthwhile and substantial. Even more interesting was the way the strike had momentarily ripped the close-knit lunchtime group apart. While six members had stayed in the meal hall, three had gone back to work. When they talked to me the next day, these tensions surfaced again. Niluka and Rena, who management identified as two major participants in the strike, said it was great that they finally fought for their rights. Kamali and Batti, however, argued that it was wrong to demand that managers talk to them as the workers desired. Vasanthi and Sujatha stood in the middle, trying to accommodate both perspectives. Throughout this discussion, Vasanthi's voice wavered and she looked as if she were about to cry. "We are not enemies of Perera san or Gamini sensei. We love them. But if they had come to talk to us, the problem would have been solved in half an hour," she said.

The group became more agitated when Ajith (the Line E production assistant) started ridiculing them on their failed strike.[13] Sujatha, who was also close to tears by that time, said, "How could you say we did not win? We wanted Perera san to come and talk to us. He did so, and we came back to work." To this, Ajith answered, "So you went on strike to take a look at Perera san." Vasanthi responded, "Yes, we love Perera san." Ajith then turned to me and, in an attempt to get my support, said, "I wonder why they have not queued up near the office to take a look at him. . . . Do you know we hooted at these people before we took them back to the lines?" Niluka shouted (somewhat good naturedly) at the retreating Ajith, "Hooted, not only hooted we were going to beat [the production assistants] if we had had a little more time."

The New Year celebrations were considered a time for peace and reconciliation, and this helped ease tensions on the shop floor. The day before the April New Year vacation started, Pushla and Sanka were conspicuously silent. They were following the traditional norms that dictated the New Year should be a time for forgiveness and friendship. At 5:15 P.M., fifteen minutes before the end of the workday, workers and supervisors alike started cleaning and covering the machines. It was also the last day at work for Batti, who started saying good-bye. Much crying ensued and both

Sanka and Pushla looked on with sad eyes. Sanuja presided over a meeting held by the Floor 1 entrance, and he bid everyone a happy New Year. Then he directed his workers to the morning greeting place where the managers, including Ando san, were waiting to bid workers a happy New Year. Sanuja spoke on behalf of Ando san and management, bidding workers a happy New Year. At the end of his speech, Sanuja greeted them with the same Japanese greeting lines as in the morning ritual. Not expecting this, all the supervisors, who usually greet on behalf of the workers, stood with the managers and an uncomfortable few minutes passed before a woman worker took a step forward and greeted the managers in Japanese. The other side relaxed and, with this symbolic act of reconciliation, the workers scattered slowly in many directions.[14] The tensions created two days earlier by the strike were thus put to rest.

Effect of the Strike on the Individuals

Although the tensions were visibly put to rest, the changes initiated for different individual workers could not be erased so easily. Just as the lunch-group members were affected differently by the experience of the labor strike and responded differently to the complexities initiated by its fallout, other workers handled the new experience and new situation in various ways. The workers who participated and were visibly active in organizing the strike especially confronted several contradictions and dangers. This initiated a process of renegotiating tolerable positions within the power structure, and women tapped into conventional roles such as daughter, sister, and obedient and good Sinhala Buddhist woman.

Madhu: Political Activist and Little Sister

During the strike, Madhu demonstrated solidarity with the workers not only by refraining from work but also by being an active participant. The day after the strike, it was Madhu who most clearly expressed an awakening to a new understanding of class solidarity. That day she got into her first angry verbal battle with Pushla, who in condemning and ridiculing the strike participants was singularly harsh on Madhu perhaps because of their former sisterly relationship. Madhu responded with angry words and later in conversation with me used the harshest terms I heard from a worker to describe Pushla. However, she said that she gritted her teeth to stop saying really mean things because of Pushla's pregnancy. This was either a genuine concern, because cultural norms demanded that people be considerate toward pregnant women even if they were enemies, or was perhaps Madhu's way of avoiding confrontation that would bar any hope for reconciliation.

Moreover, Madhu said, "There is no point in working like dogs. I will have patience for these two days, but if she says anything after the long vacation, I will go home directly." Although this statement was bold, it included a defense mechanism. The vacation was for eight days and Madhu knew that it would surely ease some of the tension. It appeared as if she did not desire to strengthen her new identity as an active rebel. The vacation did lessen the tension, but Madhu was never able to regain her former privileged position. Within three months, she was transferred to two different stations where sewing was not as easy as the work she did in her former position. This considerably constrained her free time and Pushla never allowed herself to become as tolerant again. Madhu eventually started frequenting another lunch group and, although she still made people laugh, she became more serious in her relations with supervisors.

The labor strike was a momentous event in Madhu's life. Before the strike, she considered work an extension of her childhood where she rebelled against authority while expecting love and affection from people who wielded authority. Through that specific role she carved out a niche for herself, which, though resented by several fellow workers, prevented her from becoming just a number in an industrial plant. The strike interrupted this easy, fun-filled life and opened her eyes to her own and others' shared oppression. Although she showed an initial reluctance to pursue and incorporate this newfound knowledge, the circumstances forced her to undergo a painful identity crisis. When I left in July, she was still in the middle of this transformation.

Lalitha: Unhappy at Work

As noted in Chapter 3, Lalitha considered herself as having the "worker position with the highest status" in Suishin and took pride in her work. Her capabilities and meticulous work gave her confidence to be vocal in everyday struggles with supervisors and thus her active and loud participation in the labor strike came as no surprise to me. When I talked to her two days after the strike, she was a disappointed and low-spirited worker. The first thing she did was to declare that she would not be working at Suishin for long. Then she added, "As soon as I find somebody to marry, I will leave." Then she went on to tell me that her long-term boyfriend had cheated on her a few years earlier and that she found contentment at the factory after he left her. Because she was happy at the factory, marriage did not seem important. Her parents, however, had been trying to find a suitable match for some time, but were having difficulties due to Lalitha being 29 years old. During our previous discussions, she had never mentioned these facts, but this day she said, "It is my *karma* that there is no suitable person for me." This sudden urgency to get married surprised me, and I reminded her about her earlier declaration that her job was prestigious and that she was proud of it.

"I know I said that earlier, but in this factory there is no status for our work. In other factories the marker's job is a staff-level position. Here even the supervisors treat us in a lowly manner. We have no rights to conduct a strike here. Everywhere in the world it is a worker's right. This dirty factory is the only one in which workers are insulted for striking. It is no use working in this factory," she further explained.

I asked her why she would not think about working at a different factory. "Even if I join another factory I will have to resign when I get married. So I thought, oh, what the heck, I might just as well suffer at the hands of the known devil," Lalitha said.

For Lalitha, an older and experienced worker, the strike was a cathartic moment that released her repressed anger toward the factory. But rather than using this anger to mobilize toward changing her work situation, she seemed to look for an escape route, which would likely only trap her in another form of oppression. But the talk of marriage gave her a tool to deal with her shame and anger by allowing her to proclaim that she would leave the factory as soon as possible.

Mangala: Empowered Absentee

When the workers received their April salaries, the tensions, which had lessened during the vacation, resurfaced. Mangala, a usually rebellious Line C worker, who happened to be absent for work on the day of the strike, picked up the voice of protest that others were forced to tone down because of their participation in the strike. Just before the salary was given, Mangala wondered about a possible salary cut. "Will they cut our salary for the strike? If they do that, we will strike again. Clearly the fault was not ours," she declared. When the checks were given out, workers who had participated found they had received a "late time salary cut" for 2 hours and 45 minutes. Rs. 49.97 was taken out of Sujatha's salary, while other workers lost different amounts based on their basic salary.

Mangala busied herself checking everybody's pay sheets, saying, "Look at the pay sheets of the ones who were inside. Do not let them cut even Rs. 50 for no reason." Noticing her loud protests, a sarcastic Sanka said, "Those are the results of your own faults." An angry Mangala retorted, "Watch your mouth, little brother [*malli*]. I was not present." Sanka acknowledged it and went away. The fact that she did not participate in the failed strike seemed to give her a certain power that was not afforded the workers who had participated in the strike.

After the initial shock, however, all workers started joking about the salary cut, though it was obvious that they were angry. Mangala again was a major participant in this inversion.

"You know why they cut fifty from us. There was not enough money to make a cage for those dogs that Ando san keeps. Those are good deeds. It is not a sin to give to charity," Mangala said.

There were jokes about how Sanka needed money to go to a movie with his girlfriend and Pushla needed money to buy maternity clothes. In a bid to save face, workers, through their narratives, turned the salary cut into a charitable deed while at the same time shaming the supervisory staff for participating in cutting their salary. Because Mangala was not present on the day of the strike, she was able to participate strongly in this inversion narrative. When the supervisors used shame tactics to silence the participants, she fought back, reminding them of her non-participation. At the same time, she strongly voiced her opinion of their right to strike and fight for their rights. If she had been present that day, she would have participated. Because of her absence, she did not have to save face individually and her efforts to do that for others were a result of her strong identification with the workers as a group.

Pramitha: Strike and Leave

Just as lunch-group members and Mangala responded differently to the complexities aroused by the strike, Pramitha, a final QC worker and a loud participant, understood and reacted in her own unique way. A few days after the long vacation, I chanced upon a disciplinary inquiry conducted by Ranjan. He was questioning and advising three final QC workers in one cubicle, while I sat in the adjoining one and listened. After advising them not to hinder their steady progress at the factory, Ranjan sent two workers back and started questioning Pramitha.

"You stood out as a major activist in the bonus strike. How did you get involved in that? Who provoked you to be like that?" Ranjan asked.

Pramitha sounded calm and forceful when she explained her role in the strike. "Sir, we were excited about getting the bonus and buying gifts for our parents. So when the council said we could ask the factory to give it early, it was like pouring honey in our ears. We thought the council would accomplish this by lunch break and because that did not happen, we stayed behind after tea. Sanuja sir came and asked me to go back to work. I said, 'Nobody asked me to be here. I am here in the meal hall because I want to be. If you want to take the others back, talk to them and try to do that.' Later, when everybody was trying to explain the problem, Sanuja sir said one person should stand up and say what was wrong. Because of my own desire and because of others' persuasion, I stood up and spoke for the group. I know that many people look at me with squinted eyes because of that speech. But I do not regret the strike. I did what was needed at that time. I am happy about it." I was struck by her choice of scholarly words and the eloquence with which she articulated her thoughts.

"It is not the factory but the [JOC] that was responsible for the workers' plight," Ranjan reiterated.

Pramitha agreed, saying, "When Perera san came and told us, we understood that it was the council's fault. It was sad the way the council deceived us. We love Perera san. They must have thought wrongly about us, too."

Ranjan continued, "You were one of the best in my section. I am very sorry that a child like you who was up for promotion harmed your own status. When XPM company [a buyer company that sometimes offered training programs locally and abroad for QC workers] asks for good people, you were one of the people we were thinking of recommending. Now we can't do that. Do you think you harmed your own progress?"

To this, Pramitha answered again using scholarly Sinhala, "I regret that this situation occurred. We love the factory, too. This is my first job and this is where I learned to work. Within one month of coming here, the factory granted me 23 days of leave to study for the Advanced Level exam. I regret that this occurred."

When Ranjan asked whether she accepted that she committed a crime against her own self by participating in the strike, Pramitha answered in a low, sad tone, and after a long silence, "Yes sir."

Ranjan further asked whether Pramitha accepted that because of the strike the company had suffered great losses, and Pramitha reluctantly answered, "If a strike happened and the factory suffered losses as a result, I regret that."

It was obvious that she carefully worded this answer. Ranjan again tried to get Pramitha to accept directly that she made a mistake and to apologize wholeheartedly by noting that the strike harmed her status in the factory. "When there are strikes, investors go to other countries. We can't let that happen to our country. We have to protect this [factory] because we can ask for rights only if we are employed," he continued.

To this Pramitha answered, "In my opinion, this has happened because of the weakness in communication between the council and us."

After giving her a bit more advice, Ranjan sent her back. Seeing me in the next cubicle, he said that it was a pity that I missed her speech on the day of the strike. "Stronger than a leftist politician's speech," he said. Because I heard her eloquence, I was not surprised by this information.

Although in the beginning she sounded righteous about her role, at the end she had to give in and accept that she had made a mistake. However, it was a grudging concession and Ranjan had to coax it out of her by using promotions and foreign training as bait. Pramitha also used the same tactic of stating love for the company and the managers that the lunch-group members used, albeit under duress. But Pramitha's use of the same ideas to defend her actions and save her job shows that these culturally sanctioned explanations helped both workers and managers reconcile contradictory tendencies.

A few days later, I obtained permission from Ranjan to interview Pramitha during work, and she enthusiastically agreed to be interviewed. She was from a southern village and was the eldest daughter in a family of eight siblings. She had been admitted to Ruhunu University and would be leaving the factory in one month to start her studies. Articulate as ever, she explained in scholarly Sinhala how the other workers asked her to speak for them at the strike because they knew that she was a good orator. "For children, I will do it again if the opportunity arises," she vowed.

Her words "For children, I will do it again" were the closest any of the workers came to conventionally expressing proletarian class consciousness regarding the strike. It was sad that, with her verbal skills and the sense of shared working and living conditions, she left the factory one month after the strike. I was sure she would sharpen her consciousness at one of the perennially left-oriented Sri Lankan universities. When I asked whether she would come back after graduation to work in a different capacity and help organize workers, she smiled with a dreamy, faraway look in her eyes.

Conditions of Possibility for Transformational Politics

It is clear from this discussion that working conditions as well as relations at the factory encouraged workers to develop an identity organized around work and gendered forms of discipline. The more experienced a woman was as a worker, the more she articulated a consciousness as an assembly-line worker who understood the need to fight for workers' rights. Not only the industrial production process and disciplinary methods but the constant informal education that the assembly-line workers received from the senior workers aided in the process of "raising of popular thought" (Hall 1986:21) among new recruits.

Workers spent ten to twelve hours in close proximity to one another everyday. This included three breaks and the time before and after work. Although capitalist labor relations oriented toward maximum production seem to allow only a little room for friendship and passion, this environment facilitated the development of strong friendships within the assembly lines and lunch groups, and it was through these friendships that the workers acquired and expressed their proletarian class consciousness. These friendships extended beyond the controlled compartments of work and broke into their private lives, and factory-worker groups participated in recreational activities and family celebrations together. Congregated in boardinghouses near the FTZ, their lives away from the shop floor did not allow much space to assume different private identities, and they therefore shared living and recreational conditions as well as the stigma attached to being an FTZ garment factory worker. These common experiences cemented their feelings of solidarity as FTZ women workers, and the workers brought this added awareness back to the shop floor.

This continuity in awareness across different spheres was further evidenced by workers' contributions to *Dabindu* and *Niveka* newspapers. These writings, generally as poetry, expressed deep anger against factory officials, owners, and the current government. Many called for class struggle against the dominant institutions. Some even went as far as to call for violent communist revolutions that would give power over production and profits to workers. However, none of the Suishin workers wrote or published such poems.[15] In my interviews, several workers expressed their desire to write such fiery critiques in newspapers. A persistent wish many workers expressed was to get involved in NGO political activities if they ever had a little more free time. They appreciated the *Dabindu* and *Niveka* newspapers and talked about how much they wanted to participate in the kind of activities reported in the paper. Several experienced workers talked about joining leftist parties at the same time that they directed heavy criticism at middle-class leftist-party officials for patronizing them both as women and as working-class people (Hewamanne 2003).

The interviews also demonstrated that most workers understood the macrostructures of power that are not always easily recognized. While they were unhappy with the government for allowing investors a free rein in the FTZ, many workers understood the global power structures that held the local government in its clutches. Although a Japanese company owned their factory, several workers blamed the United States for their problems. As Rena put it, "It is the Americans who are responsible for all this. They [*un*] are trying to suck the best life [*saraya*] out of us and the country." Although the workers rarely participated in NGO activities, their words and intentions showed the influence of ideas and rhetoric that regularly appeared in *Dabindu* and *Niveka*. One day the lunch-group members talked about the need for an organization of their own that would plan ways to tell of their anger and resentment to the Sri Lankan and Japanese governments. My efforts to pursue this matter further were unsuccessful, and the workers talked continuously about their anger and how they did not have enough free time to do anything about it.

In these ways it became clear not only that factory work influenced awareness of macrostructures of domination but also that the workers brought their outside experiences to bear on their factory experiences for a more complex awareness of their situation. At the same time, significant cultural, structural, and spatial circumstances impeded the development of their micropolitical activities into a transformative political struggle.

Difficulties

Although many workers manipulated conventional perceptions of hierarchy, religion, and cultural sentiments regarding work and tools and existing discourses on women in their political activities, these same influences hampered the process of these workers coming together to engage collectively in long-term transformational politics.[16] In addition, structures of production relations themselves presented problems for such an endeavor.

Structural Barriers

As previously stated, the organization of assembly lines offered the possibility for developing class consciousness. Because garment production included non–assembly-line sections, the differences in workplace arrangements ensured the different articulation of class consciousness by the respective workers. As my brief discussion about the cutting and *matome* sections demonstrated, the workers in non–assembly-line sections experienced different working conditions than did the assembly-line workers and, as a result, found it easier to enjoy work and follow rules. While most assembly-line workers participated in the strike and generally expressed solidarity with one another, fewer of the women workers in other sections participated and, in general, did not express anger against management or clamor for working-class activism.

Among assembly lines, too, there were tensions over production targets. The factory initiated an efficiency incentive for the line that displayed the best efficiency rate for the month. This meant an additional Rs. 200 for all members of the line, and workers as well as line supervisors coveted this reward. In addition to the official incentive, lines received frequent informal treats like ice cream, yogurt, or chocolates from management for short-term increased efficiency levels. These incentives promoted intense competition among lines, which resulted in increased production for the factory as a whole. Some workers' daily conversations showed that they coveted not only the monetary reward but also the emotional satisfaction of competing and winning. This occasionally united workers and supervisors into a common front against other assembly lines, further hindering the overall solidarity among workers as members of a single class. On this shop floor, I detected several sudden worker-inspired accelerations as opposed to "go-slow" tactics (Pena 1997).[17]

Among assembly-line workers, there were divisions because of the structure of production. When workers at the beginning of the line made mistakes, it affected the effort workers at the end of the line had to put in. Sometimes damages were hard to detect, and when discovered toward the end of the process, a worker who had not caused the damage might be presumed to be responsible for the damage. Often a worker had already been unfairly reprimanded for the damage by the time the real culprit was detected. As a result, workers resented those who were prone to making damages, and constant verbal battles erupted between the workers who made mistakes and those who were blamed for them. On a general level everybody resented damages because correcting them was difficult and could fall on any worker's shoulder. Regular arguments between those who produced damages and those who had to correct them harmed the overall goodwill between workers that was a necessary condition for unity.

SPATIAL BARRIERS

As stated earlier, workers formed the closest bonds of solidarity with other members of their particular sections. Not only different working conditions but also the close proximity in which they spent the workday affected this spatial division among workers. Sections and lines competed against each other for efficiency incentive bonuses, for the praise and treats of managers, and for my attention. Tensions and jealousies arose between groups in their efforts to attract such attention.[18]

The relentless work pace of the garment factory inhibited workers from associating not only with workers in other sections but also with workers stationed in different places in their own sections. Workers who spent all day standing around one table or sitting on stools placed next to each other talked, joked, and fought together and subsequently formed close relationships with one another. They intimately shared working and physical conditions (temperature, dust, and fumes) and developed solidarity that they sometimes expressed against other such groups within the same section or assembly line. These shop-floor spatial groups generally spent their breaks together and formed their own lunch groups. Over time, each line and lunch group developed rituals that intensified their solidarity as separate groups. When lines organized pleasure trips, most workers came together as a line. It was rare for these private trips to be organized as interline or factorywide excursions. It does seem that more ground-level political organizing must happen under a group of politically active women workers for workers to get together as a political group catering to the factory as a whole. Because the obligatory trips to funerals of workers' family members drew workers across lines and because the labor strike was linked to a cultural celebration, cultural concerns seem a good place to start organizing workers into matters of common interest.

Circulating Experiences

This chapter has shown that FTZ work generated class consciousness and that it was intertwined with preconceived cultural understandings. These existing identifications affected the workers' responses to specific situations, and the awareness generated through experiencing these situations affected the subsequent negotiation of new identities.

Although the conditions of possibility for transformative politics were more or less present, the chance of women workers organizing themselves to change the structures of domination in the near future appeared slim. One thing was clear, however; their learning and negotiation processes did not occur in isolation on the shop floor. Workers brought experiences from their lives outside to bear on their experiences in the factory. In the same way, their experiences at the factory influenced the way they perceived and responded to situations outside the factory. I will discuss the way the workers negotiated identities in their boardinghouse living environment and in their public and recreational activities in the following chapters.

Chapter 5

Politics of Everyday Life

"These are made with boarding children's money," Neela *akka* said while spreading her arms to indicate the nice houses lining both sides of the road. Neela, Sujani, her sister Shamila, and I were strolling along Vijaya Avenue so that they could familiarize me with the area. This was during my very first days of field research, and it was only a week earlier that a Dabindu Center activist introduced me to Neela and her friends and asked them to help me with my work.

"If you go behind the side of that house, you will see the old house and then the boarding rooms. That's how people in this area became rich. They made those shacks behind their small houses and filled them with FTZ workers, six or seven to a room. When the boarding girl's money started coming in, they built these nicer houses in the front and then got boarders into their old houses, too."[1]

"When the FTZ started, they too were as poor as our families in the villages. But now that they have some money, they think they are better than we are," said Shamila, joining the conversation. "Some have even left the area, saying they can't live with FTZ workers because their children go astray and their daughters cannot get good marriage proposals if they live here," she added, puckering her face for further emphasis.

"Boarding Anties think that we are out to get their sons.[2] *Apoi*, like we want them. The only thing they do now is hang around boardinghouses, at grocery shops, and on the roadside or the junction and make passes at us," Sujani interjected.

"This is not all. Let's go to Amandoluwa," said Neela even as she waved to a passing small bus that immediately grinded to a halt in front of us. Neela had already bought tickets for all four of us by the time the conductor squeezed my lower body into the bus by firmly pushing on my legs. Three stops later, we were in Amandoluwa, an area filled with even more crudely built rows of boarding rooms.

"These are cheaper. But look, you can even see inside the rooms from this far. Those locks can be broken very easily. No security for women here. Not that ours are much better. Even about a month ago, a thief took all the clothes we had hanging from the outside lines," Neela said.

Just before the bus turned around for the return trip, we all got seats and Neela sat down with a sigh and said, "Now, I can show you better. See those small grocery shops in front of all the boarding places? Those are run by the boardinghouse owners and they want all the boarders to buy their groceries from their store even if they are always pricier than the cooperative shop."

"Now, Saman has that shop in front of our boardinghouse. We call it the *saban kade* (soap shop) because most of the time it only has soap there. But if he sees us going to the next-door grocery shop, he becomes angry and yells at us using obscene words," Sujani commented.

"Whatever one says about having more freedom since Anti left, I think she ran the boardinghouse better. And the shop had more things and she looked after us well. If any boarding girl was in trouble, she would never turn her back. Not that Saman would do that, either. But it is not like having an older woman around," commented Neela. Sujani curled her lips as if to disagree, but she did not say anything.

During the following eleven months, I learned on my own what it is like to live in Saman's boardinghouse. It was located about 200 yards along the railroad tracks from the main road to Colombo. One could get onto the airport road, which connected the Colombo-Negambo main road to the airport, by walking along the tracks. The houses along both sides of this little avenue featured boarding rooms built in their compounds. Typically, clotheslines prevented people from viewing the rooms directly. Sometimes there were three to four clotheslines in front of the boarding rooms, and if one peered closely one could see young women engaged in various activities behind the clothes. Located at the intersection, Saman's house was a four-room structure that had boarding rooms built at the back. Three of the rooms were also rented out to workers, while one was occupied by Saman. There were three toilets, one bathing well, and one tube well in the compound, which was shared by the owner and the boarders. The boarding area consisted of six rooms, each of which was shared by four to six workers. The number of occupants usually fluctuated between forty to sixty workers. The rooms were made of cement and the roofs were covered with tar sheets. All the rooms were unpainted and the inner walls of some rooms were not even plastered. Each room held three or four beds that the workers shared, sometimes with as many as three boarders in one bed.

Clouds of dust escaped from the old coir mattresses on the beds every time someone sat on them. Some residents bought mosquito nets, while others lit coconut husks in their rooms to escape from the hordes of mosquitoes that invaded the house in the evenings. Saman had furnished several rooms with small tables, but other rooms stood bare except for the beds. Occupants improvised by using cardboard boxes as tables and storage spaces. Clotheslines on which workers hung their half-dried clothes for the night or on rainy days ran from one corner of the room to the other. Women kept their jewelry locked up in suitcases, which were usually stored under their beds to save space. In fact, the space under the beds was used to maximum capacity, with big pots and pans and other boxes that the women were collecting to take home in a "book hire van" in April or December.[3]

Although I visited several other boardinghouses in the area, Saman's place intrigued me the most, probably because it was run by a young, unmarried man without the help of any elderly women. Not only did some workers, including Neela *akka*, Sujani, and Shamila become good friends, but Saman also took some pride in my regular visits. It was after about three weeks that I asked if I could become a boarder with other workers. Saman refused, saying all the rooms were occupied. But he offered the front room in the house and said I would have to wait until he arranged alternative space for its current residents. Neela *akka* immediately doubted his motives and said, "*Nangi*, Saman is not a good man. Otherwise why does he want you in the front room right by his room when you asked for space in a boarding room? For your own safety, I need to tell you this. Some days around midnight he comes and knocks on boarding room doors. Even the other day he did that. I got so mad and asked, 'What do you want at this devil of a time?' and the man said he needed to go take a pee. I said, 'Then go pee without bothering us.' He said he is scared to go alone and was trying to see whether any of us were up so that he could have someone with him. *Ane*, see this man's shamelessness." Neela was ironing her clothes as she talked. The very old iron, provided by Saman, was fueled with dried coconut shells and it generated such heat that made everyone inside the room sweaty.

"We are lucky because Neela *akka* is here. The man is scared of Neela *akka*. But we hear of some fancy stuff that goes on around here," Sujani said this with great enthusiasm, almost prodding me to ask for details.

Before I could say anything, Shamila blurted out, "His current girlfriend stays in the third room. So early in the morning, he goes to that room. Other boarders know he sleeps with Chuti while the others are also there. You will be as spoiled as we are before you leave this place."

Saman, however, was not happy with the idea of my spending nights in the boarding rooms and continued his efforts to convince me that the front room in the house was the ideal place for me. While these negotiations were in progress, I took up residence in another boardinghouse, located half a mile away in the Liyanagemulla boardinghouse cluster area.[4] Though I was not an official (fee-paying) resident in Saman's boardinghouse, I spent most of my days in the rooms and in the compound socializing with workers. The rooms always had one or two free

Figure 4. Ironing clothes at Saman's boardinghouse. Photograph by the author.

spaces because of workers visiting their villages, and I spent nights there when the workers invited me to, which was quite often. Saman either did not care that I stayed or, as many residents claimed, was too drunk to notice whether I left.[5]

I mostly stayed in the so-called Pollonnaruwa room, which was shared by Sujani, Shamila, Neela *akka*, and three other women from the same village in Pollonnaruwa district. Soon I started making friends with several women staying in a room called the Kurunegala room. The residents in this room came from villages in the Kurunegala district and worked together in one factory, which provided transportation for workers who did night work, a rare luxury. Pollonnaruwa residents did not much like my association with the Kurunegala room residents. However, the Kurunegala room residents worked on rotating shifts and the few workers who were doing the 2:00 P.M. to 10:00 P.M. shift had unrivaled access to me during the mornings. Consequently, I became very close friends with the few workers in that room and tried to be a bridge between the rooms, albeit with minimal success. There was general goodwill between the occupants of these two rooms. Yet each regarded the other with a little contempt and did not mingle too much. The Kurunegala women saw themselves as less rural than the Pollonnaruwa women and felt, therefore, that they knew more about how to behave in a modern, urban environment. The Pollonnaruwa women, for their part, alluded to Kurunegala women's lax morality.

Although there were divisions based on regional differences, caste did not play a part in their social and recreational activities. Most workers belonged to the majority govigama caste, while Saman's family belonged to the karawa caste, one of the so called middle castes. Several residents belonged to castes considered very low in the traditional caste hierarchy (potter, washer, and *bathgam*). Caitrin Lynch (2000) notes that caste played a part in village garment factory workers' social interactions. The nonsignificance of caste among FTZ garment factory workers indicates that the FTZ enabled a powerful space that erased traditional differences and created new kinds of distinctions among workers.

Most residents worked from 8:00 A.M. to 5:00 P.M. The boardinghouse generally became quiet around 8:30 A.M. Some workers, including the ones in the Kurunegala room, worked shifts from 2:00 A.M. to 10:00 P.M., 10:00 P.M. to 6:00 A.M., and 6:00 A.M. to 2:00 P.M. This helped my research in that there were people to talk to at almost any time of the day. Workers on the 8:00 A.M. to 5:00 P.M. shift came back home about 5:15 P.M. However, they often had to work overtime and therefore often came home after 9:00 P.M. Most factories were open only for half a day on Saturdays, and the residents returned to the boardinghouse around 2:30 P.M. This was the night they usually got together to sing songs and tell jokes and stories. These Saturday night gatherings also brought regional tensions to the fore in that there were two different gatherings in the two rooms. Usually these gatherings consisted of about fifteen residents. Others engaged in different activities such as entertaining visitors, reading books, or watching Hindi movies shown on the television in Saman's living room.

Figure 5. A boarding room. Photograph by the author.

On some weekend nights, we laid on our beds and talked until late into the night. Unlike at some other boardinghouses, where the board-inghouse owners switched off the power to the rooms at 9:00 or 10:00 in the evening, Saman had no rules about when the lights should be out, but residents went to bed around 10:00 P.M. except for Friday and Satur-day nights. Usually the boarding rooms were provided with electricity using a wire connected to the owner's house. Saman's rooms, however, had their own light switches even though there were no electric outlets.

Saman also provided a better kitchen than those provided by many other owners. A long room located to the side of the boarding rooms served as a kitchen. Women installed their kerosene stoves on the crude brick counters in the kitchen and stored their pots and pans under the counters. The room was big enough for a few people to cook together, although the smoke from the stoves sometimes made it difficult to do

the preparatory work inside the kitchen. Women devised ways to minimize the time spent in the communal kitchen. Both Pollonnaruwa and
Kurunegala women had cooking schedules. One resident cooked for the
whole room each day, which meant that each occupant had to cook only
once or twice a week. Almost all the residents cooked just once a day and
used the food for all three meals.

"This way, both time and money are saved. *Nangi* must have seen by
now that we girls only cook vegetable curries. The most we will do will
be to fry some sprats. The other day we cooked a fish curry because you
were coming to eat with us.[6] We wanted to cook seer fish for you, but the
fish vendors don't even bring those to this area. They know that we cannot afford those high-priced fish," Neela explained.

"These are the times I miss my mother's cooking. When she makes
white rice, *pol sambol,* and *polos* curry, ahhh! Like heaven. Here it is rice
and *parrippu* and *parrippu* and rice, day in and day out," Kalyani complained, sitting on the bed eating rice and dhal curry straight out of a
clay pot.

"Rice and *parrippu,* rice and *parrippu,* but look at how you look. Like a
rice sack. Why, all you do in your free time is eat rice," Shamila joked,
poking at Kalyani's belly. "*Ane,* Sandya *akke,* we may look like little rice
balls, but we have no strength. We feel tired all the time. Why, because
we always eat rice and lentils. No fish, no meats. We don't have time to
make green leaves *mellun.* We must be lacking all the vitamins from A to
Z," continued Shamila, who was apparently zeroing in on one of my
comments that suggested many workers looked well fed and plump.

The bathing well partially prevented anyone by the railroad or the
front of the house from looking into the rooms. But the well, where
women spent considerable time washing clothes, bathing, and socializing, was in full view of other onlookers. Because there was only one well
for forty to sixty workers, the owner, and (sometimes) his friends, there
was always a crowd around it. It was common on Sundays to see four or
five women wearing the watercloth washing their clothes and cooking
utensils while two others took baths. The former were the ones who were
immediately next on the waiting list for bathing. Residents reserved a
place in this informal list according to the time they woke up. Usually a
woman who signed on around 10:00 in the morning would get to the
well only around 3:30 in the afternoon. Because workers did not usually
go out on Sundays without having a bath, this wait irritated many.

On weekdays residents rushed to work without taking a shower. The
first thing they did after coming home, regardless of the time, was to
take a body wash and wash their underwear, which was then hung on the
clotheslines. They tried to wear their outer dresses two or three times before washing them and, therefore, just hung those out to air. There were

Figure 6. A boarding room without furniture (author second from right). Photograph by Premani.

three dilapidated toilets behind the boarding rooms, and the workers bitterly complained about the condition of the toilets. Saman also used these facilities, though he never cleaned them. The women, therefore, had to periodically clean the toilets. At the end of my research, I asked Saman whether I could videotape his boardinghouse. He refused, saying that it would be humiliating if other people were to see the tape. When I told this to several residents, they angrily commented that they were not surprised by Saman's refusal because if the government health officers saw the conditions of the toilets, they were bound to close down the boardinghouse.[7] Most mornings workers had to wait in line to use the toilets and residents devised a way to minimize tensions by respecting an informal waiting list that they signed onto each morning.

DOMESTIC SPACE AND RESPECTABILITY

There have been several studies on factories that provided living quarters and thereby controlled workers' social lives (Dublin 1981; Fernandes 1997; Cravey 1998; Striffler 1999). Sri Lankan FTZ factories, however, rarely provided boarding facilities. Workers, therefore, lived in rooms rented by neighbors, enabling them to have a life without any direct interference from factory officials. These boardinghouses were more or less organized around patriarchal values, and both the owners and neighbors acted as agents of control. Unlike the situation within

factories, however, women constantly and strongly challenged these disciplinary measures. It is within these constraints that they negotiated
their identities as women migrant workers.

Most boardinghouse operators became a major agent of dominant
cultural forces and filled in for these women's parents in ensuring that
they did not lose shame-fear and instead followed protestant Buddhist
ethics in their daily lives. In the FTZ area, most migrant women were
presented with conditions not conducive to upholding these values, and
the women gradually (on different levels) lost their fear of subverting
sexual norms and the shame they felt over what others thought. It is
within this process that I was able to examine the way migrant workers
created and negotiated new positions within and against the forces that
sought to constrain their movements. It was while focusing on the forms
of control, narratives of changing values, processes of becoming desiring
subjects, and the resultant violence that I analyzed their daily cultural
struggles.

Home Away from Home: Life at Saman's

"*Nangi* must remember when you visited in 1995 and 1998, Anti
[Saman's mother] ran the boardinghouse." Neela *akka* started the story
of Saman's boardinghouse with those words. I visited this same boardinghouse for short periods of time in both 1995 and 1998. I had not had
a chance to talk to Neela then, but she remembered seeing me talking
to other workers. When I arrived for my long-term fieldwork at the
boardinghouse, this time to stay with them, Saman was running the facility. To satisfy my curiosity and to inform the newcomers, Neela, a six-
year veteran at the boardinghouse, agreed to tell us what had happened
since I last visited.

"Anti is a very strong woman. I heard she ruled over uncle and the
children like a queen. In the early 1980s, she went to the Middle East to
work as a housemaid. She went there several times and built three
houses, one for each child," said Neela, pausing for better emphasis.

"The boardinghouse you visited last Sunday, where your friend Rasika
stays, belongs to Saman's sister. She is married and now has two children.
She is another nutcase. The house right across the road belongs to
Saman's younger brother. He is also married and has one child. This
house is for Saman. But uncle and Anti also lived here. Saman didn't
like his siblings having their own houses while he was burdened with the
old couple. When I first came here in 1994, Anti was taking care of a little baby and I asked whose baby it was. She would not tell me. But the
neighbors talk. The last time that she was in the Middle East, Saman
started dancing the devil with boarders here and got one of them preg-

nant. Anti came back just in time and took care of the mother and baby. That girl now works in a different factory and lives in another boarding-house. Anti adopted the baby girl she had, and that was the baby she was tending to. In that way, she is a good woman. Of course, the right thing would have been to force Saman to marry that woman. But at least she saw to it that the woman was provided for. Anyway, Saman was drinking a lot and there were fights almost every day. You know why Saman was angry? Because he could not dance with the boarding girls the way he wanted to because Anti was keeping an eye on everybody. His brother had an affair with a girl in his boarding rooms and some of his friends have these romances, too. You know how uncivilized [*kamakata nethi*] this one is. One day under the influence of liquor, he beat Anti. The next day, she packed her things and went to her ancestral village with her husband and the little girl. She vowed that under Saman, this board-inghouse will soon be called a whore house [*ganika madama*]," Neela *akka* lowered her voice while saying this last sentence.

"And that is exactly what happened," Sujani interrupted in her usual excited voice that provoked the listeners to ask for more details. Even before we started prompting, she elaborated: "No, it is true. The other day someone said we live in Saman's harem. Why, Sandya *akke*, when you and I visited Kusuma Anti's boardinghouse, she also warned you of Saman and said that you need to find a respectable place where an older woman was in charge. The things this Saman does, no wonder people say such things."

"*Ane nangi*, it is embarrassing for me to even tell you these things. But this man is now sleeping with Chuti, right. But before starting with Chuti, he slept with both her older sisters," Neela said. "First, he started with the eldest sister. Then, when the next sister came, he started with her, too. When the third came, he started sleeping with all three of them. One day I talked to the girls and asked, 'What is this shameless spectacle? There are little girls coming from villages everyday and they get spoiled because of your shamelessness. Not even animals do what you are doing. Why do you waste your lives like this? Leave this useless man.' A few weeks after that, the two older sisters went to a different boardinghouse and left Chuti here. I think they are still hoping that Saman would marry her. Her mother visited a few days ago, I think to persuade Saman to marry one of the girls. What a disgusting situation," continued Neela, while blushing furiously.

"Chuti is cooking and cleaning for him on that side and Saman is making passes at women on this side. Even today he bumped into me and pretended it was an accident," Kalyani added.

"Why, Saman sent all those letters to Sujani when she first came here, begging her to become his girlfriend. The letter were full of '*Ane*, my little fair one,' and '*Ane,* my little doll.' If we had not advised her in time, she would have fallen in the same hole as Chuti," Shamila noted, affectionately ruffling Sujani's hair. A blushing Sujani bent over her suitcase and came up with several ruffled pages of paper. All workers in the Pollonnaruwa room had fun reading Saman's elaborate declarations of love.

The boarders did not show much fear that the boardinghouse's reputation would tarnish their own reputations or that Saman might be a danger to them. None of the residents was looking for other boardinghouses, and many had stayed there for years.

"If he behaves so badly, why do you stay here? You can always move to another boardinghouse, right?" I asked.

"If you stay in a boardinghouse with an Anti, you will know the difference. They supervise your every move. In a way, it is like you are still in the factory and she is your supervisor. The owner of the previous boardinghouse I stayed in wanted to be our mother. For that reason, if she does something bad we are not supposed to criticize her. With Saman, we are free," Nadee said.

"Yes, he says he is continuing his mother's rules, but he is too drunk to care. Now he lets boyfriends visit inside, but he wants them to sleep with him in the main house. You have already seen several men sleeping in boarding rooms with their girlfriends. If the roommates do not complain, you can do anything here. You also like this place for your research mostly because Saman does not follow you like Kusuma Anti did the other day, right? He lets you be," Neela commented.

"*Apoi,* if he finds out that a man slept in the rooms, he gets mad and you can learn all the pure Sinhala words [obscene words] then," Kanchana added. In fact, I have seen several such brawls between Saman and some workers. Saman screamed obscenities at residents on such occasions and more often than not the residents screamed back, defending themselves and swearing that the young man who stayed over was a brother or a cousin. Everybody disliked women who betrayed their fellow residents and there were incidents in which such women were socially ostracized until they left the boardinghouse.

"Whatever his indecent ways, he would never turn his back on one of his residents if she needed help. Once one girl lost her salary envelope and he let her stay free for that month. If a resident's family member dies, he hires a van and takes all of us to the funeral. I mean, we collect money and pay for the van later, but he takes care of all the food and drinks on our way. You will see when he takes us on the *Poson* pilgrimage to Anuradhapura in June. He spends with his hands outstretched. We just need to enjoy the trip," Shamila joined in to defend Saman.

During my research, I visited a number of boardinghouses that displayed different levels of patriarchal control that seemed to correspond roughly to the changing values the residents displayed and expressed. Workers frequently moved from one boardinghouse to another given their differing expectations. These moves brought them in contact with varied owners and roommates and affected their awareness and values in different ways. Not only the boardinghouse owners but also the neighbors and visitors to the area stood in judgment and imposed restrictions on the movements of the workers. How much control or show of control a boardinghouse offered was important to workers and their parents who frequently referred to such control as an affirmation of its residents' morality. According to De Alwis (1995), upper-class women were able to assume public roles because of their firm association with the domestic sphere. Some families insist that their daughters live with relatives or under an elderly woman. This points to lower-class people's attempts to allow their daughters to negotiate the public domain in at least a marginally acceptable fashion. However, the control that the agents and boardinghouses exerted on their residents differed in many ways. The workers' responses to such constraints also varied, depending on the form and level of control, their experiences at other spaces, and their personal traits. The following section attempts to capture the complex and dynamic process in which migrant workers crafted their identities against and within the hegemonic cultural forces that sought to make them docile industrial workers who still embodied shame-fear.

Control and Play

While every boardinghouse owner had rules that were enforced to varying degrees, there almost always was space for play. Especially at Saman's, control came in the form of kind, elderly concern as well as in the form of playful, male surveillance. A few months after his mother's departure, Saman made up with her and arranged to divide the boardinghouse income between them. Anti, who was a plump woman in her early fifties, visited once a month to collect her share of the rent. She talked loudly and used terms like *umba, ban, bolan*, and *tho*, which were considered rough terms of address, when talking to the boarders. People usually used these terms in anger to verbally abuse others as well as to denote the lower status of the person or the group being addressed.[8] Anti, however, used them in a way that indicated kindness and affection, although her use of them also accentuated inequality. She questioned and advised women about their boyfriends, and many times likened having a boyfriend to an act that showed the lack of shame-fear. She also made it a point to inform the women's parents of these relationships and advised them to discipline their children or get them married. Many women responded to Anti using lighthearted banter but in general tried to escape her prying eyes.

When Anti came to the boardinghouse, she swept the compound and tried to clean the ditch that ran from the well toward the railroad. While doing that, she invariably berated all the women for living like pigs. A few workers would jokingly tell her that it was her son and his friends that dirtied the place. Anti would then retort that, unlike men, women should notice uncleanliness and keep wherever they live clean. She also took jibes at the residents' mothers for not rearing them right.[9] Residents talked back and half jokingly presented their grievances against Saman to Anti.

Saman's relations with the residents were also characterized by this kind of play. He too used those rough terms daily. When he was angry, he used obscene words to address the residents, and some of them responded in the same way. Although he did not enforce rules as strictly as some other owners, his control was enacted in a roundabout way through his constant presence in the boarders' rooms and in the kitchen, at the well, and near the toilets. He also brought his friends inside without asking permission from the women, and he seemed to assume that the residents should entertain them.[10]

Perhaps as a defense mechanism, many residents did not consider Saman's abusive words an affront. Rather, they thought it was a result of his crazy ways and his constant drinking and spoke about him with pity and even affection. This ambivalent loyalty toward the boardinghouse and the hesitant affection toward Saman seemed to result from the unique circumstances surrounding the boardinghouse that allowed the boarders to claim a marginal respectability through Anti and explore new ways of living and acquiring new knowledge through Saman. The latter's lifestyle and his constant presence in the residents' lives did more to create a setting where women could overcome internalized norms of shame-fear than to protect them.

Saman not only allowed his friends to enter the boarding-room area freely but also organized trips to famous places for these friends and his residents. As Shamila predicted, on Poson Poya day in 2000 Saman arranged an overnight trip to Anuradhapura. The trip started from his boardinghouse at 10:00 P.M. and reached the holy city of Anuradhapura about 7:30 A.M. the next day. No elderly person accompanied the women and throughout the journey men and women visited night cafes and other landmarks along the way. There were sixteen women and seven men in the bus, and the whole trip was characterized by sexual jokes, puns, and innuendos. There was much flirting and physical contact between men and women.

Moreover, several young women laughingly confessed that they were only able to satisfy their curiosity about the male anatomy because of Saman. "*Aiyo,* Sandya *akke,* this Saman has no shame. He always wears that skimpy pair of running shorts and walks around the rooms bare-chested. And whenever he wants to, he changes and does not care that girls are around," said Kanchana, while giggling uncontrollably. I focus more on Saman's sexual escapades later in this chapter, in "Politics of Desire," to show the way his behavior and the setting influenced a fast fading of shame-fear.

Although many seemed to appreciate the freedom and fun enabled by Saman's boardinghouse, they resented it when this very situation resulted in their being labeled women without shame-fear and generated humiliating incidents. One Sunday morning, Saman and his friends started cleaning and decorating the house and garden. The women were asked to clean their rooms, too. There was talk about a ritual ceremony that circulated for a few days, but many workers were surprised to see the baby coconut frond (*gok kola*) decorations, which heralded an elaborate ceremony. Anti was visiting for the weekend and was overseeing the work. Women were not invited to participate in the ceremony, but some circulated near the tall windows and reported to others. It was a ritual ceremony to drive away the evil forces that supposedly prevented Saman from improving his life. A ritual specialist chanted over Saman and his mother at the little shrine made of coconut fronds. About 10:30 P.M. we settled down to sleep and were surprised when the ritual specialist, an assistant, and Anti came with a big pot and started to sprinkle water inside the rooms. Then the ritual specialist sprinkled the boarders, who were sitting on the beds, with water. While leaving to go to the next room, Anti said that it was to wash away the impurities (*kili*) and protect the rooms. The mention of *kili,* an impurity particularly associated with women's sexuality, annoyed all the women. We started quietly criticizing what took place and Neela said, "Until she cleans her son and the toilets, *kili* won't disappear from this place."

Premasiri Uncle's Boardinghouse

Premasiri uncle's boardinghouse is the house where I was a fee-paying resident during most of my time researching the FTZ. This boardinghouse in many ways exhibited a completely different home culture from Saman's. Premasiri was a retired government employee and also worked as a three-wheel taxi driver and was not financially dependent on the boardinghouse fees. He and his wife, Susila, kept the house neat and clean so that this was the best-kept private boardinghouse that I encountered in Katunayake.[11] A happy, contended family man, Premasiri, together with his wife and two grown children, seemed intent on providing a warm, safe, family environment for their boarders and any other young women residents at neighboring houses.

The boardinghouse consisted of two long rooms annexed to Premasiri's modest three-bedroom house and did not exceed twelve workers at a time. The family's television, stereo, and telephone were freely available to the boarders and their visitors. In fact, the family had built a reputation for being wonderful boardinghouse owners. Boarders lived in this boardinghouse for long durations and there was an informal waiting list to get a space in one of the rooms. As several women confided, they felt more cared for and protected at the boardinghouse than in their village homes. This made them loving and loyal to the boardinghouse owners. This sense of belonging came with a price, however. The owners, especially Premasiri, showed a playful, parental possessiveness toward his boarders. Premasiri and his wife took the surrogate-parent role seriously and boarders' attitudes in turn were heavily influenced by the boardinghouse owners. Premasiri or Susila did not ever talk in a derogatory manner about women's employment or their having boyfriends, but they firmly believed that women should get married soon. Premasiri was friendly with many young men from a nearby diamond-cutting factory and tried to match his boarders or boarders in neighboring houses with these men. Many boarders expressed the same urgency their beloved uncle and Anti expressed about marriage. At least four women told me that they could trust uncle to make a good decision about their lives and would go along with his wishes for a marriage.

Having a nice, loving environment in which to spend their leisure time meant that these boarders did not go out as much as residents in other boardinghouses and, therefore, missed out on many recreational opportunities and the vibrant social spaces that were constructed by and for FTZ workers. Because Premasiri and Susila's boarders lived a cozy life within the owners' paternalistic embrace, one would expect these boarders to be relatively unconcerned about class struggle. But these boarders often expressed more militant ideas than boarders elsewhere. This was, again, a tendency they developed under Premasiri's influence. He was a trade-union activist for the Ceylon Transportation Board before he retired and still expressed militant, leftist ideas. He helped workers who were engaged in labor strikes and provided meeting space, food, and free transportation for the leaders. Whenever he talked about his support for worker struggles, he used a militant, leftist vocabulary and the boarders participated in these conversations and used the same words to describe their own experiences at the factory.

About two months before I started staying at his house, Premasiri and the boarders got themselves involved in yet another labor strike. This time it was at an FTZ garment factory and the factory owners forced out all the female residents living in the factory-maintained boarding facility the moment they started the strike. Premasiri opened his house for these strikers and said that about a hundred women lived in his house for nearly two weeks, and he allowed the workers to cook meals for close to five hundred strikers in his two kitchens. Although the numbers sound a bit exaggerated, Anti and the boarders also described the exciting time they had in the house painting banners and shouting slogans. When I asked the boarders whether they felt resentful about this intrusion on their space, they sounded aghast and said it was their duty to unite with wronged workers and support them as much as they could.

The boarders were influenced by two contradictory cultural discourses they encountered at Premasiri's boardinghouse. One corresponded to the family's attachment to dominant notions of marriage and family; the other, to Premasiri's attitude toward worker struggles. Unfortunately, the former influence seemed to take primacy, while the militant ideas did not proceed beyond rhetoric.

MANY FACES OF CONTROL

I spent a week in a boardinghouse owned by a retired civil servant who said he separated his house from the boardinghouse compound by keeping bare land between them and putting up a fence, specifically to give both parties their privacy. Although this allowed some privacy, the boarders seemed to be constrained by the mere presence of uncle on his veranda. During my stay, uncle came out twice and stood silently looking at the boarding rooms from his verandah. Visitors were present on both occasions, including two young men, and as soon as the residents noticed uncle, they admonished each other to be silent and took their visitors inside.

In one case, the owner found FTZ jobs for eleven related women from his village in Kekirawa and provided accommodation for them in a hut built just outside his house. Because their uncle played the roles of boardinghouse owner as well as job agent and father figure, these women seemed to be enmeshed in an interconnected web of power that imposed control over their movements. According to the owner, he and his wife were responsible for the young women's safety and reputations and therefore had a set of rules for the boarders to follow. He expected the women back in their rooms within one hour after their work shifts ended. On Sundays if they wanted to go out they could do so as a group, and his wife or another elderly woman went with them. When a man expressed interest in a woman, the woman was to send the man to meet her uncle and if the man were suitable uncle arranged for the two to meet at his house and later got them married. "I don't like girls going to parks and movie halls. These are innocent children brought up in a village. There was one child who started going out with a boy. As soon as I got to know, I took her home and gave her back to her parents," he explained. This strict control and discipline did not allow the residents much space to move away from their subject positions as "obedient daughters." That one woman's disobedience evidenced the inevitable changes that were slowly occurring. However, the way she had to leave the job showed how difficult it was to consolidate such changes within a living environment where the boardinghouse owner held so much power over his residents' jobs and their social lives.

In another instance, the women's factory supervisor was also their boarding mistress and she controlled the women at both spaces. She imposed tough rules that included coming home with her after work and being home before 7:00 p.m. on weekends. Neetha encouraged the women to visit their villages over the weekend and also talked about her responsibility to save these "innocent, rural girls" from "crafty city men." As with Premasiri's boardinghouse, Neetha's boarders too seemed happy and contended in this protected and restricted environment.

INSTITUTIONAL CONTROL

Upeksha was a hostel maintained by a foreign-funded labor organization that provided about thirty to forty FTZ workers a clean and peaceful living environment. Located close to the FTZ, the hostel had two two-story buildings. The ground floor of one building was an assembly hall, which was used for workshops and other educational programs for the residents. The matron, as the woman in charge was called, was a motherly, kind-looking woman who stressed that she encouraged cleanliness and organization. According to her, these were women from different parts of the country and it was difficult to keep them under control. She had posted rules for the boarders on the front door, in the upstairs corridor, and in the kitchen. The first rule required that workers and visitors take off their shoes before entering different parts of the building.[12] A schedule that assigned women different days and times to do the cleaning hung on the kitchen wall.

The matron kept everybody's work schedules and closely monitored the times they returned to the hostel. If a woman did not comply with her individual curfew or cleaning schedule, she was asked to leave. The matron kept a close watch on rebellious workers. Those who complied had a warm, close relationship with the matron and expressed their happiness at finding such a clean, comfortable place to live. However, several senior residents resented the fact that they could not go out in the evening like other FTZ workers. According to one woman,

Renuka, "The Jayalath cinema is so close to us, but I have never seen a movie there. On weekdays we work and on most Saturdays and Sundays we have classes and workshops in the hostel." While Renuka was apprehensive about moving to another boardinghouse, she was also excited about it.

Women expressed their desire for comfortable living conditions, but many noted their doubts about finding better conditions in government- or factory-owned boarding facilities. Several pointed out that in a few such places, rules and regulations about mealtimes, bedtimes, noise levels, and visitor rights were more strict than in even junior school dormitories. "I don't want to be a slave during the day and be ordered around like a child at night," one woman explained.

A clean and comfortable boardinghouse run by nuns belonging to a Christian denomination was pointed out as another example of such strict rules and undesirable practices. According to the women, boarders were asked to make plastic flowers during their free time so that the nuns could sell them to benefit the church fund. Although almost all the residents were Buddhist, they all were required to participate in daily morning and bedtime prayers as well as Christian story-reading sessions. According to Kathy Peiss (1986), residents in church-run boardinghouses at the turn of the twentieth century in New York heartily complained about forced female sociability and the restrictions on their independent leisure activities. Many preferred commercial boardinghouses even though they operated under appalling conditions (73–75). In the same way, FTZ workers' preference to stay in boardinghouses such as Saman's also pointed toward women's desire to have more freedom in their social lives.

Several factories also offered boarding facilities for some of their workers. Although my attempts to gain entry into one such facility were unsuccessful, several *Dabindu* reports on the Ishin Lanka labor strike provided some insights into the factories' rationale for investing in such hostels. According to one report and several strikers' descriptions, the workers who lived in the factory hostel were warned not to get involved in union activity. But in 2000, all workers participated in a strike and within a few days the residents were forcibly removed from the hostel while the matron threw their belongings out. According to Altha Cravey (1998), establishing single-sex worker dormitories was crucial for some Maquiladoras on the U.S.-Mexico border because the local labor supply was unpredictable. The dormitories helped to quell the investors' concerns about the political controllability of the workforce (102–3). In the Sri Lankan case, too, the hostel facility usually ensured a new, younger, dependent and, therefore, loyal, section within the factory-worker population. The denial of such facilities once the residents got involved in a labor struggle demonstrated how the factory intended to use the hostel facilities as a deterrent to a total walkout of its workers.

ABSENCE OF CONTROL?

Caitrin Lynch (2000) describes how, when several women who had worked in city factories found jobs in a village factory, officials were concerned about them corrupting the "good village factory girls" by pulling "stunts" learned in the city. The "stunts" described by officials were lying to their parents about factory "off time" and spending the extra hour with their boyfriends (72–73). This clearly marks the difference between transnational corporations at FTZs and locally owned village garment factories in their philosophy of disciplining their workforce. While FTZ workers left behind the transnational discipline when they left the factory gates, village factories spread their tentacles over women's social and family lives, even as familial concerns were allowed to reach the factory.

The earlier discussion has made it clear that there were enough controlling agents who sought to discipline the FTZ workforce outside the factory gates, primary among them the boardinghouse owners. Ironically, however, the absence of direct control by boardinghouse owners did not set the workers free. Some people built boarding rooms on empty land they owned in the FTZ area, while living elsewhere themselves. Showing the strong influence of dominant cultural discourses, even these boardinghouses were organized more or less in the shadow of the dominant discourses. Ambepussa Boardinghouse was one such place that did not have owners or any elderly people living with the workers. Although women seemed to have relative autonomy within the four walls, the responsibility of living alone seemed to have instilled in many workers a strong sense of duty and self-policing. Even while happily talking about how, unlike others, they were free from boardinghouse owners' despotic rules, the women expressed a need to maintain the boardinghouse's good reputation for future workers.

Mangala, a worker I met at Suishin, also lived in a boardinghouse whose owners lived elsewhere and visited only to collect the rent. In this case, however, the boarding rooms were built inside a large coconut estate and had no close neighbors. Surrounded by coconut trees and hidden from the road by tall bushes, the women in this boarding environment were somewhat relaxed about their dress and demeanor. There was no house or shop for about a mile on either side of the entrance and women sat outside until late into the night with their boyfriends. However, there was an ongoing advisory narrative within the rooms where, older, experienced residents advised others about not abusing their freedom and maintaining the honor of the place. Although there were no tangible mechanisms to morally or physically supervise women as in other boardinghouses, the way the women themselves kept men out of the gates showed that they were still controlled by their own internalized notions of sexual and behavioral norms.

Politics of Everyday Life

FTZ workers chose, or got assigned, to boardinghouses that imposed various forms of control on them. However, this new field of everyday life was mediated through their experiences in villages, work, and the new consumer culture surrounding the FTZ. They played politics of everyday life through changes in lifestyles, bodies, sexuality, and communication.

Typically the boardinghouse owners did not object to women building on the political awareness gained in the factories. The daily conversations within the rooms easily moved from shopping and movies to factory bosses and NGO political activities and then back to mundane activities. Whenever there was a price hike on an essential item, which happened frequently, their discussions concentrated on the national political scene. Dissatisfaction with both major parties and a subsequent longing for a third force was evident in those discussions. Furthermore, they talked freely about their own poor working conditions, cruel supervisors, and heartless, exploitative foreign employers. Some factories were known for poor conditions or cruel supervisors. Residents who worked in such factories shared their experiences and everybody present criticized these factories and their officials. Workers advised each other on how to behave when certain incidents occurred at the factories. While younger and newer workers encouraged others to leave the factory, experienced workers always cautioned against angry and precipitous reactions. They noted that in order to fight for workers' rights one had to remain a worker. In these discussions, older and experienced workers demonstrated a feminist awareness in that they advised the younger ones not to run home at the slightest provocation and become dependent on parents or husbands. Each boardinghouse had several older, experienced workers who advised others on their rights and how to fight for their rights within the extant rules and regulations. Some women achieved a certain respect from supervisors and managers through their long, loyal service and had crisis-solving leverage within their factories. They influenced younger workers to curb their pride and anger and to realize that they were nonentities without factory work.

These women's influence, however, did not prevent other workers from engaging in conversations about communist revolutions that would purportedly allow them to become the owners of their factories. Although the workers mostly expressed their ideas as wishful thinking, they at times used explicit Marxist terminology. Class struggle (*panthi satana*), revolution (*viplavaya*), exploitation (*sura kema*), and the proletariat (*nirdhana panthiya*) were some terms that came up frequently when their conversations turned into discussions of political activity. Recall that in the factory environment even the most rebellious workers did not verbalize their feelings in clear Marxist terms. At Saman's boardinghouse, residents claimed that they learned these terms at school or through reading books.

An older, married woman worker who lived in a different boardinghouse visited Saman's boardinghouse every Sunday to meet two of her friends. Affectionately called *akka* by everyone, she had a way of getting the younger workers' attention. Women formed a circle around her to listen to her hilarious stories. These stories about incidents in her factory or other factories figured around micropolitical activities in the factories and showed how important it was to creatively use verbal and nonverbal language while resisting.

Saman's boardinghouse was a frequent stop for Dabindu workers who came to distribute the newspaper and other materials. Their library was located close to the boardinghouse and they made a point to come and talk to Saman's residents whenever they visited the library. Because of this close connection, some workers closely identified with the mild militancy that the *Dabindu* newspaper espoused. However, the Dabindu workers were not successful in ensuring the residents' participation in their educational and political activities mainly because of time constraints faced by the workers. As stated earlier, at Premasiri's boardinghouse, the residents were influenced by Premasiri's ideals and consequently engaged in some organized political activities. But the rhetoric of residents in other boardinghouses did not lead to collective political activities. While they told Dabindu workers about labor-rights violations at their factories, none at Saman's boardinghouse wrote to *Dabindu* about the incidents. When I asked them about this inaction, many talked about the futility of political activity when even the Sri Lankan government had no control over foreign forces. Several workers showed a reasonable understanding of globalization processes. With all that understanding and rhetoric, the hardships of their daily living limited their participation in broader political movements. However, the enthusiasm and agency they showed in cultural politics was evident in their narratives of value changes and mechanisms of constructing difference.

Politics of Desire

Desire is revolutionary in its essence
—Deleuze and Guattari 1983:116

According to Deleuze and Guattari (1983), desire is decentered and dynamic. Operating within a "domain of free synthesis" (54), it seeks more objects, connections, and relations than any society can allow, leading society to repress desire within closed cultural codes. Liberation of desire through overcoming repressive cultural codes is a requisite for reversing traditional structures of subordination (139). Workers' narratives show how the FTZ provides a potentially liberating space and how workers in different ways were involved in a process of becoming desiring subjects. Compared to what was permissible within the village environments the workers had left, the vastness and anonymity of the FTZ afforded a considerably freer space to seek connections and relations, romantic and otherwise. While their accounts certainly did not boast of a sexual liberation in an absolute sense where they would have achieved sexual pleasure free of any constraining cultural, moral limits, the women showed gradual changes in the way they thought and acted since coming to the FTZ.

At Saman's boardinghouse, I saw the way migrant women workers situationally adjusted their notions of love, sexuality, and marriage in narratives and in practice. Sujani's story clearly evidenced the contradictory cultural forces they balanced. Sujani creatively combined these cultural influences in responding to most situations as she struggled to fulfill her desire to enjoy all the new possibilities FTZ living presented.

"My parents sent me here because I got friendly with a boy from a low-caste family," Sujani started her story with a shy smile. "I was just sixteen and had finished my O-level exam [General Certificate of Education ordinary-level exam—equivalent to a high school diploma]. My sister was already working at the FTZ, so my mother and brothers thought this was the best place to send me. Then *akka* found me a job here and I started sharing the Pollonnaruwa room with her and others. I do not want to get married early. Especially I won't marry anyone my mother chooses for me. Why? Because she can only find someone from my village and he will most probably be a farmer. I don't want to marry a farmer and spend my life under the scorching sun,"[13] Sujani used both facial expressions and hand movements to show her dislike of farmwork.

"When I came here, my plan was to work in the FTZ, accumulate enough money, and then marry my village boyfriend. We exchanged letters for about six months and I pleaded with him to come to Katunayake and find a job in the FTZ or somewhere nearby. But he did not want to do that and was angry with me for even suggesting it. Once I suggested that he should visit me on a weekday so that we could go to a movie or to the beach. And he accused me of absorbing the city's evil ways. A few months back, I went home on a long three-day vacation and learned that he had found a new girl," Sujani shook her hands to show the hopelessness of the situation and then added, "Not that I minded much. He is like a frog in the well. He did not want to come to a new place and learn new things. He was jealous that I was learning all these new things and said that I had changed and was trying to boss him around," Sujani said. "He will now spend all his life as a farmer," she predicted with a smile.

Although factory work was hard, Sujani said she liked FTZ living. A Dabindu activist who was with me that day predicted that the novelty would wear off and Sujani would soon be fed up with this life. I spent about a year with them and it seemed she found the life around her more exciting every day. "I like living with other girls like me. [Saman's] boardinghouse is more exciting than all these nicer places that they talk about. It is so funny to see all these fights and scenes, you know, with Saman's old girls and his brother and sister." Both Saman's brother and sister did not work and, like Saman, lived off the income gained from renting out rooms. The two brothers drank together and sometimes started verbal duels that ended in violence. Almost all the boarders enjoyed these drunken episodes and watched from their compound. This sometimes made both brothers turn their wrath on the boarders. When this happened, workers retreated to their rooms but analyzed the obscene words for their meaning and joked about how they would now have to pay Saman for the extra education he was giving them.

"Sandya *akke*, do you know whether there is any connection, you know, like something psychological, between beating a woman and washing her dirty clothes?" Sujani once asked me in a lowered voice.

Sujani was referring to the many days when we saw Saman washing Chuti's clothes at the well after beating her senseless. According to some senior residents, he had done that with his earlier girlfriends, too. There was an ex-girlfriend living in a nearby boardinghouse with whom Saman was thought to still have a relationship. He boasted about visiting her and beating her up for the rumors she was spreading about him. Women in the Pollonnaruwa room claimed that although there were many disagreements over property and agricultural matters, they had never heard such constant obscene words or seen physical violence in their villages. I gathered that what they were trying to tell me was that they had not experienced violence associated with sexual matters before.[14] The conscious distancing from "marginal sexual and behavioral norms" aside, this situation offered them greater freedom in their boarding-house lives.

Knowledge of the sexual violence did not affect the women's desire to fall in love. Sujani was especially forthcoming about this. "I can't wait to fall in love with a good man and enjoy life in the FTZ," she once gushed.

"I want to attend all the night musical shows and go on as many trips as I can. But *akka* is not going anywhere and not letting me go with friends. If I have a boyfriend, I can say that I have weekend work and then go places with him. Thankfully my sister works in a different factory, so she wouldn't know. Really, Sandya *akke*, I feel sad when I see couples walking hand in hand. I think to myself, 'They are going to the movies or to the beaches.' How good would it be if I could do that, too?" The dreamy look in her eyes changed to annoyance when I reminded her that there are many incidents of married or opportunistic men cheating on women. "It is women's own fault that they get into trouble. Don't you have common sense to see whether a man is married? And there is no reason to jump into bed just because he wants to. We need to know how to set limits," Sujani said. On several occasions, she said that she was ashamed by the way some women behaved in public with their boyfriends and noted that if their parents had brought them up properly they would not have demeaned themselves with a boyfriend.

On other occasions, however, Sujani said she would like to experience being kissed. She had yet to enjoy her first kiss. "My village boyfriend and I never got a chance to be alone. We held hands many times and once he touched my face while walking to the temple. I want to know how it is to be kissed," she once said with a faraway look in her eyes.

According to Sujani, there were no real barriers to falling in love with a boy in the village. "But as soon as the parents found out, the boy and the girl either had to get married or forget about the relationship. And there is not even a movie theater in our village. The Pollonnaruwa town is about ten miles from the village. It is rare that I saw a movie before coming here," Sujani complained.

However, she said that it was not considered bad to go to the movies as long as women went with other women and family members. "But if you get caught going to a movie with a man, your future is destroyed. The whole family would be disgraced. Once a letter from a boy was found inside a girl's textbook in our school and she was publicly berated and was almost expelled. So we had to be very careful if we wanted to have a boyfriend. Now you saw what happened to me. They stopped my schooling and sent me here. I was underage. They forged my birth certificate so that I can work here—all because of one silly boyfriend,"

Sujani laughed with a wicked glint in her eye, knowing that her parents ended up providing her a better environment in which to enjoy life.

Sujani had seen several movies since coming to the FTZ. She had also gone on a day trip to a temple and she went to the fair almost every Sunday. "Just walking back from work I see many things and I learn many things. Everything around here is colorful. In the village it is always green and brown. We rarely saw yellow, pink, or blue," Sujani wrinkled her face again as if to show how dull her life there had been.

"Why, the sky is of any other color in our village," Shamila said to Sujani with a laugh but also in a tone that protested Sujani's description of their village.

"It was blue all right, but how often did we notice it? We were like frogs in the well. We had only the village, so we liked the village. But here I have so many friends already. They come from all different parts of the country. And you, you come from America. Would I have met you if I did not come here?" Sujani also pointed out that she had taken several friends from the factory to her village and hoped that she would be able to visit their villages soon. About three months later, she took me to visit her village and then came and had lunch with my family at our home in the Colombo suburbs.

A few months into my research, Sujani found a boyfriend from the village. The man was an army soldier from the same village as Sujani. "Jagath had first seen me in the temple and sent me many letters through Kalyani. You know, she is his niece-in-law. I like him very much. I love him so much, it is like we wished for this in our last birth. All I want to do is to spend all my life with him," she gushed two days after consenting to his request to become his girlfriend.

That same day Sujani pleaded with me, saying, "*Ane*, Sandya *akke*, can you tell my sister that you want me to accompany you to Rasika's boardinghouse? I need to go to the junction to make a phone call to Jagath. If you tell her, she will let me go." That was the beginning of many such trips in which I had to (with conflicted feelings) help her get away from her sister's watchful eyes to engage in long-distance phone conversations with Jagath.

By this time, Jagath had deserted the army and was hiding from the military police. Within a month into the relationship, Jagath's parents sent a matchmaker to Sujani's house and her family agreed to their marriage. Jagath was working in their paddy lands at this time and I asked Sujani how she, who hated paddy field work, agreed to be a paddy farmer's wife. "He said they have enough people for paddy work. What he needs is someone to do the housework," she quickly answered.

Sujani defended her decision to be Jagath's wife not only through familiar cultural tropes on becoming a wife and a mother but also through a modern vocabulary of love and commitment acquired through romance novels, movies, and audiocassettes she discovered in the FTZ. Once I accompanied Sujani to a famous shrine in Negambo where she got her palm read by a well-known palm reader. He predicted that Jagath would have to go back to the army and Sujani should do a ritual to ensure his safety. The ritual required a live chicken, three limes from the same stem, and other expensive and rare items. Sujani was ready to perform this ritual and soon adjusted to the idea of Jagath becoming a soldier again. "Sometimes I feel like he has given me some hypnotic medication [*ina beheth*] to make me love him so much," she said.

Barely two months into the relationship, there were already signs of strain. Sujani pleaded with Jagath to come to visit her over the *poson poya* three-day vacation. Her sister was planning to go home and Sujani was planning to stay in Colombo, citing overtime work at her factory. Sujani was unhappy when Jagath refused to come to Colombo and instead asked her to come to the village with her sister. He incensed her more by saying that they were soon to be married and there was therefore no need to "squeeze into corners" to talk.

"He tried to act like my big uncle, the fool," Sujani commented angrily. On the *poson* three-day vacation, she did stay back, with her sister's permission, to join the Anuradhapura trip with Saman, several other workers, and me. Jagath sent her a letter admonishing her and stating that he did not expect that kind of stubborn behavior from his "little fair one," but this time he would forgive her because she went to help the "researcher girl," who needed a companion for the trip.

This letter irked Sujani, but she did not clearly express reasons for it. She stopped exclaiming about her love and talked about Jagath only when someone asked. I guessed that she suddenly realized becoming his wife in a patriarchal agricultural society was not what she had hoped for from the relationship. I became further convinced of this when on a Sunday she came to visit me at Rasika's boardinghouse. I had just started staying at this new boardinghouse, which was a bit closer to the main road from Saman's house.

"*Ane*, Sandya *akke*, can you come with me to our boardinghouse and tell my sister that you want me to go with you to the junction?" Sujani pleaded. "The boy that I was friendly with in the village, he has come to Katunayake. He has cousins in a boardinghouse down by the eighteenth mile post. He is there and one of his cousins came to tell me that he is dying to see me again and that he had broken that relationship with his village girl because he wants me back," an extremely excited Sujani blurted out, forcing me to remind her that she was engaged to another young man. Sujani looked aghast and told me that she just wanted to hear what he had to say and she denied wanting a relationship with the man. When we went to this particular house, several residents and an elderly man were sitting in the compound talking. The young man also stood outside. We spent about an hour there, but Sujani did not get to say a word to the young man because of the presence of the elderly relative. Rather, they communicated through body language.

Within a few weeks, her engagement to Jagath ended. Sujani's exboyfriend had boasted about meeting Sujani in Colombo and exaggerated what went on between them. The rumors had reached Jagath's family, and accusations and counteraccusations ensued. Soon all parties agreed to put an end to the engagement. Sujani seemed relieved and vowed that she would not have anything to do with village men anymore. This news reached me toward the end of my research, and the first letter Sujani sent me after I returned to the United States was mailed from another boardinghouse. Her family thought it was best for Sujani to live in a boardinghouse with an elderly woman in charge. This was one step they took toward repairing Sujani's "spoiled reputation." Sujani vowed that she had had enough of men and would never marry. But five months later, she sent another letter gushing about her new boyfriend, a worker in her new factory. She had other happy news, too. Her mother had found a suitable partner for her sister and soon she would leave the FTZ to get ready for her marriage. For Sujani this meant unsupervised time in the FTZ with her new boyfriend. Since then her letters became infrequent and were devoid of the youthful candor I had come to expect from her.

Sujani's story illustrates the contestatory potential of desires created by the new consumer culture surrounding the FTZ and the ambivalences inherent in its expression. Her actions marked transgressions of cultural codes at the same time as she condemned versions of such actions by others. She desired all the possibilities available to her while dreading possible adverse outcomes. It was when those conflicts confronted her that she combined aspects of several cultural discourses to construct an in-between personality, not quite modern, not at all nonmodern: in short, a modern woman with the brake pads of rural upbringing. The emphasis on sexual reputation, evident in the restrictions on her movements and the failed engagement, shows how strategic a move this was for managing reputations.

Janaki's story shows how this play of cultural tropes provides rural, poor people an avenue to reconcile dominant cultural discourses with economic realities of the changing rural society. Janaki lived in the Kurunegala room and came from the city of Anamaduwa in the Kurunegala district. She worked at a big FTZ factory with 3,000 other workers. She had a boyfriend in the armed forces and had known him for about six months. They had met only twice but kept in contact through letters. Janaki's mother worked as a housemaid in a Middle Eastern country and Janaki was the eldest daughter in a family of five.

"My mother always writes to me about how I should be a good example to my younger siblings and about protecting my good name. And I also think that nobody could harm a woman unless she gave consent," Janaki thus started her narrative.

"To tell you the truth, there are no real barriers in my village about girls finding boyfriends if they have stopped schooling. In fact, I would say that some families even subtly encouraged finding one's own partner; why, then the parents do not have to give a big dowry. But for the parents to give consent, caste, family status, job, education, and everything has to be matching and the boy should want to get married soon. The couples are not allowed to hug and kiss until they get married. He can visit the girl's home and talk to her and that's about it. Why? Because if a man declined to marry a woman after visiting her at home and taking her to movies, her reputation would be tarnished. Afterward it would be hard to find her a good man. To tell you the truth, some parents even act like they are so strict and they don't like their daughters finding boyfriends. They beat the girl and make a big scene so that everybody will know they are proper. Why, it is good for the girl because her boyfriend's family thinks that she is really a sheltered girl. Sometimes some parents act as if the marriage is arranged by them so that it will look good on the younger daughters," Janaki said. She also pointed to the class differences by mentioning that girls from village elite families had strict rules and their parents prohibited them from having anything to do with boys because they would have to go through arranged marriages in the future.

"Everybody's nervous about FTZ romances. Why? Because here it is very hard to really know a man's background. It was easy in the village because the men were either from the same village or the same district, so the parents could easily check their family background. [In the FTZ,] men are from all over the country and they can disappear to anyplace in the country. That is why I chose a man from Kurunegala district." Janaki said this while showing me several photographs of her soldier boyfriend. But her choice turned out to be not much better than some of the other women's supposedly faulty choices she criticized. About two months later, her boyfriend came to the boardinghouse and demanded that she leave with him to go to his house. When she refused, the man publicly broke off their relationship. Janaki was sad for some days and confided in me, "One good thing came out of this. Now I am not scared of finding a boyfriend from the FTZ. Truly these men, wherever they come from, have only one thing in mind."

If rural, poor people encouraged their daughters to find their own partners and be married within a reasonable time, many workers' narratives I collected or heard about seemed to appropriate this and transform it to suit the specific conditions at the FTZ. The women considered having a boyfriend who did not want premarital sex and wanted to get married in the near future as the ideal situation while women who could keep a man interested without resorting to sex were considered the "talented ones [*daksha*]." Nadee's story aptly illustrates this narrative construction. She was from Anamaduwa and worked at the same FTZ factory as Janaki. A short time after she started working in the FTZ she found a boyfriend, and they spent almost all their days off together going to parks, temples, and shopping malls in Colombo. "He would like to marry me even tomorrow if I so desire. I just want to have bit more fun before getting married," she claimed, and added, "It is only a clever girl who can keep a man loyal. It needs much maneuvering. Pride, submission, fights, and tears all help. You can control a man on tears alone."

Nadee also talked about Shamila and Neela, who were twenty-six and thirty-five years old, respectively, and said that in her opinion women should be married before they turned twenty-five. "I don't know about Neela, but Shamila just does not know how to keep a man interested," Nadee said.

"Neela had once told another girl that Ajith is so much in love with me because I give him everything he asks for. I don't care for such jealous talk. I can leave him just this minute as pure a girl as I came from the village," Nadee further explained. Neela, however, thought otherwise and said, "You know why Nadee is trying to go to a Middle Eastern country? So that she can earn money to cover what she lacks [virginity]. Can any number of gold sovereigns cover that lack?" Neela seemed to compensate for her inability to achieve the "ideal romantic relationship" by undermining Nadee's achievement. Voluntarily explaining why she did not have a boyfriend, Neela said, "Even if Nadee has not done the big thing [*maha wede*, sexual intercourse], any relationship involved some hanky-panky.[15] Boys do not want good women like us who do not like such things." Neela later elaborated in a hushed tone that there were many ways to have sex without damaging the hymen. "One is, you know, the hand job. There is another thing that men call "stone cutting" or "lapidary [interfemoral sex]," she explained in a hushed tone.

"I am waiting for my parents to find someone suitable for me. To tell you the truth I have not met anyone that I like here or in the village," Shamila said. An eldest daughter in the family, she was good at school and passed her General Certificate of Education advanced-level examination with the best results from her school. She lacked just two points to enter the university and thought the government would give her a teaching position. She was a volunteer schoolteacher for four years and kept applying for a permanent position. Because of corrupt local politics, she failed to get a permanent position. Three years ago, she finally decided to come to the FTZ and earn some money. Although she did not say this, it became apparent that she did not find the people she met at the FTZ equal to her. The teachers' favorite student when she was at school, Shamila followed rules and seemed to have internalized the dominant cultural ideals in school. The time she spent as a teacher disseminating these ideals further strengthened her adherence to the proper behavior for young women. She constantly talked about protecting women's reputations, innocence, and virginity. She wanted her sister, Sujani, to adhere to these ideals and she set many barriers to Sujani's movements.

Geethi was among the few FTZ workers who confided that she had had sexual relations with men. She belonged to Line C at Suishin and we became friends during my research there. She bore her life story out by responding to a survey questionnaire on reproductive health and later, when I met her at her boardinghouse, by elaborating on her trials and travails at the FTZ. "*Aiyo,* my parents were just crazily protective. When I was in the village, they did not even allow me to talk with males if they were not related. Not only me, it was the same for many girls in southern villages." Geethi thus began her story and proceeded to tell me how her village depended on unpredictable paddy farming income and the families had no choice but to let their daughters leave for the city when FTZ employment opportunities opened up.

"The first day I came here, both my mother and father came with me. Before they left me at the boardinghouse, they advised me a lot and asked me to protect my good name and the honor of my family. They cried a lot and I cried, too. I was just so sad and I promised myself I would never do anything to shame them and that I would never abandon my rural values (*gamekama*). *Ane,* Sandya miss, I myself can't even believe how fast I forgot all that and became just like any other FTZ girl," Geethi laughed as she said this.

"I just loved everything about Katunayake. I loved working in the factory. I liked all my new friends. Just walking to work and back one learns a lot. Those days everything looked rosy to me. I felt adventurous as if I was finally living life and not just looking at it. I have to tell you about the other residents in my boardinghouse. They never left me alone. Included me in everything they did. I liked to spend time with them at the boardinghouse. Those days I just counted my fingers to the day I got my salary. The first thing I did was to go shopping and buy things that all the other girls here seemed to own, you know, dresses, shoes, colorful hair braids, perfumes, and, of course, gold rings. I just love to collect gold rings. I have two more at home," said Geethi as she spread her fingers and showed off seven gold rings of various designs. "But after about one year of this buying frenzy, I started feeling like I am one of the "in crowd" at the FTZ. Then I started helping my parents more. I bought school supplies for both my brothers every year. I gave money so that my father could add two more rooms to our house. They really appreciate this help. Now that I have been working here for six years, I have all my jewelry and I also bought some furniture for my dowry." Geethi also mentioned that with her accumulated EPF payment, she would have a substantial dowry when she decided to leave the factory to get married. But she had mixed feelings about marriage and was contemplating whether to stay unmarried all her life.

"The reason, Sandya miss, is that I have had four boyfriends over these past six years. I can tell you this because you are like a sister to me and you have gone to different countries and know the world. I even slept with three of those boyfriends," Geethi dropped her voice to a whisper when she related this last bit of information. The next day early in the afternoon we sat under the mango tree by the well and I asked her whether she could tell me more about these relationships. It was a hot Sunday and nobody except for one woman sweeping the garden with her back to us was within hearing distance. Geethi hesitated and then sought my right hand and squeezed it tightly. She did not let go of my hand until she finished telling me about all four of her boyfriends. "I was crazily in love with my first boyfriend," she said with a dreamy smile. "I mean, those first few months I thought that I was in heaven. I loved it when he kissed and touched me. So when he asked me to go to a rooming house, I went willingly and I also did not object to having sex. I just hated the whole sex experience. It was so painful and I was sick with fever for five days. After that I did not even want to look at his face again. But I do not blame him for what happened at the room. I can tell you, miss, that maybe in my own heart I wanted to experience sex. I mean kissing and hugging were great. And you know how one leads to the other. But oh, man, were my eyes opened, or what? It was a bad, bad experience. And then I was without a boyfriend for about three months. But I felt lonely and felt as if I were missing out on life, so I found another boyfriend. I did not like him much and did not even like the way he looked. But we were okay; in fact, we were happy for awhile. Then surprise, surprise, he wanted to have sex. And I was thinking, well, what is there to lose now? Hymen (*kanya patalaya*) is already gone and nothing for me to protect now. So we had sex. *Apoi*, this time too it was painful. He felt it, too, and soon he abandoned me. Not that I cared. I was relieved," Geethi laughed and stood up, still holding my hand and forcing me to stand up with her. Two women had moved near the well and were trying to focus on what Geethi was saying while soaking their laundry in big basins.

Still holding my hand, Geethi started walking toward the railroad. "I tell these things to you because you are an educated woman. You can understand why sometimes we do things that we are not supposed to do. I don't want everyone to know these details," she said, taking a quick glance at the two intruders. "Now the third boyfriend was younger than I and he came from a very remote village. That boy treated me with lot of respect and love. We went to many places together and were very happy. *Ane*, look at how bad my *karma* is; as soon as I started thinking about marrying him, some people told him about my old boyfriends and soon that relationship also ended."

Disillusioned with finding love again, Geethi lived alone for about one year and still enjoyed going on trips, shopping, and engaging in other fun activities in the area with her girlfriends. Some rumors reached Geethi's village through another FTZ worker from the area, but because there were such rumors about all the workers this did not make much difference. "Besides, the way I acted at home, like everybody's innocent little girl, nobody really could believe such things about me," Geethi said. "About a year ago, a boarding friend's cousin came after me, saying that he would forget all my past misdeeds." My friend cautioned me about this man, but I thought that because there is nothing more for me to lose I would just enjoy the relationship. From the first day, we started sleeping together. Now is the good part. I finally started liking sex. I don't know whether that is the reason, but I fell in love with him. When he left me for another woman, I cried for days. I vowed that I would never have a boyfriend again. I have been in this area for a long time now. I don't need a man to go places anymore. You must have already seen that it is I who organize groups of women to go to musical shows and other trips. I am an old hand here now." She again laughed, and I made a mental note of the fact that Geethi did not say that men forced her to have sex or that she felt guilty or impure because of having had premarital sex; a strategy many women used to claim a victim position.

"Now my parents are pressuring me to get married. But I am worried. You must have heard about things that are done to brides who are found to be nonvirgins on their wedding night. One bride we knew was sent back to her parents with wilted flowers. In the groom's house all the pictures on the wall were turned upside down like at a funeral house. Even if such brides were kept in the groom's family, they suffer humiliation at the hands of in-laws and the villagers. The husbands walk all over them using the virginity problem to justify everything. It is much better to live alone helping my family to develop more," Geethi said, still holding my hand as we walked back to the boardinghouse. A few days later when we were talking along the same lines, she said, "With this talk about the 30 percent I might even get away with it." She was referring to the interviews with gynecologists, published in women's magazines, that claimed about 30 percent of the female population did not show "signs of purity" at the first sexual intercourse.[16] "But it is risky. I am not sure whether I want to take [that risk]," Geethi mumbled rummaging through her old tabloid collection to find an article on the 30-percent situation.

Two other FTZ workers confessed to having had sexual relationships with men. Both women were still angry about their deceiving boyfriends and frequently cursed them for ruining their lives. One woman said that she consented to sexual intercourse when she "went crazy." She claimed, "I forgot my obligations to my parents, my siblings, my good name—everything. I was blinded by his love. I forgot the way my parents brought me up, according to village virtues [game hadiyawa]." Although she took responsibility for the situation, she used the terms "destroyed my life [vinasa kala]" and "made me destitute [anatha kala]" to describe being abandoned. The other woman said that although she willingly went to his boarding room, she did not want to have sex. He promised to marry her and threatened to go to prostitutes if she did not fulfill his needs. She said, "I was so stupid, I believed him. I am sad because I only had sex to keep him with me."[17]

Kishali, another FTZ worker that I became friends with at Suishin, was thirty-six years old and still unmarried. She said she had had a number of boyfriends after coming to the FTZ. She always had the best intentions and wanted to get married. She had such bad karma regarding relationships that all her boyfriends were "opportunistic crooks." As soon as she started a relationship something made her trust them completely, and she spent her hard-earned money buying them gifts and providing other financial help. When I talked to her she was in the process of fighting to get back her last boyfriend who, she learned, had maintained relationships with two other women while dating her. She was using sorcery to lure him away from these other women. Although she was forthcoming about her relationships, she did not volunteer information about sexual relations while I was there. In her first letter to me after I had left the FTZ (congratulating me on my marriage), she offered advice as to some common problems that could occur during sexual intercourse and how to keep a man interested. A few months later, in her second letter, she informed me that she broke her leg in a motorcycle accident that occurred when her new boyfriend was taking her home. She said that she was keeping this new relationship a secret because the man was married and also rumored to have had relationships with other women. She further said that it was hard to find unmarried men at her age and that even if there were no future in this relationship this was the only way she could have her "human desires [*manussa asavan*] fulfilled."

Kishali was the only one who clearly expressed (in writing) that sexual desire was a reason for having boyfriends. All the women I talked to expressed a desire to have romantic relationships that did not include sexual intercourse. With younger workers, the yearning to enjoy the new life seemed to have been the major reason for starting a relationship. In fact, maintaining a romantic relationship without sexual intercourse that eventually led to marriage was considered the ideal and such women considered themselves talented, self-controlled, and successful. The other women recognized this as an ideal achievement and hoped that one day they would be lucky enough to find a good man. They also maintained that the men who flocked to the FTZ area came specifically looking for short-term relationships because of the bad publicity some women's stories attracted. At the same time, workers did not consider women as victims. They held that date rape was rare because women knew why they were asked to go to a rooming house. Only women who decided that it was fine to have sex would go to such places, they claimed.

Many agreed that it was easy for women to believe men's promises that they would not attempt to have sexual intercourse but observed that it was still a woman's responsibility to take that risk. As the few narratives of women who had had premarital sexual intercourse showed, love, sexual desire, self-interest, and many other economic, social, and cultural reasons were involved in their decision. It was when the man abandoned them that the women started to express the situation in terms of "victimhood" and "defiled woman." Many workers who said they never had sex used the vocabulary in mainstream discourses on morality, traditions, and family honor to describe their reasons for this decision. These words, however, were used in a narrative of agency where they claimed "authorship" of their situation in the FTZ through self-control. Most workers agreed that it was fine for people to have premarital sex if they so desired. But they also cautioned that young people, especially women, should be aware of the consequences of such actions. They held that because Sri Lankan society mandated that a bride be a virgin, it was up to each individual to decide how one should deal with physical desires.

Surprisingly, however, I did not find instances of homosexual relationships or verbal expressions of homoerotic desires. Boardinghouse living forced women to share beds, bathing and toilet facilities, and cramped living quarters. They dexterously changed clothes in the presence of others and huddled together on the beds for jokes and storytelling sessions. They held hands as many other Sri Lankan young women did while walking and engaging in conversation. This was a habit of all women, irrespective of whether they had boyfriends. In almost all cases, it was evident that timidity and self-consciousness propelled them to seek courage from each other.

A Dabindu worker once said that she had heard about homosexual relationships. She had a difficult time choosing words to explain "this shocking behavior." In 2005 the officer in charge of the Katunayake police station had the same difficulty in describing the homosexual activities of several FTZ workers as reported by neighbors. I also found it difficult to discuss the subject due to the absence of acceptable everyday terms referring to homosexual desires and activities.[18] I briefly discussed the topic with several close friends, and one woman said that she once heard boys taunting a group of women, saying that they were "making hoppers."[19] This is a term used mostly among male youth to refer to lesbianism. The term carried a heavy stigma and women displayed an extreme aversion to talking about it. The absence of an everyday vocabulary for homosexual activities prompts me to speculate whether this had any relationship to the seeming lack of homosexual eroticism and activities.[20]

None of the workers I talked to suggested that having sex with a man made one a victim. At the same time, however, they used a language derived from mainstream discourses to explain why they would not have sex. Their ambivalent reactions to so-called promiscuous behavior by others evidenced deep inner conflicts. They condemned such behavior while at the same time mixing a certain admiration and longing for the freer sexual behavior they were condemning. The middle-class categories of "respectability" and "promiscuity" did not adequately encompass the complex realities of migrant working women's lives, prompting them to engage in intricate tactics of negotiation. Consequently, women constructed their narratives both through and against the dominant cultural narrative. Balancing cultural expectations, female desires, peer pressure and the allure of the new consumer culture in the FTZ resulted in creative ways of reconciling their desires with dominant cultural discourses to arrive at a strategic stance that would be most beneficial in that specific context.

Empowering Spaces and Controversial Practices

"There, there, that army *aiya* [elder brother] is looking at us, look he will say something now." In her excitement, Kanchana almost pushed my head to the left so that I could take a good look at the lone Air Force sentry standing by the green barrels of the checkpoint. The group of women seemed to tense in happy anticipation, and uncontrollable giggles erupted as we neared the checkpoint. That's when two more Air Force soldiers emerged from behind the bunkerlike structure of the checkpoint grinning widely. They too were tensed for an encounter. "Ah, *nangi,* seems like you are off shopping?" a soldier called from his place beside the barrels. "Tell them to go and protect Jaffna instead of dozing around in Colombo," said Kalyani, pretending to talk to Kanchana but saying it loud enough for the soldiers to hear. "*Ane,* is there a better job than protecting these sisters?" the next soldier chimed in just as our group passed the checkpoint. "No wonder we are losing the war," Nadee turned back for another shot at the soldiers. We heard their catcalls for another few minutes while we giggled our way toward the Averiwatthe junction. "Today they did not have time to give addresses, some days they pass address notes so quickly you don't even know who gave what," Kalyni explained to me while turning back to wave at the three soldiers who looked on smiling.

NGO activists usually refer to such incidents as the sexual harassment FTZ women have to face in the Katunayake area. During my studies in the FTZ area in 1995, 1997, 1998, and in the early part of my 1999–2000 research, I also documented such incidents as sexual harassment and as one of the most-difficult experiences for workers and researchers. After spending much time with workers during my last research stint, however, I felt the need for a revised approach. FTZ workers' perception of harassment differed somewhat from the middle-class perception, which is borrowed from western discourses. The workers disagreed that all catcalls represented harassment. According to many women I interviewed, a woman might like such catcalls because it showed that the man was interested in her. Catcalls have initiated many a romantic relationship, they informed me. "I would prefer that a man approach me directly or maybe send a letter, but men are shy, too. If a woman says no to a man, other men make fun of him. So it is good to first make sure that the woman likes him before approaching directly," Janaki explained.

Many men who frequented the area congregated in groups and the advances toward women were initiated as a group project.[21] Usually the catcalls were limited to funny remarks and jokes. Women showed their interest or noninterest through body language and the men proceeded accordingly. When women were in a group, this process became easier because the particular woman's friends started communicating with the male group. While the two groups stood or walked within a respectable distance, they also communicated through jovial remarks that more or less informed each group about both the man and woman's intentions, wishes, and, if necessary, where to meet again. Even when no such long-term interests were expressed, groups of women enjoyed and even encouraged catcalls, as well as sexist and cruel jokes. Some women shouted back in a jovial manner and others just laughed, making eye contact with the men.

When I was walking with groups of women, men who traveled in buses, in trucks, or on bicycles slowed down to shout a compliment or make a cruel joke. While this annoyed me, my companions giggled or shouted back at those in the vehicles. They related these stories with enthusiasm to other boarders once back at the boardinghouse. The police officers stationed in this area and the military men at the checkpoints did not hesitate to make remarks when groups of women walked past them. These remarks were always reciprocated with smiles or words and were regarded with happiness and pride. When I discussed this situation with a Dabindu worker, she said that she once confronted a policeman who made a pass at a group of women and the policeman replied, "If we do not say anything, they would hit us with a banana skin or something to provoke us."

Although they enjoyed and looked forward to catcalls, jokes, and sexual innuendos, all the women I talked to thoroughly detested men who whispered obscene words in their ears. Men do this in crowded places and it happens quickly; the women felt doubly harassed because they cannot respond in kind. They also said they disliked any uninvited physical touching. But what I observed while spending time with them was that there was a fine line between what was encouraged and what was opposed. For example, when group exchanges, as described above, occurred at the Sunday fair, temple festivals, and on trips home, women typically enjoyed being touched, squeezed, or having other such physical contact initiated by men.

However, if a man did the same thing while speeding by on a motorbike, women usually got angry. It appeared that their approval or disapproval of such behavior was based on the possibilities of further association. As shown earlier, FTZ workers desired having boyfriends and experienced much peer pressure to have a boyfriend. Because their factories employed only a few male workers, they could only meet men through their leisure activities in the area. Therefore, unlike middle-class women, they considered catcalls and some other acts generally termed sexual harassment fulfilling a necessary social function. Catcalls provided a space for young people in a nonpermissive society to express their initial interest in each other and to enjoy cross-sexual communication. This did not mean that the workers welcomed every comment or every physical advance. They contextually decided what actions demanded a favorable response and what was reprehensible behavior. While the major criteria for their decisions were the intention and space for further relations, women's particular character traits and how invested they were in projecting an image of themselves that was similar to ideal expectations also figured into the decision-making process. Creating this new space for cross-sexual communication showed how these women combined different cultural knowledge in responding to the new demands and needs of their lives as factory workers.

The communication, through the safety of gendered groups, is probably influenced by village experiences where most verbal exchanges occurred across gendered groups. However, the use of such communication as a stepping-stone for male-female relationships and the acceptance of physical contact that occurred within these exchanges evidenced the way they re-created this culturally accepted communicative space to fulfill emotional and physical desires that flourished under conducive conditions of their lives around transnational industrial production. Although the FTZ brought them new knowledges through NGO educational activities and media exposure, FTZ workers appeared to reject the middle-class understanding of sexual harassment. Instead, they have chosen a modified version in which they contextually decide what sexual harassment is. Because sometimes women eagerly awaited these cross-group communications initiated as catcalls, it appears that what a middle-class feminist considered "instances of sexual harassment" marked a part of the process toward empowerment for FTZ workers in which they actively engaged in a communicative process through which they found their boyfriends.

Another activity that challenged dominant cultural codes was the FTZ workers' involvement with two magazines that contained pornographic stories. The workers not only enjoyed reading these sexually explicit accounts but wrote their own stories of premarital sex for these magazines. This engagement with pornography undermines the normative models of sexual behavior for unmarried Sri Lankan women and thus represents a contestation. In that sense FTZ workers reading and writing pornography is an emancipatory feminist activity despite being constrained by multiple hegemonic forces.[22]

Workers' newfound sexual freedom was also expressed in their Saturday-night gatherings at boardinghouses. Sexual activities and body parts were a recurrent theme in the jokes they shared and the parodied songs they sang at these gatherings. Most also focused on their experiences with their factory bosses, and they used the names of their bosses in some popular jokes and songs. In one case, they changed the words of a popular Buddhist devotional song to talk about the way they would show their private parts to different bosses and make them speechless. This particular instance captured the deep complexities rooted in their new practices: They challenged traditions by substituting words of Buddhist songs or revered classics to depict sexual scenes, but this subversion occurred in a private and gendered space, thereby not initiating long-term changes.

Women without *Lajja-Baya* and Violence

The women's narratives showed their values change with FTZ living and the way the FTZ environment became a louder, expressive space for their desires and changed selves. Women desired romantic relationships with men for many reasons, including as a way to attain an easier social identity as someone's girlfriend. In narratives none of the women stated physical and verbal abuse as a reason for not wanting to get into relationships. Yet I observed much violence associated with relationships and their FTZ living. They took much verbal and physical abuse from factory officials, neighbors, boardinghouse owners, family members, and boyfriends.[23] Pradeep Jeganathan (1997) writes that when women do not practice (norms of) shame, it produces a space for sexuality; the practice of fearlessness produces a space for violence (115). He further elaborates that it is more disconcerting when women inhabit "the cusp between *lajja nethi* [without shame] and *baya nethi* [without fear]" than when they directly projected themselves as *lajja-baya nethi*, in which case they could be easily marked as sluts (117). As shown earlier, FTZ workers inhabited this in-between space and aroused deep anxieties in many people. The women workers, however, faced and responded to the resulting sexual exploitation and violence in contradictory ways.

Deepthi was from Kurunegala and worked at a large FTZ factory. She and her sister were among the first few boarders to befriend me. Within a few days of getting to know each other, we became good friends and shared confidences about our love lives.

"My parents had found someone for me and were pressuring me to leave the job. I begged and begged and begged and finally they said 'Okay, then complete your sixth year at work and come home,'" Deepthi informed me during one of our early discussions. "He is a good man. He owns a van and takes tourists around the country. He is building a big house in the village. He trusts me and let me be free here. I like that very much. But after marriage these things will change," she mused. She further confided that she had a boyfriend for three years and her parents forced her to stop that relationship because they wanted her to marry a man who was financially stable.

About a month after I started my research, Deepthi suddenly fell crazily in love with an "army deserter"[24] who was staying in a room in the house. He was a married man with a child but had abandoned his family to live with another FTZ worker. As soon as that relationship fell through, he started this affair with Deepthi. It surprised many of us how lightheartedly Deepthi started sexual relations with him. She started spending nights in his room from the first day of the relationship and also went wherever he wanted her to go with him. Within seven days she missed work three times. She stopped talking to or spending time with the other women and began behaving as if she were living in a dream world.

Deepthi could enjoy this sexual adventure for only six days because her parents came on the seventh day and took her to their village. Deepthi refused to leave Katunayake, and her angry parents and an elder brother slapped and manhandled her for hours while demanding that she get ready to leave. Ultimately, when they literally dragged her to the vehicle, she screamed obscenities vowing that she would marry only Nihal and that she would rather die of hunger than go along with her parents' plans. When Nihal came back from work that day he went berserk, cursing everyone around and trying to break household items. He vowed that he was somehow going to get Deepthi back and within a week went twice to Kurunegala with the intention of abducting Deepthi from her home. But Deepthi was kept locked in a room mostly because she kept screaming about her sexual experiences with Nihal and looked as if she had lost her mind. The parents suspected that she may have been given a hypnotic medicine to fall so crazily for Nihal and they started administering an antidote. Within a week, it was reported that Deepthi started behaving as if she did not know a person named Nihal. About six weeks later, we heard that her marriage to her parents' choice was legally registered and that Deepthi was enthusiastically getting ready for the marriage ceremony.

According to other workers, the young FTZ worker, Inoka, with whom Nihal lived before meeting Deepthi, had barely turned seventeen when she came to work in the FTZ. After dating several boys, she moved in with Nihal. As soon as Nihal abandoned her to pursue Deepthi, Inoka started a relationship with a young man staying at the house. He was eighteen and had come to Katunayake only about three months before he met Inoka. A few months into this relationship, Inoka became pregnant and they got married and moved into another boardinghouse. Because of the pregnancy, the factory fired her and she became totally dependent on the meager salary the young man received. He soon grew tired of the responsibilities and avoided Inoka by spending as much time as he could in Saman's boardinghouse. He started this habit around the time I began my research. Within a few days it became routine for him to come to the boardinghouse early on the weekend and have his wife come looking for him. Typically, verbal battles erupted between them and often these developed into physical violence. Many times it was Inoka who started the physical violence, but when the husband responded it was she who ended up badly bruised. This situation continued for about three months until Saman prohibited both of them from coming to the compound.

Jayani lived in the Kurunegala room and was Deepthi's best friend when she was there. Some time after Deepthi's departure, Jayani got involved in a whirlwind sexual relationship with Manju, a young man staying in a room in the house. One day Jayani announced to the whole boarding room compound that she and Manju had started a relationship. From then onward for about a week she spent nights in his room and cooked and did his laundry. She also appeared to be living in a dream world for that week. The first weekend after they started the relationship, she took Manju to her village and introduced him to her family.

The day they came back, however, Manju broke up with Jayani during a public argument. During this fight, he told her that he had slept with her only because Saman made a bet for Rs. 1,000 that Manju would not be able to have sexual intercourse with Jayani, a virgin. A wailing Jayani confronted Saman and he, together with some of his other friends, corroborated Manju's story. A full-blown verbal battle broke out between the men and Jayani, resulting in Jayani's departure from the boardinghouse. Although many felt sad for her, nobody supported her during the fight. Jayani left the boardinghouse a shamed woman. Nevertheless, because of her hasty introduction of Manju to her village, she could not easily let go of him. Jayani was twenty-four years old and was feeling pressure to get married. Damage caused to her reputation as a result of the relationship with Manju made it hard for her to find a suitable partner. Therefore, she began visiting Manju every weekend to try to win him back by pleading, cooking, doing the laundry, and performing sexual favors.

The urgency many women felt about getting married caused them to become involved in extremely exploitative relationships. On the many occasions that Saman's different girlfriends came looking for him, they recounted stories about Saman giving them slim hopes of marriage as a prelude to sexual activities. Kamani's woes also seemed to result from this same urgency to get married to someone from the urban or FTZ area. Kamani was a tall, thin, beautiful woman who stayed in Saman's boardinghouse for more than six years. She worked at the same garment factory during those six years. She stood out among other boarders because of her reluctance to talk to me. Every time I tried to talk to her, she backed away to her room smiling sweetly. She in fact did not talk with anyone in the boardinghouse unless she really had to. According to Neela *akka*, this was because Kamani had already had two abortions and was now involved with an army soldier. Following her second abortion, she had complications and bled heavily. Fortunately, Anti was home and took Kamani to an ayurvedic doctor and saved her life. But Kamani never gained her weight back and thereafter looked gaunt and anemic.

I was at the boardinghouse when Kamani returned following her third abortion. For two days she again lay in her room moaning loudly. Neela reported that this time it was only a high fever resulting from postabortion pains. Kamani, in one of her weak moments, confided in Neela and confirmed what the others suspected. After three days, she went to work and fell back on what the other boarders called "*baka vatha*," her pact with silence.

Kamani's reasons for engaging in unprotected sex and then having abortions at illegal, substandard abortion clinics remained a mystery to all of us. While these incidents kept happening all around us, my friends insisted that they had no intention of having sexual relations before marriage. In our discussions, they verbalized these incidents in terms of dominant cultural discourses on the proper upbringing of girl children and on the ideal self-restrained behavior of women. This expressed loyalty to traditional cultural values sometimes prevented some workers from acquiring the knowledge that made the reconciliation easier. For all the rapport I cultivated with the boarders, I was unable to discuss with them the need for reliable contraceptive methods.[25] Although mainstream media focused only on such sad stories and portrayed FTZ workers as innocent victims, I perceived these incidents as risks of independence and freedom. The FTZ living offered women opportunities to taste life on their own, and this resulted in an unchaining of their desires from some of the restrictive rules and regulations on female behavior. Many dived into this life without much experience or maturity. Some adverse structural configurations exacerbated the pitfalls of freedom and personal responsibility.

Although women changed their values and adjusted to a new way of life in the FTZ, the structure of the FTZ was such that workers had to leave their employment within five to eight years. This temporary character of their employment ensured that women had no way of achieving long-term empowerment through FTZ employment. Consequently, they had to rely on the traditional means of leaving their "daughter" status behind: by way of marriage. Moreover, as in many poor rural and urban neighborhoods around the world, FTZ workers seemed to use having a boyfriend as a measure of self-esteem in a difficult and oppressive environment. For many women, having a boyfriend had become not just a choice but also an important part of their social identity. Although their living conditions drastically changed at the FTZ, the dominant cultural codes surrounding women's behavior did not. Therefore, signs and rumors of their transgressions in the city tarnished their reputations and hindered their chances in the village marriage market.

It is this combination of changed modern lifestyles and unchanged cultural codes that made the women hold onto their boyfriends under extremely exploitative conditions. The abuse and violence they faced within these relationships were simply dismissed by onlookers as resulting from lack of shame-fear. Still I am reluctant to call FTZ workers a victimized group. Despite constant media attention on their trials and travails, many women leave their villages each year to work in FTZ garment factories. Their desire to be financially and otherwise independent itself marks a challenge to the existing patriarchal structures. Their daily transgressions of traditional values within this urban, industrial milieu, while generating shock and indignation among the middle classes, contribute to changing the dominant values. Furthermore, positive FTZ experiences outweigh the shocking experiences discussed so far. Many women managed to achieve their ideal of "talented, good women" who kept their boyfriends under control. If they engaged in premarital sex under the guise of this narrative construction, they did so safely and discreetly, thereby maintaining relatively unspoiled reputations.

It is important to note that women who were involved in abusive and degrading relationships did not downplay their own agency. In all such cases, women seemed to make choices after weighing many available possibilities in a way that benefited them best. In Deepthi's case, after failing in her attempts to bend her parents' will, she seemed to engage in managing her damaged reputation by embracing the symptoms common among victims of hypnotic medicine.[26] After being given the antidote medicine for a week, she conveniently forgot all about Nihal, convincing others that she was a victim of magic and thereby "blameless." Jayani, Saman's girlfriends, and even Inoka seemed to make their decisions after weighing all the other options. Their relationships ending in such sad circumstances was more symptomatic of the poor choices available to them as women from marginalized sections of society than of being victimized by someone else.[27] Silence, a willful refusal to speak, can be an act of resistance (Visweswaran 1994:51). The silence of Kamani, who underwent three abortions within six years, speaks volumes about how women can express agency through their actions. By not talking to me or anybody else about her life, she avoided having to reconcile her actions with cultural ideals. Through her silence, she spoke of her agency as well as of social cultural expectations that held her back more eloquently than she could have with any number of words.

Constructing Difference

This analysis shows that the FTZ area is a transformative space that enabled working women to become desirous subjects who strategically moved back and forth between the subversion of cultural codes and their expressed loyalty to dominant cultural discourses. In their everyday lives within their FTZ area boardinghouses, the women situationally expressed and performed their differences from rural women who had not migrated, middle-class women, and male industrial workers. It is within these constant politics of everyday life that they creat an in-between identity as modern women with traditional brake pads who can enjoy all the new opportunities that the transnational culture offers while being able to set limits.

The agency they demonstrate in changing their lives and then creatively accommodating the cultural constructions on women's lives forms the basis of the difference they express from unified, static identities as rural women, young Sri Lankan women, or industrial workers. It is through performances, narratives, and writings that they emerge as new persons who are not quite rural, not quite urban. The following chapter focuses on the way they create and negotiate an identity as a gendered group of migrant industrial workers through cultural production in their public recreational activities.

Chapter 6
Performing Disrespectability

Unawatuna beach was already full of male vacationers when we disembarked from our van around 11:00 A.M. The sun was high in the sky and the gold and silver beads on the women's *shalwars* and *gagra cholis* glittered in the sunlight as we made our way to the beach. The purple, orange, and green silk material swished upward in the strong sea breeze giving way to fits of loud laughter as women struggled to keep them modestly down while balancing on high-heeled sandals. Holding hands in groups of three to four we walked to the far corner of the popular beach, passing men in bathing suits and women in shorts and T-shirts. While men laughed and made catcalls, the middle-class women curled their lips in disapproval.

Amila was the only worker who chose to dress differently from the easily identifiable FTZ dresses that the others wore. I was not surprised by this choice because she continually refused to be identified as an FTZ worker, insisting that she worked only because she was bored at home. By constantly pointing out that she came to work from her family home, which was located close to the FTZ, she had emphasized the fact that she was not a migrant worker from a rural area. For the trip to the beach, Amila wore tight, black jeans with a black-checked shirt and only a little jewelry. She used make-up sparingly and applied a soft, pink lipstick, in stark contrast to the bright shades of reds the others wore. Perhaps the biggest difference in attire was her simple pair of beach sandals, which were popular among Colombo youth. But with many of us wearing bright-colored party dresses (I wore a burnt-orange *shalwar kameez*), we attracted much interest from the numerous men at the beach. The indirect, group flirtations between men and the workers climaxed when a group of men surrounded the women and dragged them to the sea in all their finery. As women ran back from the sea, men tossed sand on their wet clothes.[1]

When the men started to drag the women to the sea, I was sitting at the back of the group; Amila caught my hand and pulled me along with her as she ran down a dirt path and up an incline that ended in a deserted temple. There were four of us who escaped this way, and we had a bird's-eye view of what was happening on the beach. After about half an hour the men's laughter and women's good-natured protesting wails ended as the groups prepared for picnic lunches on the beach. When we finally came down, the other women had taken showers and were opening their lunch packets. As they saw me they started happily reporting how often each was dragged to the ocean and how some managed to exchange mailing addresses. Their raucous laughter made me feel a bit sad about missing out on the experience.

When Amila sat down with her lunch, a conspiratorial air enveloped the excited group. Sanka and Nuwan (Line C quality controller), who accompanied us on this trip, grabbed Amila by her arms and dragged her to the sea. With all her clothes soaked with salty water, Amila came out cursing everybody, only to be dragged back to the ocean. After dipping her three times, the men allowed her to pay Rs.10 and take a shower. As soon as she finished the shower, they again dragged her to the sea. The workers, obviously enjoying the scene, encouraged the men with clapping and whistling. Their comments focused on how they had all gone through the forced drenching and that Amila ought to suffer the same experience. But I was puzzled as to their focus on Amila because there were at least three other women who had managed to escape the drenching.

"Look, Sandya miss, my nice blouse has shrunk in size because of the seawater," Amila loudly complained when she came back to eat. Ever ready with a combative rejoinder, Mangala answered, "Our clothes are nice clothes, too." Although she motioned to Mangala not to aggravate Amila further, Vasanthi whispered, "Whatever we wear, we all are garment workers."

The punishment meted out to Amila who willfully refused to be identified as an FTZ worker demonstrated the importance of collective identity to FTZ workers and the role clothing and style play in expressing this identity. The incident showed that workers consider adopting FTZ fashion to be a necessary step in community identification and solidarity. The abuse that Amila was subjected to was a rebuke to her refusal to identify herself with the workers in narratives and in clothing and fashions. The choice of clothing not only signaled a woman's willingness to be identified as an FTZ worker but also signaled her membership in a stigmatized women's group and paved the way for "humiliating" incidents at the hands of men. Workers, however, refused to acknowledge the incident as humiliating or as an act of violence against them, opting instead to recognize it as a mutually pleasurable game. In this way they not only refused to be victims but embraced the consequences of being identified as FTZ workers—in other words, as women who transgressed.

New Cultural Practices and Identity Performances

Toward the end of my research among the workers, I once asked those at Saman's boardinghouse why women workers wanted to buy expensive FTZ clothes when they can easily buy cheaper pastel-colored dresses and try to pass as university students or other middle-class women. Sama succinctly expressed what many workers tried to explain in many ways. "This is the situation, Sandya *akke*, however much we try to be like them, they always brand us as lower class. Only when you realize that do you start seeing the stupidity of those hi-fi [westernized, middle-class, snobby] fashions. Then you start to think, hmm, there is value in what we do and what we like."

When I related this sentiment at the Suishin lunch group, Niluka said, "That's exactly what I would have said. They say our fashions are third class. Well, third class is my class and that is just fine with me."

Many Sri Lankans use the term "third class" (in English) when referring to working-class tastes and in general try to dissociate themselves from such tastes in public.[2] As a group, FTZ workers celebrated this stigmatized identity by unhesitatingly claiming stigmatized tastes and engaging in counter hegemonic cultural practices as well as creating transgressive public spaces. Women were keenly aware of their subordination along class lines and consequently developed their own tastes, cultural practices, and spaces to contest such subordination. These new tastes, practices, and spaces contained many elements of what middle-class people consider disrespectable.

As Willis (1993:206) states, the symbolic creativity of young people in endowing their immediate life spaces and social practices with meaning and their selective use of subcultural styles are crucial to creating and sustaining individual and group identities. In this chapter I demonstrate how women workers collectively expressed their difference from the dominant classes and males and articulated their identities as a gendered group of migrant industrial workers by cultivating new tastes, engaging in oppositional cultural practices, and creating and participating in gendered public spaces. In the urban, modernized, and globalized areas of the FTZ, women developed unique tastes in the realms of music, dance, film, reading material, styles of dress, speech, and mannerisms. By performing subcultural styles that are subversive critiques of dominant values in public spaces, they posed a conscious challenge to the continued economic, social and cultural domination they endured. In this regard, my analysis of counterhegemonic trends in workers' practices corresponds to José Limón's assertion that the carnivalesque cultural performances of Mexican American working-class men in South Texas "represent an oppositional break in the alienating hegemony of the dominant culture and society" (1989:478). The conscious oppositional character of the workers' emergent class and cultural contestatory narrative became evident in the journal notes they wrote about me.[3] In several journal entries they criticized my taste in clothing, music, and movies and termed my preferences middle class. In their boardinghouse conversations, they also attempted to construct a difference between their own recreational activities and those of urban, working-class youth by pointing to the latter's desire to follow middle-class customs when they could afford to do so. It is this cognizant critique that allows me to assert that their creation of subcultural styles is a conscious challenge to the continued economic, social, and cultural domination they endure.

Significantly, my focus on cultural practices and styles also situates them as gender critiques in that the workers refused to perform the ideals of respectability sanctioned for women by middle-class men. In claiming that FTZ workers' performance of their recently developed preferences in the realm of aesthetics was central to creating both working-class and gendered identities, my argument resonates with Dorinne Kondo's notion that "the world of aesthetics is a site of struggle, where identities are created, where subjects are interpellated, where hegemonies can be challenged" (1997:4). Kondo's study is one among several works that demonstrate the role played by music, performance, dance, dress, and style in constituting identity (Gilroy 1993; Tarlo 1996). In summary, FTZ workers' insistence on unique tastes and their play with established categories of style, language, and demeanor subverted middle-class values and tastes, on the one hand, and enabled them to register distinctive identities as migrant working women, on the other.

However, some of their subversions in beauty, fashion, and demeanor were directed toward creating intimacy with working-class males. In fact, the activities led to women workers having asymmetrical and even abusive personal relationships with men. The subversions in fashions also depended on and fed into a materialistic consumer culture around their lives, which represented an accommodation to different hegemonic forces—the predominant one being capitalist. Thus while FTZ workers' participation in stigmatized cultural practices was explicitly transgressive and critical at some levels, their demonstrated acquiescence to different hegemonic influences marks the inseparability of resistance and accommodation.

Consumption and Creating Community

It was a Sunday afternoon when I first took a walking tour of the bazaar, holding hands with four friends from Saman's boardinghouse. The bazaar seemed to come alive with colors, smells, and sounds, giving way to a different feel than what one experienced when passing through it in a vehicle. The space was bustling with women factory workers walking along the stalls inspecting the cheap, colorful goods the merchants offered. The stalls were filled to capacity with fancy hair ornaments, handbags, wallets, religious statues, audiocassettes, posters depicting movie and sports stars, shoes, baby items, household products, and ornaments, which spilled onto the walking space between the road and the stalls. The musical toys, audiocassette sellers, and ice-cream sellers made quite a clamor trying to peddle their wares. The prawn *vada* and chick pea vendors constantly threw chilies and prawns onto the boiling oil making a very pleasant *chrazzz* noise that was accompanied by a smell that made our mouths water. The *aluva* and *rulang* cake vendors waved free samples of their sweets tantalizingly close to our faces, challenging us to abandon our resolve to not eat anything at the bazaar. Women passing by us biting into *ambaralla* or mango pickles straight from *kenda* leaves or messing their faces with pineapple slices drenched in chili pepper mixture did not help our resolve much. Finally throwing all caution to the wind, we decided on pickled olives and some prawn *vada*. All this while the pavement hawkers praised their wares by personalizing their comments onto each passing group. "Ahh, *kohila* is good for this *nangi* from England," one vendor shouted even while pushing a bunch of *kohila* onto my face. The reference to England was apparently inspired by my wearing jeans.

This open-air market was located on the right side of the road just as the Friendship Road passed the intersection. People sold their produce for cheaper prices on weekends and on certain other evenings. This place doubled as what workers called a "bazaar," a bigger fair with many itinerant merchants spreading their wares on the pavement. The line of traveling merchants stretched for almost a mile from the intersection. It was hard to decide who attracted whom, but on Sundays women flocked to the area from morning until evening. Many items on display were handcrafted, produced on a small scale, and priced low.[4] As we walked along the line of merchants, we saw a young man who had wrapped multicolored nightdresses around his body, shouting, "Come sisters, buy these nightdresses. No question, you will look like Sangeetha.[5] How would it be to wear this and show a leg here and a leg there? No doubt the 'lover boy' would be hypnotized. If you wear this once, no abortion, no suicide, lover boy will be caught." We passed him red faced while commenting on the women who surrounded him. But after many walks down this same path through the bazaar, I now know that almost all vendors used eroticized language in their attempts to attract women's attention and that with time one ceases to become embarrassed. Mayol

(1998) writes about a vendor at a Parisian market who used eroticized language while selling vegetables to women customers. While this particular vendor talked about "mounds of lettuce" and "well-hung onions" (29), vendors at the FTZ market shouted how women could look like "jack fruit" or "breadfruit" if they ate vegetables from their stalls.

Often merchants offered one-size night attire and slips and hung these on the barbed-wire fence. Made from flimsy, pastel-colored material, they found favor with the women. All commodities have social uses and cultural meanings assigned by the dominant cultures. But a group can inflect these assigned meanings by using the commodity in a different way (Hall and Jefferson 1975:55). Pastel-colored nightdresses were designed for middle-class women to go to bed in style. With all the media hype about the sexual activities of FTZ workers, it made sense for the vendor to focus on the hidden meaning of sexual seduction as the young man described above did. But workers undermined both sets of meaning by using the nightdresses as an essential part of same-sex socializing within the boardinghouses. Many wore a nightdress and a matching robe in the evening after bathing and went on doing their errands, including going to the nearby grocery shop or to the main house to watch television. They also did not hesitate to entertain any visitor in this attire. When they gathered in one room for paper readings or gossip it seemed as if many butterflies were invading the drab surroundings, and it afforded the women much emotional satisfaction.

According to Schiller (1989:31), economic activity and its symbolic content or cultural importance cannot be separated. Much of the literature on commodification focuses on resistance by local populations to its contaminating character (Toren 1989; Comaroff 1990; Umble 1992). However, studies have been done on its positive aspects that celebrate the way communities may appropriate the possibilities represented by consumer cultures for their own ends (Hall and Jefferson 1975; Hebdige 1988; de Certeau 1988, Gilroy 1993). Miller (1995) holds that communities "with a particular experience of rupture and dislocation may use commodities to embody more extreme forms of modernity such as radical freedom or transnational identity" (150). Following this, I argue that FTZ workers' enthusiastic participation in the consumer culture built around their lives is an important foundation to building community and creating identity. They learn what is needed and appropriate for an FTZ worker through this space and, by choosing to consume the same commodities as others, they express their willingness to be a member of the community. These goods in turn signal to outsiders their membership in the community. The following section examines the way FTZ women workers contributed to structuring a specific commercial space surrounding their needs and demands and then use it as a major instrument in expressing a different identity as a gendered migrant community of industrial workers.

I Consume, Therefore I Am

About seventy yards from the heavily guarded entrance to the FTZ was the four-way intersection popularly called Averiwatthe Junction. While one road ran toward the main bus terminal, the other connected the Colombo-Negombo main road to the suburbs. For about three hundred yards along these roads, except for the fifty-yard strip leading to the FTZ, were lines of shops that catered to FTZ workers. In the morning and after 5:00 P.M., as well as all day on Saturday and Sunday, the area was filled with FTZ workers. Especially on Sundays, women flocked to the area to shop, meet friends, and enjoy what the new consumer culture had to offer them. On that first Sunday walk in the area, Sujani, Shamila, Neela *akka*, and Janaki took me on a tour of this shopping space, too.

About ten crudely built little rooms stood near the intersection and Sujani explained, "These are called bag centers. We can leave our traveling bags or shopping bags in these for a little fee, like Rs. 5 or 10, and then go to work unburdened." Next we passed many small eateries selling breakfast food and snacks, crowded with workers buying rolls and pastries. The smell of baked and fried food was tempting, but before I could suggest a snack break, Shamila drew our attention to flies buzzing around the stalls. We then spent a few minutes inspecting goods at some pavement stands erected on the sidewalks that sold fruit, fabric, thread, needles, umbrellas, handkerchiefs, and cosmetics.

Then we came to the bigger and nicely decorated shops that sold gift items, dresses, and audiocassettes. "We visit these shops to buy dresses and gifts for home.[6] They say these lampshades and knives are from Japan. And they are cheap. But *ane* these things, they only have color and gloss. Don't last long," Neela *akka* mused.

It was considered a great achievement to save some extra money to buy something such as a glass or brass ornament, a tea set, or a fancy household item. Colorful dresses with flowing skirts adorned the glass windows of dress shops, beckoning women to spend their hard-earned money on the FTZ's "in thing." Women usually bought material from the numerous pavement stands and got dresses made by neighboring seamstresses for their everyday use. For annual parties, trips, and other functions, though, they bought elaborate and expensive dresses from these shops.

The burning desire among most women was to acquire gold jewelry. This was also the most difficult to achieve because of the high price of gold. Yet, everytime we went to the shopping area they visited these shops and lovingly caressed the glass showcases holding jewelry. Some shops, however, catered to their special needs by using an installment plan through which a woman signed up to pay for the jewelry over six months or a year. The jeweler held the item while the woman saved enough money to make the purchase.

Along the way, all four of my friends gave money to beggars and talked to them as if they had known the beggars for awhile. "Ahh, they are our friends. Wherever we go they are there, too. That blind man I just gave Rs. 5 to was at Gal Vihare temple near our village during the Vesak vacation. And over there his eyes were fine, but the legs were crippled," Shamila said, laughing loudly. "But why would you give them money if you know they are crooks," I asked. "This is the case, Sandya *akke*, they are owned by *mudalalis* (businessmen). They have to perform many tricks to get the daily target. In a way they are just like us. Besides that man reminds me of my father just days before he died," Sujani explained sadly.

This attachment to certain beggars who frequented the area also represented a form of commodified sentiment and a source of cheap emotional satisfaction that characterized their lives. Many beggars, mostly old men, were (or appeared to be) blind, disabled, or otherwise challenged, and they habitually frequented a particular place in the area. Women enjoyed giving them money and food and sometimes engaged the beggars in conversation. Further complicating the already blurred distinction between gift and commodity, the beggars belonged to businessmen who ran highly organized begging operations. This notwithstanding, giving these beggars money brought the workers immense emotional satisfaction because they could not afford to perform almsgiving for dead relatives, as they would have liked to. Judging by the beggars' long, convoluted praises on the givers' dead relatives, the beggar operators seemed to know how to manipulate this emotional need in workers to commercial advantage.

Sujani's sadness quickly dissipated as she pointed toward the nearest portrait studio with a big banner announcing "photographs with movie stars" and a smaller one announcing "photographs amidst beautiful scenery." A life-size cutout of a western woman in a bikini stood at the front steps of the studio, beckoning women to a world of fantasy modernity. "There are big pictures of Nirosha and Jagath [famous young singers] and one of Ranjan [a movie star]. We can sit by any of these pictures and then we have a photo with the stars. And there are pictures of beautiful waterfalls, mountains, snow, and castles in there. That is what I want, a photo beside a castle. Let's go inside, let's go and see," Sujani was already climbing the steps when her sister Shamila stopped her by reminding her that there was a lot more to show me. Sujani reluctantly climbed down. Later I got to know that almost all women desired to have their photographs taken to send home and to give men with whom they were corresponding. Most women liked to own such portraits, which gave them a sense of getting closer to a desired world of beautiful people and places. While not many listed owning studio portraits as a priority, workers generally liked to pose for photographs and collect them. Because it was rare that a worker owned a camera, it was at the factory parties and trips that they got a chance to fulfill this wish. But on these occasions, they finished numerous film rolls. Selling and printing film rolls brought huge profits to these studios.

Many buildings displayed notices advertising boardinghouse facilities as well as vans and drivers who could be contacted to rent vehicles for various trips or to "book hires." They also displayed notices about famous shrines and sorcerers in nearby towns. We also passed several dark, dingy rooms occupied by horoscope and palm readers. We went inside one room and both Janaki and I got our palms read as the other three sat in the front of the room with four other workers waiting for their turn.

In fact, FTZ workers provided many employment opportunities for area youth. The musical shows held every month at the FTZ outdoor stadium provided periodical employment for youth. Some others engaged in providing cheap entertainment for the workers by performing snake and monkey dances or basic acrobatics. Women enthusiastically participated in this vibrant consumer culture built around their lives. Although at times it seemed as if they were becoming slaves to the newest fad in the area, they also shaped the structure of this commercial space through their specific demands and needs. While their participation in FTZ consumer culture marked a challenge to patriarchal and middle-class values, it also guaranteed their immersion in capitalist markets that mostly benefited the rich merchants and ensured the flow of foreign goods to the country. Acquiring colorful commodities gave women a false sense of empowerment while preventing them from taking steps to initiate long-term empowerment, such as acquiring land or building houses in their home villages.

However, it is these new and unique consumption patterns that allowed them to display their difference and to register their identification as a gendered group of migrant workers. They did this by developing gendered social spaces and practices of everyday life. More important, this happened through and against the capitalist cultural discourses surrounding their lives. In the following sections, I focus on how the creation of new public spaces and new tastes and fashions facilitate the expression of new identities.

Creating Public Spaces and Expressing Public Identity

The stigma attached to the very characterization of migrant workers' in-dustrial employment, as women living away from their families, had a two-way relationship with the dynamic commercial, cultural, and public spaces they created. While these spaces became marked and degraded because of their association with the workers, the very nature of the newly created spaces added to the stigma of being away from one's home. However, FTZ workers enthusiastically consumed the public space created around their lives. On weekends they went to Averiwatthe junction to shop or to get their horoscope read. The area became full of women, with venders catering to them and groups of young men follow-ing them. Women gathered in circles, by the roadside, at bus stops, and in front of shops to engage in loud conversations. Young men gathered near these groups of women and communicated via jokes from two to three yards away. This appropriation of public space for a group's activ-ities had always been contested and when the groups are socially margin-alized ones, it generated fear and jealousy among middle-class people. According to Schiller (1989), "the uses of the public streets in the city has been a site of social struggle as far back as the early nineteenth cen-tury" (103). Middle classes always contested the rights of the people who congregated on streets to socialize or participate in parades.

Dabindu maintained a street drama group comprised of FTZ workers and it regularly performed on the crowded streets near the bazaar on Sundays. Women gathered in a circle that took up more than half the street space. Registering how unique the FTZ area and FTZ Sundays are, the police turned a blind eye to the obvious violation of traffic laws. FTZ workers' appropriation of the streets provided them only an ambiguous and contested space for social participation. While their presence was tolerated, the ways they utilized the space, for assertive behavior and flir-tation, was similarly feared as a sign of moral degeneration and as a test of the nation's purity. Workers contested the prying eyes and eroticized language of male participants in the commercial sphere to continue consuming this public space as well as several other spaces, including the railroad tracks.

Boardinghouses were attached to all the homes along the railroad tracks for at least three miles. In the evenings and especially on week-ends women left their crowded boarding rooms to sit on the railroad tracks and socialize.[7] They sat on the tracks in groups to comb each other's hair, sing, gossip, and quarrel. When family and friends visited, it was along the railroad tracks that they sat and talked. Lovers walked hand in hand back and forth along the tracks, making visible that they were not up to any "hanky-panky." Petty traders, food vendors, palm readers, snake dancers, monkey dancers, and NGO music groups visited the railroad tracks providing women with cheap thrills.[8] Every hour trains threateningly rushed toward them, tooting their horns continuously. Women waited until the last moment to get off the tracks and then stood dangerously close to the tracks to reclaim their seats. This silent battle with the train extended to its passengers, and women stared back at suburban office workers who looked on disapprovingly.

Male neighbors and visitors to the area sometimes stopped to talk to women, but the tracks remained predominantly a women's gathering area where they had more room to stay away from contending forces. This relatively isolated gendered social space was significant in educating newcomers to the FTZ way of life. "Propriety" would seem an inappropriate term to describe FTZ workers' lives, but that is what they learned within this space—how to present an image that is understood, recognized, and approved by all who consumed the public space. "Propriety is simultaneously the manner in which one is perceived and the means constraining one to remain submitted to it. . . . That is why it produces stereotyped behaviors, ready-to-wear social clothes, whose function is to make it possible to recognize anyone, anywhere" (Mayol 1998:17). Strangely, it seems highly appropriate to use this same term to analyze a space characterized by transgression to dominant culture.

Not only the shopping area and the railroad tracks but wherever they went in groups—to shrines, temples, or movie halls, with their colorful clothes as well as social clothes displayed through language and demeanor—the women rendered these urban social spaces arenas of expression that celebrated their new identities. This creation and celebration stirred intensely ambivalent responses from different sections of Sri Lankan society, again characterizing the conflicts generated by modernity. On the one hand, the creation of gendered social spaces as well as new cultural practices were resented for the contamination they brought to Sinhala Buddhist culture. On the other hand, people across classes were relieved that the FTZ workers were creating exclusive differences, thereby keeping intact the extant categories of respectability. In the next section I will analyze the way FTZ workers learned, performed, and registered an exclusive identity as migrant women industrial workers through the symbolic functions of the body, its adornment and its accessories (words and gestures), as well as through their aesthetic preferences and cultural practices.

Body Adornment and "Garment Girl Tastes"

Toward the end of my research, Sujani and Janaki visited my parents' home in a Colombo suburb. While Janaki wore a maroon tunic over a

Figure 7. Drama group performing street drama on Sundays, and women enjoying the performance. Photograph by the author.

long maroon skirt, Sujani was dressed in a bright yellow and orange blouse with a black skirt. They both wore almost all the gold jewelry they owned. When my mother heard that we were planning to visit two temples in the vicinity after lunch, she asked me to loan them some of my clothes that were "appropriate for the temple." Because Janaki and Sujani had no qualms about their dresses, I did not offer them different clothing as my mother suggested. We had talked about taking some photographs at the temples, and it was clear that they chose these prized clothes in anticipation of photographs. At the temple we drew many angry looks both for our choices of colors and for their exaggerated poses for the camera.

Kathy Peiss (1986) writes that "dress was a particularly potent way to display and play with notions of respectability, allure, independence, and status and to assert a distinctive identity and presence" (63). Similarly, the colorful dresses and other accessories FTZ workers habitually chose to wear on special occasions registered for them a distinctive identity as garment factory workers. They wore bright colored *shalwars* and *gagra cholis* that were embroidered with gold or silver beads, combined with dark red lipstick, nailpolish, and heavy make-up. They also wore high heels (even if going on a trip to a beach) and frequently wore multicolored dots (*pottu*) on their foreheads. Such choices loudly proclaimed a difference from other women and made it easier for people to recognize them even if they were hundreds of miles from the FTZ.

Their dresses could be loosely divided into two types: work clothes and party clothes. Their everyday work clothes were of different styles because they wore their old party dresses to work. This habit also ensured that they were easily recognized no matter where they went. These dresses included a flowing skirt (called a flared skirt), with puffed sleeves and round necklines, and skirts and blouses in several different lengths and patterns. Most of their work clothes suggested popular urban fashions modified with elements from favored rural fashions. Their party dresses, however, were a combination of several past middle-class fashions and their own color preferences. Haney (1999) writes that the creation of a hybrid style called fantasia by female performers in Mexican American tent shows asserted Mexican American identity while marking the performer's entry into "newly public female roles" (437). The hybrid styles among the FTZ workers similarly marked their newly acquired public role as urban factory workers who are different from middle-class or rural women as well as from other urban factory workers.

At the boardinghouse I often observed workers bringing their newly made work dresses from the nearby seamstresses. One by one they acquired "Titanic dresses,"[9] which were the fashion craze at the time. In the film *Titanic* the dresses were made of light colors, but the FTZ workers preferred bright and dark colors. They especially favored yellow, maroon, magenta, dark green, purple, and black.[10] This choice of colors was especially significant given that Anagarika Dharmapala considered the white sari the optimal dress for respectable ladies because it signaled their chastity and purity (De Alwis 1997:98–99). Incidentally, many FTZ workers liked to match black skirts with bright yellow or bright pink blouses even though middle-class people associated such color combinations with prostitutes. The workers' choice to sport these stigmatized colors as well as other marked fashions[11] could not be attributed simply to an ignorance of middle-class "dos" and "don'ts" because they pored over the fashion pages of various magazines. However, these colorful dresses were sometimes more expensive than "simple, accepted fashions," thus ruling out affordability as the reason. This play with the prostitute image seems a particular mediation of culture and style by women who have found themselves between the categories of "respectable" and "promiscuous." If this play pushed them further toward the latter category, the workers did not seem particularly concerned about it.

FTZ workers could easily buy or make pastel colored dresses of the kind that were fashionable among female students attending Colombo's higher education institutions. By doing so, they could have passed for belonging among those who congregated at "respectable public spaces," but they showed no interest in this. When I visited some seamstresses near Saman's boardinghouse, I noticed that they mainly made "Titanic dresses" and a two-piece dress that most urban women tried to stay away from because of its association with FTZ workers. Once when we were discussing workers' fashion choices, a male visitor interjected that, even if the workers wore the same dresses as other women in Colombo, their jewelry and various colored hairpins would give them away.

Neighbors as well as factory officials talked about workers wearing excessive gold jewelry to work. Some women wore up to four rings to work at one time and sported thick, gold chains with pendants.[12] Others wore long, gold earrings. During my research, many women wore a plastic hairband that featured the English alphabet. Their favorite hairstyle necessitated the use of braids, bands, and pins, and the workers experimented by combining different colored or patterned hair accessories. The hairstyle was called the "bump," which was created by combing back a portion of the hair in the front into a puff and then using hairpins to keep it in place; they then used a braid to catch their hair in a ponytail or they wore their hair loose. Some women had bangs cut on the sides; others permed the front of their hair into curls. Although some women at the FTZ had short hair, they too used many popular hair accessories for ornamentation as well as to hold their hair in place. Other accessories, such as cheap handbags, sandals, and fake brand-name watches that the women bought at the FTZ bazaar, also contributed to their identity.

I attended four parties at different factories and several wedding receptions at workers' homes. On these special occasions, women proudly displayed FTZ party clothes and jewelry. They also wore makeup, perfume, bright lipstick, and nailpolish. They took many photographs at these parties in all their finery, especially while posing with their superiors. Women showed photographs from past annual parties, and it was easy to see that their fascination with the brightly decorated *shalwar* and *gagra choli* as a party dress had been present for at least five years. Those photographs presented an ongoing story whereby women's wear evolved over the years from pink and blue "flower-girl dresses"[13] to colorful *shalwars* or *cholis* and the gradual addition of other accessories, including gold jewelry. This material change coincided with another transformation—from confused, wide-eyed young girls to self-assertive, animated women posing for photographs holding beer cans while seated on men's laps.

FTZ workers used make-up when they went on trips or attended special functions. Refusing to follow the barrage of middle-class advice about beauty that they were subjected to in the media, the workers almost always chose bright-red lipstick. None of the workers I knew even considered shaving her legs. They kept using soap on their faces and in their hair even though billboards around the FTZ were filled with advertisements for shampoos, conditioners, facial cleansers, and scrubs.[14] Their skin took on a deathly pallor (a thin, white layer over the dark skin, probably caused by the bleaching agents contained in the soap) for a few hours after applying soap to their faces. Mirroring standards of beauty in other postcolonial societies, Sri Lankans consider fair skin to be essential to beauty and consequently fairness is invested with a considerable amount of social prestige. Although they never acknowledged it, the workers also craved fairer skin through ways that made sense to them. While this preoccupation with fairness is rooted in the racist construction derived from British colonial-era ideologies that claimed the Sinhala are Aryan (and therefore fairer) and the Tamils are Dravidian (and consequently darker), it is elitist to condemn this obsession on senseless racist prejudices alone. As Kondo (1997) writes, it is only the dominant and unmarked sections of society that can afford to be unconcerned about appearance. She also warns that it is a mistake to think that being unconcerned about appearance is a politically innocent position because this apparent lack of concern itself is a preoccupation with appearance (15). Interestingly, FTZ workers who wrote journal entries about me identified my unconcerned attitude toward appearance as the very mechanism through which I registered my difference from them.

New workers who came directly from their villages learned the appropriate attire, fashions, and behavior within the FTZ through an intense socialization process at the factories as well as in their boardinghouses. After a few months of FTZ life, workers acquired dresses and accessories that conveyed their membership in the community. Many workers confided that they were determined to uphold their ruralness when they first came to the FTZ. But they reported that the strength and happiness derived from following other workers and the gentle prodding from senior workers soon made them change their minds. According to Lynch (2000), village garment factory workers spoke disparagingly of the way rural workers first came to work "dirt dripping from their clothes" (234) and celebrated the newcomers' gradual transformation in hygiene level and style as a mark of modernity. Marking the difference between the two fields, FTZ workers did not talk disparagingly about new workers or the way they slowly acquired the styles and habits of the FTZ. They all came to the FTZ as rural women and had to collectively suffer the stigma of being "unhygienic, backward, ignorant, and tasteless rural women." This instilled an "us" against "them" mentality that focused on whether a woman wanted to be identified as a FTZ worker, as opposed to what her appearance or conduct was when she first arrived in the FTZ.

Figure 8. Workers dressed up for a factory party. Photograph by the author.

Disrespectable Language and Demeanor

Four women wore saris, two wore *shalwars*, and one wore a two-piece dress when we went to Kandy by train to attend a wedding reception. The saris were neither bright colored nor expensive (as were the Indian saris that middle-class women favored). For this special occasion, they abandoned their standard bumps and braids and got their hair done in big buns at a salon in Katunayake. On the return trip that evening, women took off their jewelry and placed it in my backpack for safekeeping. With their make-up worn off by sweat, they looked like any other group of working-class women returning from a wedding reception. However, from the interest our group generated at the railroad station, it was soon clear we were recognized as FTZ workers. As soon as we entered the station, a man asked, "What garment [factory] are you from?" Several other young men gravitated toward us and started talking about garment factories among themselves. One reason for our being recognized may have been the absence of an elderly individual in the group, although the women's demeanor and language definitely played a role as well.

The women entered the station in two groups, holding hands and talking loudly among themselves. Workers were usually gregarious when in groups, and on this occasion the beer they had consumed at the reception intensified this behavior. They talked to the men without hesitation and responded with glee to their uninvited comments. They played verbal games among themselves and frequently erupted into loud laughter. Starting indirect group communication with some young men, they proceeded to hide one man's traveling bag. The man jokingly threatened to bring the station master over to strip-search them. Sujatha replied that this was the whole point in hiding the bag. This provoked an elderly woman to spit on the tracks and comment, "There is no worth in these garment girls [*ganna deyak ne*]." When the train arrived, several young men managed to get into the same compartment with us, and the women immensely enjoyed their company until the journey's end. Several other people in the compartment looked on with, I thought, sad eyes, probably wondering what was in store for the nation when its women behaved so shamelessly.

Generally, behavior and language worked as identity markers for women in the FTZ. Not only were they loud, but their speech was also heavily interspersed with "rough terms," such as *umba* (you), *varen* (come), and *palayan* (go). They also used the masculine terms *machan* (best buddy), *ado* (you), and *malli* (younger brother) among themselves and with men. Although some women claimed that they used "rough terms" with friends in grade school, all the workers I talked to said they never used masculine terms in conversations before coming to the FTZ. Appropriating masculine language was a powerful subversion of middle-class notions of feminine discipline and respectability. Workers learned the creative use of regional dialects and phrases in the factories and at their boardinghouses, which they then used to get back at superiors as well as to get out of difficult situations at the factories. They also used this knowledge during everyday conversations at public places. Much of this language bordered on what was considered obscene, which attracted the interest of young men but caused older people to react with disgust and frustration. Workers also used familiar technical phrases from the production process to talk about everyday occurrences, making it difficult for outsiders to understand what they were referring to. They used the term "target" for someone's love interest and "in *karanawa*" to describe when a man or woman first expressed a love interest. They also used the term "damages" to identify losses suffered from a broken relationship, which ranged from money and jewelry to one's virginity. They incorporated other factory jargon into their everyday language, including the term "issue girls" for women who provided materially for boyfriends, "trimmers" for scheming men who cheated women out of money, and "QC manager" for women who bossed others around at the boardinghouses.

Men and middle-class people censured FTZ women's behavior and their new linguistic practices. Women nevertheless kept using such language and showed off their newly fashioned rebellious demeanor.

Figure 9. Workers dressed in colorful clothing during a trip. Photograph by the author.

After a trip to the beach or a temple, women laughingly talked about people's reactions to their particular actions and how they deliberately did things to anger onlookers further. Women workers usually became loud and animated when they were in a group, further demonstrating the strong links between their behavior and their identification as FTZ workers.

Celebrating "Third-Class" Tastes

"This is the situation, *nangi*. These girls come from villages and they get into these romances. All they get to read here is these silly novels with such silly conversations. If we try to advise a young girl about not seeing a particular boy because he has no future or something, they give us these big ideas like, 'Begging for food with him is better than kingly comforts' or 'We will live in a shack and eat rice and salt,' all learned from romance novels," Neela *akka* commented, wrinkling her nose to show her disapproval of the situation. She said this after I asked the residents at Saman's boardinghouse about their frequent use of terms such as *raththaran* (golden), *patiya* (little one), *sukiri* (fair one), *rosa mala* (rose), *kollo* (boy), *lamayo* (child), and *babo* (baby) in their everyday conversations. "It is true, *akke*," Janaki joined the conversation. "These girls call even those men who cheat them out of their salary packets 'prince' and 'precious.' 'Sacrifice' is the most popular word when your boyfriend is a good-for-nothing bastard," she laughingly continued.

During the time I stayed at Saman's boardinghouse, I also noticed that women used words and phrases from romance novels to resolve their continual attachment to hopeless or abusive love affairs. I, however, see this as a creative re-centering of dominant cultural constructions on the "sacrificial mother/wife" roles to understand their participation in doomed romantic relationships. Just as turn-of-the-twentieth-century factory women in New York developed a penchant for dime novels (Peiss 1986; Enstad 1999), FTZ workers at the turn of the twenty first century also wanted to read romance novels in their free time. Both Dabindu and Mithurusevena maintained libraries and they contained readings on labor and human rights, history, and politics, as well as readings considered good by schoolteachers and middle-class parents, but workers usually borrowed "silly romance novels." They laughed at their own choices, saying that after a hard day at work they did not want to read difficult novels about social and political problems. This choice signaled a form of worker alienation in that the workers tried to temporarily escape their drudgery by reading romance novels rather than reflecting on exploitative working conditions during their leisure time.

Craving romance novels was not unique to FTZ workers; young women belonging to many social backgrounds read these during leisure time. What was unique to the FTZ workers is that they developed a reading community in which they read and discussed these books in their boarding rooms. Tabloid magazines published serialized novels and workers collected all the episodes, bound them, and then exchanged the bound copies among themselves. Because these readings were so closely shared, discussed, and extended within an intimate social space, their effect on workers' daily conversations was significant.

FTZ workers registered their difference in other leisure activities and tastes they developed in the FTZ. Reading tabloid magazines, some of which contained pornographic material, was one pastime they indulged in after beginning their employment in the FTZ. On weekends, when they usually found time to relax, women read magazines with pornographic content that catered to urban youth and FTZ workers. Middle-class people looked down on these magazines, claiming they only catered to "stupid women" or women in the FTZs. Teachers and parents encouraged young women to read mainstream weeklies, such as "The Young Woman" (*Tharuni*), "The New Woman" (*Nava liya*), and "Goddess of the House" (*Sirikatha*), and they made it clear that possessing tabloid magazines seriously jeopardized one's reputation as a "good and intelligent woman."

Some of these magazines are considered filthy (pornographic) papers and FTZ workers claimed they read them for juicy accounts (*pani kelli*), which typically dealt with sexual adventures. Many workers claimed their interest in the magazines was educational and that the material provided much-needed sexual knowledge. A spokeswoman for the Women's Bureau contradicted this, saying, "If they read good books and magazines like *Tharuni* and *Sirikatha*, rather than reading these filthy papers, they will be better equipped to deal with the problems they face in the urban environment." Dabindu members also bitterly complained that the workers read tabloid magazines rather than reading the *Dabindu* magazine. Workers knew that middle-class people looked down on those reading such magazines. However, even while emphasizing the magazines' educational value, workers claimed that they did not care what other people thought. Many workers mentioned that they had never seen or heard about these pornographic magazines before they came to the FTZ. This demonstrates that, by providing a space where transgression was the norm, FTZ employment played a crucial role in the development of new practices among women workers.

"Gallery Movies" and Class Stigma

While I enjoyed going to movies with my friends from the boarding-house, I cringed when buses and cars slowed down near Jayalath Hall, causing traffic jams while we stood in line to see movies such as *Where Are You, Darling?*, *Miguel at Day and Daniel at Night*, and *You Belong to Me*. While reading the disapproval and amusement in the eyes of people who peered from passing vehicles became a preoccupation for me, the workers laughed and joked as if to better press the difference home. People gawked at the FTZ workers, dressed in their colorful party dresses, with *pottu* on their foreheads and gold jewelry adorning every available space, snuggling with their boyfriends. The cinema was located right by the main road, and the lines of FTZ workers clamoring to see "gallery movies" easily became another marker for FTZ workers' lifestyle and identity.

One movie I saw twice was titled *Here Comes Alice* (*Menna Bole Alice*), a copycat of the Robin Williams movie *Mrs. Doubtfire*. On both Saturdays, there were long lines of FTZ workers wearing their best clothes, in groups or with their boyfriends, waiting to buy tickets. The movie was filled with songs, dancing, and hilarious comedy; the latter was generated by a well-known comedian playing a character who falls in love with the man disguised as Alice.

With regard to Sinhala cinema, people acknowledged a division between good, artistic movies made by acclaimed directors and Hindi copycat (*anukarana*) films or lovers' dream world (*pemwathunge sihina loka*) movies.[15] There was another distinction made with regard to "middle path" (*madha mawatha*) movies because of their family-oriented character. Although the educated, "socially conscious, disciplined people" were supposed to like artistic and middle-path movies, the other category was identified with low-income people and was known as "gallery movies"—a term that describes the cheapest seats in a Sri Lankan movie theater. Even if one enjoyed segments from gallery movies shown on television, one was not supposed to go to a theater to view such movies. Growing up in a Sri Lankan middle-class family, I was socialized into disparaging gallery movies. The stigma associated with such movies is also gendered, as it is widely considered more disrespectable for women to go to such movies. Gallery movies and the theaters used to screen such movies are considered low class, masculine spaces where youthful lovers also go to engage in transgressive sexual acts. Nevertheless FTZ workers, most of whom confessed that they rarely saw movies when in the village, flocked to the nearby Jayalath Cinema to see lighthearted romances and comedies replete with song-and-dance sequences and intensely followed trivia about such movies. Workers also loved to see subtitled Hindi movies shown on television. Middle-class wives and youth also enjoyed these movies. But watching them at home or at the boardinghouse prevented the class stigma associated with lining up by the main road to see gallery movies.

FTZ workers, however, displayed a conflict between what they desired and what they thought they were supposed to desire by planning endlessly to go to see celebrated artistic movies. During my research at the FTZ, they never went to see what was considered an artistic movie. Several women sarcastically talked about their fellow workers who continuously expressed a desire to see artistic movies by saying that those workers were trying to impress me. Yet, in a clear break from their tendency to openly critique middle-class values, none of the workers talked irreverently about acclaimed films. They instead engaged in a silent critique by spending their leisure time going to movies deemed "disrespectable" by the middle classes.

Popular Music and the FTZ Workers

Averiwatthe junction also was home to several record bars (where one can buy audiocassettes and CDs), and I visited two of them often to buy cassette tapes and to make phone calls using their booths. I became friends with the young man who operated the Rani Record Bar at the top of Sumithrarama Road. One day at the beginning of my fieldwork, he showed a glass case full of audiocassettes by singers unknown to me.

"Amila Pushpakumara is now known among other young people too, but he started by producing cassettes for FTZ workers and selling them himself at the junction," he informed me while pointing to several cassettes by the singer. Inspecting a cassette by K. Chnadima, I asked who he was. "I really don't know. I heard this name only after I came to Katunayake to run this record bar," Thushara answered with a sheepish smile.

Workers' preferences in music, songs, and vocalists also marked a break from both the "acceptable" as well as the new youth pop culture. Indian classical music had long influenced Sinhala music. Vocalists and music directors trained in that tradition or who combined this with Sinhala folk rhythms dominated the music scene via *sarala gee* (directly translated as "simple songs," but generally meaning nonclassical or soft). Older and middle-class people valued these songs as well as soft rock and classical western music. The younger generation, however, favored western popular music, and a movement that began in the mid-1990s saw new bands recording celebrated old songs to fast, western rhythms. These remixed songs were fast enough for dancing and, when played at popular musical shows, attracted youthful crowds by the thousands.

This was preceded by an Afro-Portuguese music genre called *baila* that was popular among Sri Lankan urban, lower-income communities and youth. Middle-class people consider *baila* music as hybrid and of poor quality, although they also played it at parties and on pleasure trips. Because this music and the attendant dancing were linked to alcohol consumption, it was considered another evil associated with modernity (Sheeran 1997:231).[16] FTZ workers enjoyed this music and certainly abandoned their inhibitions when they joined dancing crowds at outdoor musical shows and parties. When asked, the overwhelming majority said they liked soft music as well as *baila* music. They also said they preferred *baila* music to slow classics at parties and on trips. However, educated in Sri Lankan public schools, many were compelled to voice their admiration of singers revered since independence.[17]

Workers' everyday listening preferences differed from those of the middle classes and other youth mostly in lyrics rather than in the choice of music. They liked soft music with lyrics that related to their lives. The difference between these soft songs and the ones favored by the middle classes was the presence of previously unknown singers and the parodying of soft song tunes with hastily written, garbled lyrics. The songs also copied popular Hindi tunes, using whatever lyrics suited the tune. New singers and lyricists, who were launching their careers, created such songs, and cheaply made cassettes were sold to workers at the Sunday fair. Indeed, on Sundays it was common to see the vocalists themselves promoting their new cassettes by blasting the songs from their vehicles.

These songs expressed sympathy for the workers as well as for the country's military personnel. The latter were close to workers' hearts, and the formulaic, celebratory terms and phrases reminded them of their brothers and boyfriends at the war front and brought tears to their eyes. Although every singer had at least one patriotic song, these new singers' songs, which I had never heard broadcast or promoted over radio or television, directly addressed the close relations the garment factory workers had with soldiers. Their focus on mothers, sisters, and girlfriends, who were waiting for soldiers to return, in fact marked a break from popular patriotic songs, which focused on masculine duties to the nation and womanly sacrifices.

Workers' desire that cultural forms reflect their real-life experiences was also evidenced by their penchant for changing the words of popular, mainstream songs to include information about their lives. They frequently sang these impromptu parodies at their Saturday gatherings at the boardinghouses. I have read several such parodies published in the tabloid magazines *Priyadari* and *Suwanda* (the latter has a feature section devoted to parodies) that were sent in by FTZ workers.

The workers' special interest in these new audiocassettes and parodies of old songs did not preclude a preference for popular *baila* singers or songs by well-known singers that spoke to their particular life experiences. According to Seneviratne and Wickramaratne (1980), paralleling the national independence movement was a movement to de-Sanskritize the Sinhala language. This simple, lyrical Sinhala style came to influence the songs of soft classics singers such as Sunil Shantha, Amaradeva, Victor Ratnayake, and others (740). These songs, however, were still composed using metaphors and creative language and their subject matter adhered to dominant cultural expectations. In the late 1990s, acclaimed female vocalist Nanda Malini recorded several songs that steered away from this standard style. One such song that the workers frequently sang in their rooms and on trips said, "Why didn't you join our pilgrimage, oh, child [*lamayo*]? I am very lonely." This song was written in decidedly colloquial, rural Sinhala, using workers' favorite terms such as *lamayo*. Nanda Malini recorded many romantic songs, but they did not evoke the same interest among FTZ workers because her other songs contained scholarly Sinhala, Sanskrit, and obscure metaphors.[18] Another song by Nanda Malini, however, caught FTZ workers' attention. Written to a popular Hindi tune the lyrics noted, "My darling, take me wherever you go. Let's build a hut by a mountain and eat only rice and salt. Let's tear saris to use as window curtains."[19] This song was also regularly sung at parties and on trips. On trips, the few males present would change the words to read, "Darling, take me to a dark place." Once when we were returning from a trip to a temple, intoxicated men on the bus started replacing the last verb of all the lines with an obscene word for having sex.

Nanda Malini was criticized for singing a song written to a Hindi tune, espousing hedonistic ideas. Ironically, Nanda Malini and the composer, a professor of Sinhala at a leading university, created the song as a critique of young people blinded to social problems because of their pleasure-seeking ways. The two also hoped to ridicule the current fascination with Hindi tunes and movies among young people.[20] Their efforts backfired when youth groups appropriated the song as an affirmation of their lifestyles. When males appropriated the tune to embarrass women, FTZ workers refused to be silenced by such masculine parodies.[21] They kept singing the song with its original lyrics while critiquing the self-indulgent philosophy even as they desired similar carefree pleasures from their real-life romances. Nationalists have "always looked down on *baila* as alien, debased, vulgar—in short, *thuppahi*" (Siriwardhene 1990). Sheeran (1997) found that it is more shameful and un-Aryan for women to sing and enjoy popular music than it is for men (235). In this context, the FTZ workers' determination to sing a popular song, which contained the potential of vulgar parodying, signaled a celebration of what is deemed vulgar, debase, *thuppahi*, and un-Aryan—that is, embracing all that which was not middle class.

Mirror of an "Evil Time": Dance Mania and Modernity

Almost all of RAC's 3,000 workers, which included a substantial number of men, too, attended its New Year party held at the spacious grounds of the Hotel Good Wood Plaza. It was a rainy day and the revelers had to run for cover twice. Women huddled together under any awning they could find by the side of the hotel. "Look, look, Miss, there is a film showing over there," Nalini, an RAC worker who volunteered to show me around nudged my elbow, pointing to a couple kissing in a dark corner. In fact, there was much physical intimacy between men and women. The couples, their wet clothes pasted seductively to their bodies, stole kisses in the rain, reminding the onlookers of the song-and-dance sequences in workers' favorite movies.

Just before dinner was served, the band played feverishly and the dancers reacted as expected. Couples danced close to each other and frequently touched hands and faces. Walking around the spacious plaza, Nalini and I came across a man and woman dancing by an overgrown hedge even as they squeezed each other to the rhythm of the music. "This woman is kind of strange. She had been drinking all day today. Once before, she went crazy in the factory because she lost everything she owned when her boardinghouse flooded," an embarrassed Nalini commented hastily.[22]

Reed (1998) states that dancing expresses relations of power, protest, resistance, and complicity (505). Examining early twentieth-century Sinhala cultural discourse, De Alwis (1998) holds that dancing—be it *bailas* or ballroom dancing—was perceived to be a particularly reprehensible form of behavior for "respectable" women (126). Sinhala Buddhist young women have been learning Kandyan and low-country dance styles and Indian classical dance in schools and private classes for decades. Dance is an important means of producing and reproducing gender ideologies, and these dance forms reflected the stereotypical gender images through their conservative movements as well as their subject matter.[23] Consequently, they were easily incorporated as an admirable aspect of the middle-class image of the ideal, accomplished woman. *Baila* dancing, the dance form that the RAC workers were engaged in, is not conservative in its movements and does not address specific subject matter. The resultant space of ambiguity offers women an opportunity to test cultural categories and control. It is this nonchoreographed and, therefore, undomesticated (Savigliano 1995:122) character along with its hybrid origin that invested the *baila* dance and its female performers with class stigma.

The way women participated in their factory parties reflected both embodiment and resistance to dominant cultural values. Suishin managers talked derisively about women dancing to *baila* tunes and noted that they were becoming women without shame-fear. By implication, the ones who did not dance signaled their allegiance to the dominant culture by avoiding certain bodily movements. FTZ workers, at different levels of intensity, used *baila* dancing to express happiness, protest repression, and invert authority. At different dancing parties, performers and spectators negotiated the discourses on shame and fear in ways that were meaningful to them.

At Suishin and in boardinghouses, workers described their attraction to dancing as "dance mania" (in English) or as "*baila pissuwa.*" "I can't wait for my first factory party. And all the other workers are counting the days, too," Sujani once informed me. "I mostly want to watch others dance and learn. I am not sure whether I want to dance in front of managers, supervisors, and everybody," Sujani continued, blushing a little. In fact, knowing how to dance or losing enough self-consciousness to dance was considered a sign of being "mod." This is not to suggest that these women learned to dance *baila* at the FTZ. Several women confided that they had danced while on school trips or at home with their siblings. "In our family we, the children, used to dance in our room to Nihal Nelson's *baila*. But it is not like jumping up and down in front of everybody. I was very shy in the beginning. But after I have a glass or two of beer, I kind of get over the fear," Nadee said.

"Many women drink beer to get over the shyness," Deepthi once confided. In fact, learning to drink beer and dance at parties, as a sign of modernity or fully embracing the FTZ identity, was a common discourse in factories and boardinghouses. I attended four factory parties (in different factories) in which many attempts were made to get new workers to drink and dance.[24] Groups surrounded reluctant young women and ridiculed or forced them to drink and dance. When a woman took her first sip of beer or tried her first steps on the dance floor, there was applause and joking.

The link between modernity, westernization, and insanity was a regular theme surrounding FTZ dancing parties. On a nationally televised youth talent program called *Thurunu Shakthi* (Young Strength), which was held at the Katunayake stadium, FTZ worker groups were frequently featured either dancing or watching others dance. On one occasion, the cameras lingered on a young woman who was engaged in a solitary dance that did not conform to *baila* or western dance routines. She convulsively flayed her arms and legs while her face alternately held expressions of anguish or ecstasy. The middle-class people with whom I watched the program speculated that she either had gone temporarily mad or was in a trance (*yakek vehila*) and the demon that had overtaken her was doing the thrashing. The next day at the University of Colombo and a few days later at the Suishin executive meal hall, middle-class people, especially men, expressed similar ideas about this woman's dancing. Obeyesekere (1978) asserts that most trance dances are highly erotic. Explaining trance experiences at Kataragama, he writes, "These women dance round and round the shrine . . . lost in ecstatic rapture, eyes shining, hands held out in an imploring manner as if yearning for his [god's] love" (468). Thus people's recognition of this dance as a trance is also a veiled reference to its erotic expression. It was significant that they claimed the dance as one performed under the spell of a demon. Obeyesekere wrote that under the traditional belief system, it is inconceivable that any god would reside within an impure body (465). Sri Lanka has seen social and economic changes on a massive scale since Obeyesekere's article was published. Women now readily occupy spaces that are considered modern and dangerous. So it is not surprising that people perceived that the FTZ woman worker, who was not just "physically impure" but also "socially and culturally impure," effectively prevented any god from even considering the idea of possessing her!

At Saman's boardinghouse, women talked about the dancer in embarrassed tones. According to several workers, the military personnel at checkpoints had ridiculed them asking whether they too performed the "*aspa* dance" (horse dance). Indeed, for months workers' referred to "excessive" physical movement at FTZ dances as "*aspaya gone*" or "*aspa* dance." "*Aspaya gone*" is a childish term describing children riding stationary horses. This allusion to horseback riding somehow seemed fitting for the televised dance. Morris (1995:584) holds that when possessed by spirits, women are permitted to take attire, gestures, and many other privileges denied them in everyday life. She further contends that within the trance women can appropriate and play with the sexual and social privileges of masculinity. Although I am unsure as to whether the dancer was in a trance, it was clear to everyone who saw the dance that she was performing many things that were taboo in everyday life.

Focusing on the subculture surrounding American dance halls at the turn of the twentieth century, Kathy Peiss (1986) asserts that dance forms "dramatize the ways in which working class youth culturally managed sexuality, intimacy, and respectability." (90). Because *baila* dancing did not require physical intimacy as did the ballroom dancing that New York working women engaged in, FTZ workers had a more difficult time managing respectability. Men and women could be totally segregated when engaged in *baila* dancing. Usually it was easy to see distinctive male and female dancing groups at factory parties. As the night progressed and the lights were dimmed, one could see more male-female couples dancing face to face or groups dancing together. There was much touching, trampling of feet, and holding hands among these dancers. The physical contact in these cases was usually designed to look inadvertent.[25]

However, much more direct physical contact took place during these dancing sessions. The Suishin New Year party was held indoors in the meal hall, and the only lights were swiveling party lights. This allowed more freedom to experiment with physical closeness than did an outdoor party or a trip. The few men workers and supervisors were in heavy demand that night as women encouraged them to join in the dancing. In fact, many women workers found the dark atmosphere a good opportunity to tease and harass junior factory officers, thereby getting back at them for the indignities suffered on the shop floor. I saw one executive officer storm out of the hall and later found out that while forcibly applying a shiny dust all over his body several women had squeezed his crotch.

In the vignette about the RAC party included in the beginning of this section, Nalini attempted to understand the transgression of dancers through the idiom of temporary insanity. This allusion to temporary insanity (brought about by drinking or other socioeconomic problems) and spirit attacks provided a culturally meaningful space for onlookers to make sense of what happened during dances.[26] However, it did not help much in managing individual reputations within the factory. What helped was that a vast majority of women were "guilty" of transgressing some rule or another during the party. The surprisingly little finger-pointing that I noticed among Suishin workers after a party or a trip appeared to be a consequence of collectively engaging in these new cultural practices. Because some women sat shyly in corners and avoided dancing, women workers were able to claim that they were among those shy ones and thereby counter the FTZ-related stigma in their villages.

It is clear from these vignettes that their *baila* dancing was much more sexually expressive than would have been accepted in middle-class households or in public arenas. *Baila* dancing was not the only form of dancing considered reprehensible behavior for respectable women; one early twentieth-century newspaper article described ballroom dancing as "drunken men, in hotels, who ride women as jockeys would ride horses . . . in the presence of large audiences" (*Sarasavi Sandaresa* October 2, 1925, quoted in De Alwis 1998:126). It was perhaps significant that the people termed the televised solitary dance by an FTZ worker the horse dance. Rather than being a horse, the woman in this case seemed to ride an invisible horse, her own desires, perhaps in an unconscious effort to tame them.

According to De Alwis (1998), early twentieth-century newspaper discourses on women identified practices introduced by Europeans such as dancing, drinking, smoking, and frequenting hotels and beaches as signs of an "evil time" (127). Suishin's annual "excursion [*vinoda yathra*]" combined all these "evil practices" for their women workers. The excursion was held annually at a famous tourist hotel on the southern coast. Workers were taken there in buses and then provided with a day of fun. This included lunch, snacks, drinks, and games, culminating in a contest to choose Miss and Mr. Suishin. Both men and women wore their best party clothes for the excursion, but some changed into special outfits (Sinhala national dress) for the contest. However, the highlight of the competition was the dance contest, and, according to Vasanthi who was the 1999 Miss Suishin (and often referred to as such), the finalists had to dance for some time and only then were two winners chosen. The factory reserved several rooms on an upper floor so that workers could change clothes and rest. But women used the rooms to spy on foreign tourists lounging on the beach, smoking, drinking, and kissing. There were photographs with FTZ workers in their bright-colored finery battling each other to take a look from tall windows down at the beach. These photographs represented a particularly poignant collapse of women's entrance to modernity with the nationalistic fear of women's attraction to *para weda* (foreign activities) and *para sirith* (foreign customs). An "evil time" indeed!

Urban, Working Class, and Gendered: Alternative Religious Practices

Women workers danced to fast rhythms and sang songs containing sexual innuendo while traveling to visit Buddhist temples in hired vans. The same women who engaged in these transgressions displayed deep devotion while they worshiped and meditated at the temples. Then again they picked up transgressive song parodies and jokes with sexual innuendos during their return journey. Even when we took a public transport bus to travel to Angurukaramulla temple, their revelries were not much different. Many workers wore their colorful and fancy dresses and became the center of attention in the public bus as well as at the temples.

Pilgrimages always fulfilled several social functions, including socializing, community building, and even serving as a venue for romantic endeavors. The award-winning Sinhala novel *Gamperaliya* depicted a pilgrimage at the turn of the twentieth century that was specifically arranged by the protagonist to create space for romantic communication with his love interest. Workers' trips to religious places could also be located in this ambiguous space characterized by sociality, pleasure, and religiosity. Two other overnight trips—to Kandy and Anuradhapura—fit into this ambiguous space. Singing, dancing, and engaging in sexual dalliances, as well as picnicking and drinking alcohol characterized both trips. During the trips, and in general, FTZ workers were criticized and looked down on for mixing religiosity and pleasure. The workers belonged to a unique group of women who occupied an already marginalized public space. Their insistence in expressing their identity through dress, language, and demeanor audaciously invaded deeply internalized notions regarding the ideal woman's behavior. The proud display also effectively closed the space for turning a blind eye and forced people to get on the bandwagon of moral purity. Undaunted by criticism, workers unmade the ambiguity between sociality and religiosity by listing the necessity to make a long, fun-filled trip and opportunities for meeting young men as two of the major reasons for their attraction to visiting certain religious places.[27]

Writing about how the great tradition and the little tradition became enmeshed in people's popular beliefs, Obeyesekere (1963) states that Sinhala villagers share the salvation idiom of the Buddhist great tradition (*karma* and *nirvana*) while believing in many gods and engaging in ritual practices that are contradictory to the great tradition (150–52).

Figure 10. Dancing in the bus during a factory trip. Photograph by the author.

With the advent of protestant Buddhism, an attempt was made to "demagicize" Buddhism or develop Buddhist avenues to achieve this-worldly benefits. According to Seneviratne and Wickramaratne (1980), the dramatic rise in the *bodhi* worship for this-worldly benefits was one aspect of the new urban middle-class Sinhala Buddhism and served as an avenue for collective appeasement of the frustrations felt by educated urban youth (737).[28] Obeyesekere (1978) further asserts that the increasing popularity of fire walking is a manifestation of the rise of *bhakthi* (devotional) religiosity among urban populations engaged in nontraditional occupations (462). He also holds that the erotic-ecstatic devotional *kavadi* dancing was first adopted by the urban lower classes (475).[29]

Not belonging to the middle classes and not exactly being urban proletariat, FTZ workers did not get themselves involved in the highly organized collective *bodhi puja* ceremonies or any other organized, scheduled urban temple events unless they happened to be there by chance. They, did, however, actively pursue ritual practices associated with popular beliefs about astrology, sorcery, and healing ceremonies. They were also highly interested in Buddhist avenues of achieving this-worldly benefits like performing individual *bodhi puja* and making vows (*bara*) at Buddhist sacred places.[30] A Buddhist temple stood at the four-way intersection by the railroad station. Many women went either to this nearby temple or to another one, two bus stops away in Seeduwa, to perform *bodhi puja* for their loved ones in the armed forces. These activities were conducted either individually or in small groups. It was through manipulating the ambiguous space where pilgrimage and pleasure intersected as they did in our trip to Varana and Atthanagalle temples that workers found an avenue to build community.

POPULAR BELIEFS

"Your stars are so bad these days," the elderly horoscope reader declared, peering closely at Ajitha's horoscope. Ajitha sat patiently with folded hands as the man took time to spit out the beetle cud and put another crumpled leaf in his mouth. The day before, Ajitha had had a major scuffle with her line supervisor at the factory. After presenting the horoscope and a twenty-rupee note to the reader, she asked the man to tell her whether she should leave her factory at this time.

"You have *senasuru dasava* [senasuru planet's influence] for two more years, four months, and twenty days. This *senasura's* main task is to agitate people and make them run around [*pissu vattala aviddavanawa*]," the man said. Spitting another wad of beetle juice into the spittle, he continued: "You know Shakra god [head among all the gods in the Buddhist pantheon]. Even he had to eat hay when he had the *senasuru dasava*." He pointed the hand that still held the spittle in Ajitha's direction and advised, "Be patient until this bad time is over. Don't run around and wear out."

Showing the intense conflicts generated by the encounter of capitalist ethics with rural beliefs, Ajitha took his advice and went back to work, though she bitterly complained for days about having to suffer through the same supervisor's scornful behavior.

Workers enthusiastically participated in deity worship, sorcery, and other devotional rituals. As stated before, the bazaar contained at least two permanent horoscope-reading places, and many horoscope and palm readers frequented the area. Just as Ajitha did, workers usually consulted their horoscopes when they had to make difficult decisions.

One Sunday an itinerant (*ahikuntika*) palm reader visited Saman's boardinghouse and about twenty women, including myself, had our palms read. The palm reader's pessimistic forecasts generated much anxiety, making the women get their horoscopes read at the bazaar. The horoscope readers in turn prescribed *bodhi puja, senasuru puja*, and even more elaborate healing rituals such as lime cutting and *bali shanthi karma*. While women wrote to their parents about the latter rituals, many went to the nearby temple to perform the simple *pujas*. This happened early during my research, and when four months later Deepthi and six months later Jayani got into trouble (incidents described in Chapter 5), panic surfaced again, sending several women scurrying back to the temples and shrines.

"You know why I like this temple? Because it is a temple for little people [*podi minissunge*]. People come, worship, and go. They don't look for other people's rights and wrongs. Don't you know these other hi-fi temples? Women are always looking to see what other women are doing so that they can criticize," Janaki said, while taking the long walk between abandoned paddy fields to the Pillawe temple. Although the number of parked cars by the main road evidenced that at least some middle-class and lower middle-class people visit Pillawe temple, I agreed with Janaki's sentiment that people seemed not to be too much interested in FTZ workers' bright-colored clothing as was the case when we visited other temples.

Residents at Saman's boardinghouse visited Pillawe temple twice while I was there.[31] Pillawe is a new temple organized around an alternative narrative to the famous Bellanwila Royal temple. In the early 1990s, a man cleared the marshland around a *bodhi* tree and started worshiping the tree. Rumors started to circulate (many suspected that they were started by this self-appointed guardian himself) that this *bodhi* tree was the original Bellanwila *bodhi* tree and that it was years later that the royal temple was built at a nicer location around a sapling of the Pillawe *bodhi* tree. This narrative caught people's imagination and the place soon drew large crowds. Considering that the small temple grounds contained nine shrines for different deities, it was perhaps not surprising that this new temple became popular.

Pillawe temple was located in the middle of an abandoned paddy field that stood on the side of the Piliyandala-Colombo road. Many times I saw garment factory workers (from the FTZ and local factories) clogging the main road by crossing in groups and flocking around the huts that sold flowers, incense, and snacks. Lights, music, and noise from these huts and the young people who milled around them added to the atmosphere's festive mood especially on weekends and *poya* days. Factory workers with their distinct clothes, hairstyles, language, and demeanor prompted many a middle-class person to talk derisively about the temple as a "garment girl temple."[32]

This newly created religious space was also popular among other urban, lower-income communities and was already invested with a class stigma. This particular stigma apparently resulted from several factors, including the temple's own alternative narrative. However, one of the major reasons was the FTZ workers' enthusiastic consumption of the space.

The bus we traveled in on a *poya* day to visit the Pillawe temple was crowded with many garment factory workers who were going to the same destination as we were. While at Pillawe, we found young men lining the main road and the footpath through the paddy field, whistling and catcalling to get women's attention. There was again much indirect communication between the groups while many new acquaintances were made. The other patrons at the temple were also from urban lower-income communities, and because of that and the congested, rushed way people had to worship, FTZ workers did not receive angry stares or whispered criticism as they had in other established temples. It is not surprising that Janaki labeled the temple "little people's temple" in a rare expression of solidarity with other working-class people regardless of gender.

Good for Mothers, Not for Daughters

Although they partied along the way, dressed differently, and talked loudly, FTZ workers' religious activities at the temples or shrines did not differ much from those of the other women present. They spent lavishly on flowers, incense, and donations and spent much time on their knees worshiping. They also prayed and made vows on matters that were meaningful to them, such as the safety of their loved ones in the armed forces or the attainment of a good marriage. However, people frowned at them and criticized them for the gusto with which they sought to participate in this "respectable" public domain. It was women more than men who showed annoyance by staring, spitting, or criticizing the transgressions committed by the workers. This particular female resentment perhaps resulted from the fear that the entrance of this highly stigmatized group of women would taint the hitherto secure public space.

As the protectors of the spiritual domain, women always claimed a legitimate place in religious activities. Women congregated at temples on *poya* days, organized women's social service societies through the temples, and in short fully used the easy access to a "respectable" public space.[33] Although attending shrines and visiting sorcerers always entailed some stigma for both men and women, the latter were able to manipulate that stigma within the purview of their roles as wives and mothers. Women were supposed to protect their husbands and children from evil influences. Their efforts to save the husbands from drinking alcohol or from bad friends or to ensure their children's health or good education through sorcery or other rituals was tolerated and continued for a long time without much social concern. Stirrat (1992) writes about Sinhala Catholic women who visited Catholic shrines in Sri Lanka to ask for divine intervention in mundane matters, such as securing a job for a son, arranging a marriage to a daughter, or curing a husband's illness. He also writes about women who visited these places to pray for their own health and happiness or regularly visited out of sheer devotion. But these activities seemed to be understood within the rubric of women fulfilling womanly duties.

Even among the middle classes, the daughters did not have as much unhindered access to religious spaces as did their mothers. The organized and officiated *bodhi pujas* attracted frustrated, educated youth who attended these ceremonies in vast numbers, mostly in the hope of meeting members of the opposite sex (Seneviratne and Wickramaratne 1980). But because of their class status, the specific conditions of their participation (with parents, with neighbors) and their "not unrespectable" position as educated, unemployed youth did not lead to rumors of suspicious behavior. Even *bodhi puja* participation did not lead to young women's temple societies or any other activities except the highly respectable *dhamma* school teaching positions.[34] It was no wonder then that the daughters who visited in groups without elderly guardians and announced their membership in a sexually stigmatized group were less welcome at temples.

But the workers still made religious sites empowering spaces by refusing to acknowledge the social repression forced on them by organizing trips and enjoying the journey with all its ritual and social activities. However, the existence of contradictory cultural discourses became evident in their discussions on the relative merits of the places that boasted miraculous powers. At the same time as they were awed by such stories, they ridiculed each other for their belief in supernatural powers. Educated in Sri Lankan public schools and, by their own account, "street wise," they were cynical about the supposed miraculous powers yet appealed to the very same forces to bring them a better future. They unhesitatingly subscribed to the major Buddhist salvation ideals but again sought to achieve this-worldly goals through any religious ritual, be it Catholic, Hindhu, Sai Baba, or folk supernaturalism.

This further demonstrated that particular groups differently intertwined aspects of religious traditions to come up with creative versions of their own religiosity. FTZ workers who were to a certain degree alienated from both the mainstream Buddhism (great tradition) and the folk tradition had been particularly busy in creating their own version by appropriating different aspects from several traditions and transforming them to serve their particular emotional and spiritual needs. This was perhaps most evident in their collective attraction to alternative commercialized temples. They seemed to find this a perfect fit: a marginalized religious space for a marginalized group of women.

Subversions That Mattered

Mills (1997) writes that Thai migrant female factory workers intensely pursue standards of modern womanhood and attempt to achieve an "up-to-date" identity through new consumption practices. Constrained by low-status and low-wage employment, however, they are marginalized within the urban consumer culture and the up-to-date identity remains unattainable. Nevertheless, workers keep trying and even the Buddhist merit-making trips they take mimic the religious practices of the powerful and wealthy (43–54). Sri Lankan FTZ workers, on the contrary, not only insisted that they did not want to follow the middle classes but expressed considerable pride in being able to follow fashions and tastes that were their own. They developed new religious and consumption practices and continually engaged in producing social and public spaces of their own. They were happy in the knowledge that their actions irked the middle classes. Their performances of FTZ garment worker identities at public places, through activities deemed disrespectable and shameful, represented a critique of middle-class and male-enforced cultural hegemony.

While these new tastes and activities represented a class and gender critique, a question worth exploring is whether these new practices are different from the practices of other working-class youth. One difference is the deeper anxieties that the FTZ workers' actions aroused, given that they were rural women temporarily living in an urban area and as such were expected to uphold village traditions and customs while living in the city. While activities of urban, working-class youth were considered "normal" behavior, similar activities by FTZ workers were considered transgressive and therefore warranted contempt and punishment. In fact, women were well versed in ideal norms of behavior and used their rural demeanors and charms whenever it was beneficial to them—especially to escape difficult situations in the factories. Workers talked derisively about urban, working-class youth and said that those men and women would do anything to be considered middle class. Although in practice individuals belonging to both groups had varied motives for their behavior, FTZ workers as a group were aware of their differences and the oppositional character of their public performances, which challenged middle-class notions of respectability. In both embodied and narrative performances, they constructed their specific tastes as unique—something not quite urban or rural, not quite modern or traditional, and definitely not male. Therefore, when FTZ workers established their identity as a particular taste community, they did so by excluding not only the urban middle classes but their rural communities and urban, lower-income communities as well.

As noted earlier, even while resisting some aspects of Sinhala Buddhist cultural domination FTZ workers compromised on other aspects, such as their desire to enter into romantic relationships and to get married. Finding boyfriends and enjoying physical intimacy transgressed norms of sexual conduct. But their somewhat uncritical acceptance of patriarchal domination within their romantic relationships marked accommodation to a different set of dominant cultural expectations. More important, their performance of alternative identities required that they participate in the consumer culture surrounding the FTZ and ensured their acquiescence to capitalist hegemony even as they sought to subvert dominant cultural values. The very acts of expressed resistance contained strains of accommodation while explicitly accommodating acts encompassed elements of resistance.

Although workers' contestatory practices contained levels of opposition and complicity, they still subverted Sinhala Buddhist male cultural hegemony. These subversions formed an important part of their daily cultural struggles that had the potential to reconfigure the terms of dominant discourses. In this sense, their oppositional activities represented subversions that mattered (Kondo 1997:26).

Sample Garments and Home Clothes

Women loved to go out in groups wearing the same color or same patterned dresses that were sold from their own factories to the bazaar because they were slightly damaged. When they went out in those garments and proudly displayed allegiance to their group, men at bus stops and in shops called after them, saying, "Ah, sample, where are you going?" Women expressed pride in being recognized as garment workers—the garments they produced being a "sample" of who they were. However, when they visited their villages, they left behind these "slightly damaged" garments in their boardinghouses and put on home clothes to make the obligatory visits around the villages. I focus on this process of negotiation and compromise in the village environment in Chapter 7.

Chapter 7

FTZ Clothes and Home Clothes

Negotiating Stigma

It was the first day of a four-day vacation at the FTZ and the train carried many workers on their way to their villages. We were taking the night mail train from Colombo to visit Mala and Karuna's home in Pollon-naruwa, in the North Central Province. A few minutes into the journey, we realized that military personnel in civilian clothing were moving to the compartment in which we sat with about ten other factory workers. By midnight, about fifteen such young men had joined us in the compartment. These military personnel were also on leave and going home to their villages. As usual the men started indirect communication with the women through jokes that were replete with sexual innuendo. By the time we reached Pollonnaruwa, several young men and women had exchanged addresses and, according to Mala, one woman whom we met on the train had fallen in love with an army soldier.

Although the train arrived on time at 8:00 A.M. at Pollonnaruwa, it was close to noon when we reached Mala's house, which was located in an interior village, by bus. Her mother, Leela, was outside in the compound talking to an elderly woman. Mala hurried along the small path and lit-erally threw herself at her mother's feet, paying respect to her the tradi-tional way. Leela started to cry while blessing Mala. Then Mala proceeded to worship the other woman present, who appreciatively commented, "Good children do not forget good customs however far they travel." This seemed to have pacified Leela, who started telling the other woman that while she had brought up her two daughters in poverty they were nevertheless taught good morals. Meanwhile Karuna also worshiped both women and everybody joined in to fuss over my comforts.

That afternoon many of their young relatives came to visit them. I was introduced as a "Miss" from the factory who was writing a book about the FTZ. Two female cousins stayed for the night, and after dinner we all sat on the patio floor to relax. Mala put her head on Leela's lap and Leela lovingly caressed Mala's hair. Leela then turned to me and asked whether Mala was too playful (*danga*). When I said "no," Leela playfully tugged at Mala's hair and said, "If she is stubborn and does not listen to sirs and misses at the factory, give her a spanking or two." Karuna, who was sitting behind Leela, burst out laughing and then quickly covered her mouth with both her hands. Mala acted as if she did not hear this, but within a few seconds managed to wink at me. In fact, the time I spent in Pollonnaruwa was characterized by much winking, many secret smiles, and many squeezing hands and trampling toes. Those were the props they manipulated in enacting a series of scenes in which I unwittingly (though not unwillingly) collaborated,[1] a series of scenes enacted to save their endangered reputations in a way that made sense to their family and neighbors in the village.

Home Clothes and American Clothes

We had planned to visit Mala and Karuna's friends' and relatives' houses as well as two temples during the vacation. In deference to rural sentiments, I brought long skirts and blouses to wear in the village instead of my usual jeans and T-shirts. When I opened my bag in the afternoon, both Mala and Karuna seemed aghast. They earnestly asked me not to wear the skirts to visit around the village. The reasons, they explained, were that the thorny bushes surrounding footpaths might scratch my legs or that the skirts might tear when we climbed over fences. "Besides, jeans go better with your short hair," Mala said. I wore jeans for the journey and had to wear the same pair of jeans for most of my stay in Pollonnaruwa, according to their wishes. Both of them, however, chose to wear long skirts whose colors were faded from constant washing. "These are what we wear at home," Karuna explained. I also noticed that they tied their hair nonchalantly into a knot at the nape.[2] Attired this way, they looked quite different from the two young women in "Titanic" dresses who also wore their hair loose at the FTZ.[3]

Walking with them among the paddy fields and small houses, I felt considerably ill at ease in my jeans. It aroused much interest among the villagers, and Mala and Karuna explained in different ways that I was an important person at the factory or that I was from the university and was writing a book on the FTZ. On each occasion, they emphasized my association with the United States by saying, "She came from America." This inspired much awe, and people milled around me explaining the fruits and sweets that they were treating me to. The second day of our visit was the full-moon *poya* day, and I visited the temple with Mala's family and neighbors. Mala wore an old, white school-uniform dress, while Karuna wore a faded blue dress that looked almost white.[4] This time, too, they insisted that I wear jeans and a T-shirt. While we were getting ready, Karuna offered me face powder and insisted that I wear some lipstick. When we joined other people who were also walking toward the temple, the feeling that the sisters were putting me on display became stronger. At the temple, I was introduced to the two Buddhist monks and my status was further elevated when the younger monk, who was a student at the University of Colombo, recognized me as a lecturer.

Mala and Karuna participated in the flower-offering ritual (*mal pujawa*) with much devotion and, perhaps reiterating the message of "pure innocence," volunteered to take flower baskets and water pots down the line of devotees, a task primarily reserved for children present at the ceremony. With downcast eyes they demurely carried their offerings with both hands and passed by the lines echoing the other devotees' cry of "*sadhu, sadhu, sadhu.*" They prostrated themselves not only before the two monks but also before other elders whom they had not had a chance to meet before the temple visit.[5] I often heard Leela tell interested villagers that I had chosen to visit their village instead of many other workers' villages because her daughters were well-behaved, obedient, and innocent girls.[6]

At each household we visited, Mala and Karuna paid respect to the elderly people and did not sit on chairs but leaned on the walls when elderly men were present. They answered the villagers' questions in the regional accent, which had a different rhythm and intonation from the city accent they used in the FTZ. Neither woman offered information on the interesting, fun-filled aspects of their lives. Once a man started telling me about the way women in cities behave and said, "They dance at *baila* parties without any shame or restraint." Before I could respond, Karuna interjected, "Yes, uncle, even at our factory party, women danced just like men. We were shamed by it, too."[7] This turned the conversation to discussing how the shameless few give all the FTZ workers a bad name. Karuna enthusiastically participated in this discussion, distancing herself and Mala from the bad crowd at the FTZ. She once said, "It [condemnation of factory workers] is like when people kill all bugs because one bug bit." Throughout this discussion, Mala intermittently squeezed my hand, which she had been holding. Karuna talked in a slow, rhythmic voice and managed to flash meaningful smiles in my direction without arousing others' suspicion. Later she explained that even though the whole village consisted of relatives, there were jealous people who were always trying to find something amiss.

Mala and Karuna took me to many houses and with each visit I became more aware of the way they were using me to negotiate a better position for themselves within the village. On the one hand, I represented someone who had achieved everything that the villagers wished for their children and, on the other, I also personified many things that they feared for their daughters: westernized, "mod," and as a result without shame-fear. I was a woman who moved in spaces formerly reserved for men. Either way, my presence contributed to a positive identity in the village for Mala and Karuna. Not only were they associating with a "Miss" who came from America but they also managed to maintain their "ruralness," their village traditions, in a space where they constantly met "dangerous" people such as the "Miss" from America. Their insistence on my wearing clothes associated with the western world sharpened the contrast they projected by wearing home clothes. The difference in clothes and mannerisms not only signified differences in taste but also other associated binaries such as westernized/traditional, urban/rural, bad/good women.

Once when returning from a neighbor's house, Karuna asked me why I was silent during the conversation. I explained that I was afraid I might make a mistake that would offend the villagers; I did not usually talk much unless I was questioned directly. However, I kept smiling until my mouth hurt and, in this timid, silent appearance I must have looked not very different from a village woman. In retrospect, I think that Mala and Karuna did not expect this from me. They either wanted me to talk on their behalf or to act in a boisterous and an aggressive manner, which would have better registered the differences between us.

I carried a cell phone with me to use only in an emergency and on the second evening, when the number of visitors seemed at its highest, Mala begged me to make a phone call to Colombo. While I was dialing the number to my home, she almost pushed me to the patio where the visitors congregated. My mother answered the phone, and I talked to her in Sinhala as I always did. I think I again failed to fulfill Mala's unspoken wish for me to show off my English-speaking skills. Several times I overheard comments among the neighbors about how I spoke English like a pair of scissors (fast and fluent) and how my whole family spoke English and that my mother lived in Australia.[8] All those comments served to register a specific class position for me.[9] Rajasingham-Senanayake (1997) argues that Sinhala youth use the term *kaduwa* (sword) to denote the use of English as well as its function of cutting off vernacular-speaking people from economic, social, and cultural advancement (16). The villagers' use of the metaphor *kathura* (pair of scissors) also captured the function of cutting others off from an exclusive class identity. In this specific instance, however, Mala's attempt to show off my English knowledge not only would have registered my class affiliation but would bring them more respect, both through their friendship with one so distanced from them and then through their clearly demonstrated unchanged good/traditional/village girl attributes.

Why was it so important for Mala and Karuna to project an image that was quite different from what they had become through their FTZ experience? Focusing on stigma-management strategies among South Indian drama actresses, Susan Seizer (2000) notes that these actresses usually do not perform at venues located within ten kilometers of their homes. According to Seizer, setting up geographical boundaries is their way of consciously separating their professional lives from their domestic lives (221). Mala and Karuna's decision not to perform their FTZ selves in their village is also a part of their attempt to maintain normative codes of behavior appropriate to their village lives. Occupying an awkward position, as temporary migrants, FTZ workers did not have the luxury of shaking off all that was associated with their village lives. They would be forced to leave their employment and retreat into the village sooner or later. Leela was trying to find a suitable match for Karuna during this time and said that when a man from another village was proposed, his family sent spies to see whether the woman had led a moral life. These spies would talk to nonrelatives, and it was important that at least some people say good things about the woman. It was in this context that their farce took meaning and became an important process geared toward repairing the damaged identity brought about by associating with a stigmatized space. According to Bourdieu (1977), our internalized sense of acceptable cultural practices and the way we express this internality may be accompanied by a "strategic calculation" (76), but he cautions that the actions should not be identified as resulting from conscious and deliberate intentions of their authors (73). I, however, attributed considerable agency to the FTZ workers for their changed responses. As stated earlier, I assert that it is their experiences at a different habitus that influenced the calculated, strategic responses to the different power relations they confronted in the villages. Through these strategic responses, they made way for the existing structures to stretch to accommodate them as women who have not changed because of their temporary employment in the city.

At the same time as the sisters tried to show that they were still "good, rural girls" they shared fascinating information about their FTZ lives with several trusted friends and cousins inside their room. They not only showed photographs from their trips and parties but also talked about how Mala brought a copy of *Priyadari* magazine the first time she came back from the FTZ. She had not done so again, but the enthusiasm they both conveyed through casual conversation aroused much excitement. The shiny eyes, happy giggles, and earnest appeals for more stories about the FTZ convinced me that many more Pollonnaruwa women would willingly trek the dangerous path to Colombo in the coming years.

Cloaks of Childish Innocence

Madhu, who became a close friend during my time at Suishin, invited me to her village home in the Southern Province during the Sinhala New Year vacation. While she went home early, I traveled on my own to her village, which was thirty miles from the city of Galle. In contrast to Mala and Karuna's village in Pollonnaruwa, this village was heavily populated and consisted of nicer houses and several public buildings. Madhu and her family warmly welcomed me and treated me with all the hospitality for which southerners were renowned. According to custom, Madhu wore new clothes during the New Year vacation, but her dresses were made to simple patterns popular among village women. However, she wore her hair as she always did at the FTZ and displayed a gold pendant with the English letters to her first name.

As described in chapter 3, Madhu had made a name for herself at Suishin as the line clown. She interacted with the supervisory staff in a way that bordered on insubordination but with a bit of humor and sarcasm. She used a rolling, babyish voice to cover the harshness of her words, making it difficult for the supervisors to be angry with her or punish her. Although this trapped her in unequal power relations, with supervisors as older siblings who should be obeyed and herself as the younger sibling whose transgressions had to be tolerated, it also provided a space to maneuver within oppressive working conditions. Madhu's tactics of negotiating the stigma of migration in the village context were also based on a similar routine. Madhu breezed through her village playing on swings with children and pulling pranks on young and old alike.

She also took me around the village and introduced me to the people who visited her house, but unlike Mala and Karuna she let me decide how to dress and how to behave. Madhu elicited both angry and affectionate smiles from elderly people by her constant teasing, which included squeezing cheeks, pinching arms, pulling hair, and so on. Once she tried to sit on the lap of an elderly male relative, making everybody present break into laughter while her mother screamed at her to desist. The elderly uncle ran after Madhu, waving a cane and threatening to beat her. Madhu ran down a footpath and vanished inside a neighbor's house. In the evening, the two picked up their mock fight again and Madhu ran around a tree with her uncle in hot pursuit. People laughed while Madhu's mother again shouted at her to stop acting crazy. Many times, Madhu's mother looked at me with laughing eyes and said, "This child . . . talking to her will only hurt my mouth."

On two different occasions, two of Madhu's cousins declared that Madhu was a "playful child [*danga lamaya*]" and that she was so even during her school days. However, their use of the term *danga* did not connote the sexual promiscuity that the same word implied in the FTZ. It instead invoked the playfulness associated with children. Madhu was the youngest daughter of a well-to-do family in the village and her married siblings along with her parents still treated her as if she were a child. Despite being twenty years old, she was physically small and her face also bore a look of childish happiness and naiveté that matched perfectly with the Sinhala idioms *podi paata* (looking like a child) and *ahinsaka* (innocent/harmless). These traits, together with her constant blurring of the child and young-woman categories, made it difficult for villagers to pin her down and apply all the social, cultural codes that are part of a particular category. Occupying this ambiguous space helped Madhu enjoy all the perks of modernity that the FTZ offered while, to an extent, escaping the sexual stigma attached to other migrant women. After all, how could any villager tarnish the character of a playful, young girl who surely was too young and immature to be sexually active?

Not only her personal traits but also her accommodation at her father's friend's house in Katunayake and her family being a respected family in the village helped sustain the image she cultivated in the village. Just as in the factory, this behavior bound her to the village and its elders in an unequal kinship power relation; at the same time, it released her from the stigma that most other migrant workers were constrained by. This release, however, did not come easily and Madhu as well as her family had to manage her reputation through regular maneuvers, both conscious and unconscious. Although it did not surface during my stay in the village, I was sure that at times the villagers managed to fit Madhu into the young-woman category and speculated on her behavior in the city. After all, her father sent her to the FTZ to break up a schoolyard romance.

"FTZ Mod" Sans the Shawls

The Sinhala-Tamil New Year vacation in the year 2000 was a busy one for me. I spent April 15 and 16 with Madhu's family, then I went to the central mountain region to visit Sujatha's family on April 18. The day was considered auspicious for anointing oil for the New Year (*thel gana avurudda*), although there was nothing auspicious about our trip. I was in charge of arranging a van for the trip and failed miserably in this task. Forgetting the high demand for rented vehicles during the holidays, I did not try to rent a van until the last minute and found that all the vans were already reserved. Because none of the other three women with whom I was planning to travel had telephones, I had no way to inform them of this situation. Therefore I met them the next day at the Averiwatthe junction as we had planned. Geethi, Vasanthi, and Niluka, who had no idea that we did not have a private vehicle, came in their most colorful clothes and jewelry. They were not happy to discover that there was no van. However, we decided to use the crowded public buses because Sujatha was to meet us at the Kegalle central bus station. During the trip, I discovered that women in ankle-length flowing skirts and long shawls could get into much trouble in buses crowded with tired and cranky people. Their skirts and shawls were trampled on and intentionally tugged at by people in the bus. I was almost happy when we got separated in the bus because that allowed me to escape their little jibes about the "person who was supposed to bring a van."

By the time we arrived in Kegalle and met Sujatha, our little group was tense and cranky. While taking a smaller bus to Sujatha's village, the women earnestly questioned her about the appropriateness of their clothes. Questions such as, "Are these fine?" "Will your relatives think badly of us?" or "Will we bring a bad name to you?" were repeated, and Sujatha, who incidentally was wearing a simple pastel-colored dress, waved their concerns aside. But the visiting women looked genuinely distressed about their clothes and kept whispering their regrets about their choice of clothing. I had never before seen them concerned about the appropriateness of their clothes and asked Vasanthi why they did not think of this before embarking on the trip. She replied with an edge in her voice, "We thought we would be traveling in a private van [in style]."

Feeling responsible for their plight, I became silent but it struck me that there was only a thin line between reputation-enhancing and reputation-weakening situations. One intentional or unintentional objective of the trip appeared to be to boost Sujatha's reputation within the village. If we arrived in fashionable "Colombo" clothing in a private vehicle, which was a rare occurrence in the village, it would have enhanced the host's reputation. Then the association with the factory miss/researcher from America also could have been registered through appropriate social markers. But when a group of young women from Colombo arrived in flashy clothing and outrageous make-up by bus, tired, and worn out, it was the inappropriateness of their attire that would be registered, and this of course was not going to help Sujatha. The visitors' appearance pointed toward all the evil things that the villagers had been hearing about and the fact that Sujatha was associating with such friends might well have raised serious doubts about her own "good village girl" image, which she vigorously promoted through dress, language, actions, and demeanor.

However, once we arrived, the visiting women immediately started repairing the damage. They asked to be anointed with oil and showed dismay that the auspicious time had passed and insisted that they go to the temple and get anointed. Especially Vasanthi and Niluka talked with elders, showing off their knowledge of traditional New Year customs. They asked to borrow Sujatha's clothing for their visit to the temple, but in a risky move to save everyone's dignity Sujatha insisted that her friends should visit the temple as they were and that they should not be afraid of what other people thought. After much negotiation, they decided not to change clothes (mostly because Sujatha did not provide other clothes), though they took off their make-up and, in a symbolic movement of dissociation, left behind the colorful shawls from their *gagra cholis*. Without the shawl, a specific symbol denoting "FTZ mod," their *cholis* looked like an elaborate version of a simple skirt and blouse. Just before we left for the temple, Vasanthi grabbed an old shirt from a clothes rack and put it over her burnt orange *choli* blouse. This started a fresh round of fretting about clothing by the other two. The accusations this time were directed at Vasanthi, and I felt a sense of relief that their criticism was not directed at me.

Wearing this watered-down version of FTZ fashion, our little group still made a spectacle at the temple of this serene, Central Province village. However, the group had several other tricks up its sleeve. They referred to all Sujatha's relatives using kinship terms and soon adopted the "stretching" regional accent. They petted and carried little children and helped elderly ladies perform *bodhi puja* by bringing them pots of water. Back at Sujatha's home, all three volunteered to help with the cooking. Despite the family's objections, Vasanthi and Geethi wrapped old clothes over their skirts and helped in the kitchen. According to Goffman (1959), social benefits result from appearing to be conforming to moral standards, and those benefits prompt people to practice "ways of the stage" (251). But the audience's interpretive activity is necessary for the performed self to be properly registered (253). By the end of the day, I could see them winning over Sujatha's family members and the neighbors and relatives who were constantly in and out of each other's houses.

This unfolding visual/action narrative that stemmed from the troubling event of not having a private vehicle came to its culmination the next day at the moment of our departure. The women paid obeisance at the feet of all the elders present. They shed tears, received invitations to return, and promised to do so. Suddenly the room was silent and people seemed to be looking at me and urging me to perform one last act on behalf of Sujatha. The air of expectancy was so overwhelming that it seemed that the only resolution was to follow my friends and pay respect to the elders the traditional way. While kneeling at the feet of the family patriarch, I thought my mistake of not providing a van had put Sujatha's reputation in danger and if by doing this I could refurbish her good name and restore my relations with the other women, then this discomfort was well worth it. While on our way back, everybody seemed to have forgotten the blunder I had committed as we kept criticizing all the other people in the bus for staring at our glittering clothes.

Stigma Management and Protest

Goffman (1963) writes that every society has rules and standards of what an ideal person should be and that these identity norms breed both defiance and conformity. When people are alienated from norms, they can either withdraw from the community, which is costly both for society and for the individual, or engage in tactics of stigma management (129).

FTZ workers who were well aware of the danger to their "good name" within the village took many steps to manage their identity. Their tactics were mostly geared to ensure that they were included in the blurred category of the "good FTZ worker" who toiled in a faraway place to keep the home fires burning but did not get swayed by the evil influences of city living. To achieve this, women had to contribute to the collective development of their natal family. Villagers constantly praised workers by enumerating the material goods acquired by their families after their daughters began working in the factories. These material goods demonstrated that the young women were dutiful daughters who did not forget the economic reasons that drew them to the city and that they fulfilled their obligations to their families. At the same time, the sexual promiscuity, modernity, and evil attributed to city living in general and to the FTZ in particular offered a clear threat to their reputations as naïve, sexually ignorant, virgin daughters of rural families. Since the temporary nature of their FTZ jobs necessitated their return to these villages after several years in the city, the management of stigma became a high priority when they visited their villages on short vacations.

Two of the three vignettes in this chapter demonstrated how women took off their "FTZ clothing" and put on "village clothing" in a conscious process of visually narrating a different self to the curious audience. Madhu put on a cloak of childhood innocence when she was with people who held different kinds of power over her. While "talking trash" with her friends and the researcher, Madhu adopted a babyish voice and childish ways with her supervisors and village elders, thereby ensuring a little space for her to maneuver. Although the alliances made and steps taken by all the women showed conformity to oppressive hierarchical values, the fact that the conformity was staged speaks to its subversive character. According to many scholars, the struggle to reconcile expectations with actual experiences is prominent in the narratives of people who suffer social and political repression (Ochs and Capps 1996:29). Women's changing narratives (through visuals, gestures, expressions, and so on) marked their response to social and cultural codes that sought to constrain them. Assuming one's expected role in the social order always entails silencing aspects of other selves created elsewhere. Taking up home clothes or cloaks of childish innocence required linguistic as well as performative suppression. Women protested against this suppression in their own locally relevant ways by smuggling "FTZ knowledges" (in the form of magazines, audiotapes, Victoria's Secret underwear) to younger vilage women in the privacy of their rooms.

Chapter 8

Made in Sri Lanka: Globalization and the Politics of Location

> Beautiful women in rainbow colored silk sheaths dance on top of a large rock. Colorful silk shawls swirl around them as they tantalizingly offer glimpses of naked legs before the visual changes to women workers in assembly lines, heads bent over sewing machines or smiling as the camera zooms in. Their faces fade quickly back to the dancers still circling a male flutist in traditional garb looking dumbfounded by the fast-dancing women and the multitude of colors whirling around him. The background alternates from softly sung Sinhala lyrics about colors, music, and dancing to sudden flourishes when the singers break into feverish repetitions of "Made in Sri Lanka" in English.

These visuals accompanied a song by popular Sri Lankan duo Bhathiya and Santhush, first telecast on national television in October 2003. Whether intended to do so or not, the visuals neatly captured public opinion about FTZ workers: carefree and colorfully attired women who dance to their own fast rhythm, thereby rendering the male flutist's traditional tune useless. Unfortunately, the visuals were not able to capture the discipline, control, and stigma that did not allow these same women to dance to their own tunes when not in the FTZ area as a group.

Earlier I noted how FTZ workers hung their white underwear from clotheslines that surrounded their boardinghouses. Most times, they placed those clotheslines to create some privacy. By covering their private spaces with clotheslines, FTZ workers acted like *lajja-baya athi* women (women with shame-fear). But by hanging their *underwear* on these same clotheslines, they challenged and protested the norms of *lajja-baya* that did not suit their lives. And by putting out *white* underwear that was washed every day, they again signaled the contradictions that surrounded their protest. White underwear spoke of their need to tell a different story to the world: "Yes, we are out here in this exposed, transgressive space, but we are as pure as one can hope for and definitely not prostitutes" (who were widely known to wear black underwear).

Why did women who claimed they did not care about what others thought of them send out a conciliatory message to interested parties? Was it because, for all their agency in moving between identities, they still could not escape an internalized common sense regarding the "evils" of premarital sex? Or, was it an attempt to avoid violence directed toward women without shame-fear? Whatever the reason, it spoke of the contradictions they faced and the complex ways they attempted to reconcile the varied discursive influences in their lives.

Once the FTZ workers were back in their villages, they performed appropriate behavior and rituals befitting innocent daughters of rural families. Not surprisingly, they also rediscovered the "appropriate place" to hang their underwear: in the corner of the kitchen. In Mala and Karuna's house in Pollonnaruwa, the designated place was a short clothesline strung in the tiny space between an old smoke-blackened set of shelves and the wall of the small kitchen. While folding dried underwear, Mala informed me that she had two sets of underwear—the one she wore in the village that hung in the dark kitchen and a set she wore in the FTZ that hung outside for the world to see. "I hate the smokey smell that comes from this underwear [hung in the kitchen]. I can't wear this in the FTZ because the girls will laugh at me. I have good ones that I bought in Colombo. I do not even bring them to the village," Mala explained. "We are not the only ones who do that. Many of our friends do the same thing," Karuna agreed.[1]

In the preceding chapters, I have frequently discussed clothing as a mark of identity or a metaphor for identity shifts. Because the book focuses on garment workers and their strategies of stitching (and unstitching) identities, it seems appropriate to highlight the importance of garments and their symbolic function. The ideal image of Sinhala Buddhist women, fashioned almost a century ago, focused on women's attire. Anagarika Dharmapala's writings centered on prescribing a public dress that symbolized the Sinhala Buddhist woman's religious and moral qualities (Guruge 1963).[2] Although these writings did not delve into the intimate realm of women's underwear, the rules and norms regarding women's underwear do not apply to men's underwear. Conformity, non-conformity, creative conformity, or performances of conformity to such sexual and behavioral norms were linked to the way FTZ workers moved between the multitude of available identities at different sites.

Commenting on women's experiences and responses at the complex intersections of gender, nationalism, and modernity, this book explores important aspects of globalization as it affects these women's lives in multiple ways. It also contains an analysis of identity formation at two levels: first, the workers' negotiation of individual identities and, second, the creation of an identity as a gendered group of migrant workers who are different both from other women and from male industrial workers.

The book weaves its way through FTZ garment factory workers' lives: in garment factories, in boardinghouses, through recreational activities, and back to the villages to explore the stitching, unstitching and restitching of identities by these women workers.

It is through their everyday social interactions and expressive practices at these different sites that the workers created and negotiated their identities—resisting, appropriating, transforming, and re-creating the images constructed for them in varied discourses. Women's migration to urban areas was the underlying factor in the changes, strategies, and creativities depicted in this account. While highlighting the importance of migration for the development of new selves, it is also important to understand the way the temporary character of the women workers' employment hindered them from attaining long-term economic or social empowerment. The realization that they have to leave the transnational capitalist culture at the FTZ and return to patriarchal villages made the women develop an identity that is between several positions with which they grappled daily. In this new position as modern industrial workers with traditional brake pads, FTZ workers were left with some space to maneuver when they returned to their villages.

Women moved among various available identities while in their workplace, in their boardinghouses, and even in their villages. The movement was between the new identities they created, such as subversive industrial worker, political activist, or desiring woman, and conventional subject positions that were already available to them, such as daughter, sister, mother, or innocent girl. Sandoval (1991) states that it is the development of oppositional consciousness that, as a "clutch of an automobile," enables oppressed people to move between different identities as best suits the situation (14). I contend that working women developing oppositional consciousness at the FTZ is key to their expression of situational identity. We have seen the way young rural women get caught in an intense process of socialization both in the factory and at the boardinghouse. Senior workers educate the new ones in everyday resistance, subversive moves, and even political and trade union activism. The work of NGOs such as Dabindu and Mithurusevene and the branches of several political parties also facilitate the workers' politicization. Although women's political activities can be termed cultural struggles in that they challenged the dominant cultural expectations, these cultural struggles are strengthened by a nascent class and feminist consciousness. This emergent consciousness enabled workers to understand the power relations in a given situation and re-center accordingly. In that sense, oppositional consciousness facilitated the movement between identity stances, and it is not by coincidence that the experienced, senior workers showed more adeptness at moving among positions. Although the likelihood of their everyday politics leading toward transformational politics in the near future appears slim, it must be noted that the FTZ provides these women an important space that is conducive to developing and situationally expressing class consciousness.

As part of their developing oppositional consciousness, workers gradually changed from rural women with shame-fear to women who frequently broke behavioral and sexual norms. Contrary to the prevalent discourses on FTZ women as victimized women, the FTZ workers I observed became desiring subjects who sought material, physical, and emotional pleasures and more or less took responsibility when things went wrong. However, their narratives manipulated varied discursive influences to construct a story about themselves that they and others could accept. Narratives of their lives brought forth the intense contradictions they faced and the creative ways they dealt with the pains and pleasures of modernity and industrial work.

As there was little space for political activism within the transnational factories, women workers found innovative ways to challenge the class and gender norms that oppressed them. Participating in the FTZ consumer culture was one such way. Ong (1987) holds that the Malay FTZ workers attempt to construct an identity based on moral piety and self-regulation (191–93). Sri Lankan FTZ workers took a different route in expressing their newfound sense of self: They performed disrespectabilty. Mills (1997) holds that Thai factory workers were unable to attain an "up-to-date, modern womanhood" through their participation in the consumer culture and remained marginalized within it. In a somewhat different context, Enstad (1999) contends that working women at the turn of the twentieth century in New York challenged the middle classes through participating in the consumer culture—by appropriating middle-class styles and "playing the lady" (10). The FTZ workers' manipulation of fashion and taste was different to both scenarios in that they did not imitate middle-class fashions or tastes; rather, they developed new and unique tastes and practices that registered their difference from the middle classes and other women.

However, workers easily and strategically distanced themselves from this group identity when back in their villages. Changing clothes and demeanors worked as a locally meaningful strategy for managing stigma. This illustrates Stuart Hall's claim that a single, coherent identity is a fantasy and that such identities exist only because people construct coherent identity narratives for themselves (1995:65). For migrant FTZ workers, neither identification was complete but nevertheless remained possible and available positions that they could situationally acquire. In addition to illustrating performances of docility, this book highlights the experiences that fell outside the domain of the "docile subject." However, it also recognizes that moving among identities is not as easy as shifting the gears of an automobile and discusses the ways structures and institutions hinder FTZ women workers in their efforts to shift identities. In that sense, this book deals with the constant struggle for identity in which women tried to acquire, protect, move, and reacquire identities as they faced complex and contradictory power relations within varied hegemonic influences.

Garment Work and Empowerment

Earlier works on flexible labor and gender focused on workers recruited from local areas who went home to their families after work (Fernandez-Kelly 1983; Ong 1987; Lamphere 1987; Wolf 1992; Pena 1997; Mills 1999; Salzinger 2003). My study focuses on migrant rural women who lived together in an urban area that provided them a decidedly conducive environment for negotiating alternative identities. Although my account also provides evidence of labor and sexual exploitation, I focus more on the way workers construct difference and manipulate all possible identity stances. I also focus on women workers' boardinghouse lives and recreational spaces as extensions of the workplace. This enables a complex understanding of the ways work and living environments together influence new identities.

This book focuses on gendered and classed cultural domination and sites of resistance from which FTZ workers expressed critical alternative perspectives and noted that several structural conditions, especially the constrained space for political expression and the temporariness of their FTZ employment, hindered activities that may have contributed to transforming existing hegemonies. However, I hesitate to dismiss the workers' oppositional activities as symptomatic of a transitional phase in which young village women are allowed space for transgression until they move on to marriage and motherhood. Whatever the sufferings and hardships they go through and however temporary this liberation from village habitus is, the struggle for identity and the resulting "stitching" of many identities in their lives, provides tremendously empowering moments for women.[3]

Other studies of FTZ work contend that marginal employment at transnational factories does not enable women with long-term empowerment (Fernandez-Kelly 1983; Pena 1997). Although I agree that the economic and social power attained diminishes once they stop working, what happens to the oppositional consciousness, the new knowledge, and the changed sense of self when they are back in their villages is not transparent and is an important point to explore. How do the women workers respond to the constraints of village life with their newfound sense of self? Do they yearn for the colorful, transgressive years they spent as FTZ workers? What aspects of FTZ life and culture are they willing to share with other village women? Do they start to work at village factories? If so, would they be able to influence a new "village factory culture?" These are the questions that drove me to extend my research to workers' post-FTZ lives in villages throughout the country. The epilogue looks at the post-FTZ lives of several workers (some of whom featured prominently in earlier chapters), further emphasizing the complexity of analyzing the effects of globalization and transnational production on the lives of third-world women.

Exclusions and Claiming Stakes: The Politics of Location

It was a day that Suishin's workers had worked overtime until 9:00 P.M. and Mangala and I were going to her Kohuwalawattha boardinghouse. Heavy rain splashed on us while we, together with thousands of other FTZ workers who got out at the same time, dragged our tired bodies over puddles of water and mud. The plastic goods inside the shops lining the road dazzled under fluorescent lights, but we found it hard to look at them lest we step into the puddles. The street was so full of women that even when we did look up we saw nothing but the backs of other rain-drenched women. The only prudent thing seemed to be to hold onto the wet clothes of the woman in front and blindly proceed ahead. Mangala continually assured me that we were heading toward the main bus terminal and that we might, therefore, be able to catch a bus out of "this mud hole." But the bus terminal seemed miles away and with each step the world seemed to get darker and narrower. My neck and shoulders ached from looking down and tears came to my eyes as I found it hard to breathe. Suddenly the air cleared and the crowd eased into the wider space of the bus terminal. Even if the buses entering the terminal splashed mud on our already wet clothes, we all seemed to relax and let go of a collective sigh.

But then . . . is it my imagination or aren't all the buses running in a circle . . . village to Katunayake to village.?

Many times, I wondered how the government could provide foreign investors with so many facilities but would not take simple steps such as making road repairs or providing streetlights that would immensely improve women workers' lives. The women live in insecure, poorly built, and overcrowded rooms and have poor access to running water, electricity, health care, and sanitary services even as they get stigmatized for living away from their villages.

Yet each year, thousands of young, rural women trek the "road to fantasy land" to become machine operators at the Katunayake FTZ. Many openly agree that they choose the Colombo garment factory over factories located near their villages under the 200 Garment Factory Program. They come hoping to participate in the modernity those in Colombo enjoy as depicted on television and through glittering commodities other FTZ workers bring back from the city. This book shows that while the FTZ work creates social and political spaces to enable women's participation, the particular gendered and classed subjectivities created in the process limited that participation. Other such marginalized groups within cities, such as slum dwellers, have the "vote," which they use to access their rights to public goods and services. Women FTZ workers did not have votes in Katunayake and did not get leave to travel home to vote. In a scenario where conventional democratic politics was not available, women enacted politics of citizenship by creating difference. They thus used the colorful performance of disrespectability to claim public space and to shape the social and commercial worlds surrounding FTZ living.

Postcolonial societies like Sri Lanka are not strangers to national mythmaking and counterdiscourses on exclusion and marginalization. Rampant urban-rural disparity ensures that rural areas remain outside the country's development trends, even as moral discourses of the nation carve out a special space for villages as the bearers of authentic Sinhala Buddhist culture. Their new sense of self and loud performances set migrant FTZ workers outside this national imagination and twice exclude them: both as rural people and as women. The workers engage in subaltern politics by creating differences and staking claims as political subjects through their association with NGOs and even party politics. The middle classes, however, have already engineered the workers' subsequent return to the appropriate places within the rural landscape—as daughters, wives, and mothers—at the inception of FTZ.

Despite powerful ideological discourses that pressure them to get married, many women express the desire to be wage earners and city dwellers. The acute economic stagnation, almost nonexistent infrastructure, and limited sociocultural opportunities make many young people yearn for the elusive city lights. However, almost all FTZ workers have to return to their villages and take on conventional roles. Arjun Appadurai (2000) notes that labor relations within globalized industrial environments enable emancipatory politics. It encourages people to consider migration, resist state violence, seek social redress, and design new forms of civic association and collaboration, often across national boundaries (6). Appadurai's notions of global scapes have come under criticism for not taking into account politics of location (Visweswaran 1994). This book shows that while Sri Lankan rural women certainly envision redress for social violence (of exclusion) by migrating to the FTZ, not many vehicles enable them to transcend the exclusion from the national development narrative as equal participants. Although globalization is touted as a wonderful phenomenon that brings people across national boundaries together via technology, the only global networking available for some FTZ workers is receiving a periodic letter or an occasional visit from an ethnographer they befriended while at the FTZ. Thus after leaving employment, being objectified as a worker and a factory beauty queen by a Japanese factory director is cause for jubilation. Indeed, seeking a job as a nanny in a developed country or taking steps to become a mail-order bride are the ways available for former FTZ workers to participate in globalization. Therefore, this book, in a broad sense, is about the unequal opportunities global flows provide women from disparate backgrounds.

Although some scholars note that the nation-state is losing its place to global flows and structures, this book points toward the importance of state structures to ensure that rural women are able to achieve sustainable livelihoods through their participation in transnational production. Despite obvious and subtle restrictions, women strive for and claim political subjectivity within masculine public spaces. Most local, middle-class feminists have thus far not recognized these tactics as worthwhile political actions. Until that recognition happens, transnational feminist networks would not be able to reach disparate gendered constituencies like former FTZ workers for collaborative political action.

Through my FTZ fieldwork and subsequent research about former workers, I found that conventional research methods are inadequate to comment on women's lives played out within varied, intersecting forms of oppression and marginalization. To discern their tactics of claiming citizenship, we need to pay attention to silences, winks, smiles, gestures, jokes, puns, poetry, journal entries, and especially letters.

On this note, I present the following four excerpts from present and former FTZ workers' letters[4] sent to me over the last six years.

My Dearest Sandya Miss,

. . . We are always talking about you. Especially at the lunch group we miss your presence very much. . . . Pushla is now so big-headed. She said the other day that we were inflated like balloons when you were with us. She is so happy that you left. But we won't let her get away with these slights. She so wanted to see the wedding photos you sent us, but we somehow managed to keep them from

her. But we showed the photos to Kasun sensei and he said you sent some photos to the office people, too. Did you? . . .
Your loving sister,
Vasanthi

Dearest Sandya Miss,

This is how it happened. From the day you left, Pushla, Sanka, and even Sanuja sir were after us to find faults. We were moved to different lines, sent to repair damages and all these bad things. So after Niluka had this big verbal battle with Sanka and Pushla, we decided to resign. Niluka, myself, Madhu, Chandani, Dammi, altogether seven of us sent word to the office that we were not coming to work. When we came to get our back pay, the managers begged us to come back to work and promised to make things easy for us. So we promised to come back the next Monday. That day, we gathered at the main gate. When the Suishin van came to transport us to the factory, we told the driver how we have been unfairly treated by people in power. We told him all what we had in our hearts and refused to go back to work.

I went to work in a different factory and Niluka found another factory. She is now a line leader. Madhu also works at another garment factory. . . .
Chamila

To our loving Sandya Miss,

. . . I am so happy miss and sir [my husband Neil] came to visit my family. It was like a dream. My parents and in-laws are all very happy. . . . It was like a dream that you came to our poor house. I still cannot believe it truly happened.

You asked about microcredit opportunities. . . . They are helpful only to a certain extent. I have obtained all the loans I can from SEDEC and the other one. The highest they give is Rs. 20,000 [US $200]. I got it three times. Twice I re-lent the money to several other women who cannot get loans as they are still paying off old loans. I tell this only to you, Sandya miss, I, of course, charged a little interest, too. We have to live, right? . . .
Your loving sister
XXXX

Dearest Sandya Miss,

When Krishan and I were walking past Wattala Food City we met Ando san coming out of the Food City. He pointed at me and said, "No: 123, Miss Suishin." I was so surprised he remembered.
Vasanthi

Epilogue
Cautious Voices

July 2005

"Is there a couple staying here with a five-, six-month-old baby?" I asked the middle-aged woman who was looking at me suspiciously. This was about the tenth house where I knocked on the door, asking the same question. "No. We don't have couple rooms. We don't even allow boyfriends in." She came out of the door, forcing me to turn back toward the fence. "Sure, you don't," I muttered under my breath before getting into the road that was teaming under the hot sun. I sometimes wished that Dilini did not leave those messages with Dabindu workers for me. This was the second time in two years that I was going door to door looking for her. Once before, in 2003, she left a message with Chamila at the Dabindu Center asking me to visit her at her then boardinghouse. When I visited that place, she had already moved to another place. When I came back in July 2005, Chamila again informed me that Dilini had visited in May with an infant and inquired about me. She was now married and living in a "couple room" in Katunayake and was running errands when she happened to pass by the center. She had said that she lived in a boardinghouse on Temple Road and asked Chamila to tell me to come and visit her. Within the two to three months till my visit in July, she seemed to have moved to another boardinghouse. I could imagine how it would be difficult for a couple to find stable accommodations in this sea of boardinghouses that cater to mostly unmarried FTZ workers. Although Dilini and her husband are married, outsiders would perceive them as a couple living together and the boardinghouse owners themselves, as newly elevated middle class of the area, would be conflicted about their role in supporting such "immoral" activities on their premises.

Dilini's decision to stay in Katunayake even after she got married intrigued me. Very few women, if any, did that even if their men worked in the FTZ. Is she finding it hard to leave behind the FTZ life? She learned to desire practices and sensations that were forbidden before, to display tastes that were stigmatized, and to play cultural politics in everyday life; in short, she learned to become a woman without shame-fear within the Katunayake FTZ. Is this her way of holding on to that fun-filled life that held promises of modernity and social mobility even as it allowed only a little space to achieve such aspirations? Did others want that as well?

In 2006, I embarked on a ten-month research project to see how former FTZ workers negotiated village lives with the new sense of self they formed in the FTZs. Questions such as those just listed had prompted me to visit the villages of several former FTZ workers during an eight-month period in 2003–4. This epilogue focuses on the experiences of seven former workers, based on information I collected during that period.

While discussing the decline in North Carolina's textile jobs on the *News Hour with Jim Lehrer*, Representative Robin Hayes stated that the flexible capital policies that allow U.S. companies to go overseas looking for cheap labor were damaging local economies. According to Hayes, "We are in the process of destroying our middle class to create a middle class in other countries."[1] The account in this book of Sri Lanka's FTZ garment factory workers shows that work in the transnational factories does not help people, women or men, to attain middle-class status. On the contrary, the FTZ has become a stigmatized space feared by middle-class people. Indeed, poor remuneration makes it impossible for women to sustain urban working lives after getting married and thus guarantees that they go back to their villages when they get married.

When I visited the former workers' village homes (most had now moved to their husbands' villages), I had the opportunity to spend time talking to them, their husbands, and their new relatives. Three of the seven women whose FTZ lives I recorded at length in previous chapters married their boyfriends, two entered into arranged marriages, and two remained unmarried. Four of the seven women—Vasanthi, Dinithi,[2] Vinitha,[3] and Sujatha—had belonged to the politically conscious Suishin lunch group that had expressed rudimentary forms of proletariat and feminist consciousness. Three of them are now wives and mothers. Even though development planners, BOI, and other government officials claimed that FTZ employment was an avenue for rural women to earn their dowry, these women expressed a willingness to continue working after getting married. However, employers' reluctance and other so-ciopsychological reasons prevented the women from doing so, and these politically conscious workers reluctantly accepted the role of village wives.

All the women lamented the fact that they did not earn money anymore. "I feel like running back to the factory when I don't have money to do what I want," Vasanthi said. "My husband does small-scale business and we don't have a steady income. Now he has gone to Italy illegally, so he cannot come and visit me. He does odd jobs there and there is not much improvement for us," she further explained. "I am so worried about not having children even after four years of marriage.[4] But now he is in Italy. So how can we conceive? If I could have kept my factory job, together with the little money he earned we could have made ends meet. But around here, there is nothing I could do. So our young lives are wasted in two countries. *Ane* miss, can you see whether there is any way we can find jobs as a couple in America, you know, like driver and nanny?" Vasanthi once pleaded.

Vasanthi, however, is not as bad off as Dinithi. "I am not ashamed to tell you, miss, the reason that I cannot visit my friends the way I want to is that I just can't afford the bus fare. My husband is a soldier, so he gets a steady income. But he only looks after his needs. He only gives me money for bare necessities. If I try to talk to him, he starts berating me and even says that, unlike other men, he was stupid enough to have gotten burdened with an FTZ worker. Look, miss, how unfair is it to say that? Isn't he the one who pursued me with love letters and gifts?" Dinithi said this with a defiant tone that lacked the spirit she showed during labor struggles and crisis situations at the FTZ.

Vinitha was the only one among the seven former FTZ workers who was engaged in an income-generating activity. She owned a small grocery shop and divided her time between the shop and her duties as a wife and mother. "My in-laws sometimes complain that other FTZ workers brought more money and material goods to their marriages [to compensate for their besmirched reputation] and I did not. You know they say it indirectly, so one cannot even question them. My only consolation is that Sumith is such a loving, kind person. We got married after a long romance, so that feels like a victory. But we are poor and my life is just the baby, our home, and the grocery store. I miss all the fun things that we did as a group when I was there," Vinitha explained in her usual calm monotone.

Sujatha's friends advised her not to leave the factory, even as they themselves left their jobs to get married. She, however, found factory work extremely difficult without her social circle. Therefore, she subsequently resigned, thinking she could find another garment factory job near her village. Eighteen months later, however, she was still unemployed, having been rejected by two village factories. "We don't have local political support, and these village factory managers believe that FTZ workers are too rebellious. That is why they try not to recruit us. Now I am thinking of finding work as an agricultural day laborer," Sujatha said. Tears glistened in her eyes as she continued, "You know that I spent all my FTZ money on my brothers and sisters. I don't have any savings, so I must work."

When I met Sujatha in July 2005, a little more than a year later, she seemed happier, having found a garment factory job thirty miles from her village. "The job is good, but it does not pay much. In the FTZ, we had bonuses, overtime payments, and other incentives. In this factory, it is Rs. 4,000 and that is it. If you are absent even a day, they cut Rs. 100 per day. So I cannot buy gold jewelry and other things like I did with the FTZ job. Also, transportation costs too much. It costs Rs. 30 a day for the bus fare. So how can I save?" Sujatha asked. Having recently visited Suishin again I was happy to inform her that Suishin will be more than happy to have her back if she wants to return. "I would like to go back to Colombo, miss, but my parents won't allow me," Sujatha said, coyly reminding me that her parents were trying to find her a suitable partner. It will not help their efforts for her to move back to the "evil city."

Employment in the FTZ clearly did not provide the environment for achieving lasting empowerment for women and only exacerbated gender inequalities. However, some former workers also showed that they were different from other women who never migrated by being adept at engaging the limited social and political space in their villages. For example, several former FTZ workers (not the seven workers I studied at length) took advantage of microfinance programs offered by NGOs working in rural development, and their FTZ experience probably helped them in this regard. In some villages, more than one NGO offered microfinance facilities, and one former worker, after taking all the loans allowed from an NGO-organized community-based society in her village, moved on to another NGO-organized society, started taking loans, and eventually became the bank manager. Some former FTZ workers are now trying to emigrate to the United States and other western countries as either housemaids or mail-order brides. They offer a sharply different image from that of the nonmigrant village women who expressed fear of moving even to an urban area to find employment.

Suppressed Knowledge

In Chapter 7, I explained how women acted naïve, shy, and timid when they visited their villages on vacations so that they would be included in the category of the "small number of innocent women" in the FTZ and not identified with the transgressive FTZ workers who have no shame-fear. When I talked to some of the same women in 2003 about their post-FTZ lives, they said it helped them to get married to their boyfriends without their families objecting or to enter into proposed marriages without much difficulty. It is significant that all the women felt they could survive in their new homes only by strictly following ideal gender norms. Some women, especially early in their marriage, exaggerated ideal behavioral traits such as coyness to counteract the FTZ stigma. As Vinitha once said, "As the cart follows the bull, the shame of spending time in the FTZ comes after us."

The two unmarried women, Sujatha and Kishali, suffered from somewhat similar problems, resulting from the stigma of FTZ work. While Kishali craved marriage to feel secure, her family found it difficult to find her a partner. She has had relationships with several men and never tried to hide the facts from anyone. Now living in her village she admitted that her carefree attitude seriously damaged her reputation and has adversely affected her marriage prospects. She is now using her EPF and gratuity payments, which she received when she resigned from her FTZ job, to pay an "international matchmaker" who has promised to find her an Italian or a Swiss husband. She had hoped that she would find a husband by December 2002, but that had not happened by December 2003. Sujatha was not only unable to find a suitable job in the village, but she was also unable to find a suitable partner for marriage. To acquire both a job and a marriage partner, Sujatha is now trying to cultivate an image of a woman who is shy and disciplined through her clothing, speech, and mannerisms. Her permed curly hair now grown long and demurely clipped back away from her forehead, Sujatha shyly declared, "My free days are over."[5]

These narratives show that it is very important for village women who must return and integrate themselves into patriarchal families to disavow new knowledge flows acquired within modern, transnational spaces. Creating and performing a contradictory picture from the worldly FTZ worker is a strategy that helped them dissociate from accusations of cultural transgressions usually associated with FTZ work. However, their pretenses to being naïve women with shame-fear meant that they had to hide their new knowledges even on subjects that mattered most to them as women: sexuality and reproductive health. Three of the five married women, including one who married her longtime boyfriend, found it difficult to talk to their future husbands about family planning before they got married. They were, therefore, unable to use any contraceptive method from the first intercourse onward and four of the women now have small children. Vinitha, who perhaps most strongly expressed her need to be financially independent and started her own village shop, had a baby in the tenth month of her marriage. "I tried to talk to him about not getting pregnant for a year or two so that we could develop our shop. But he thought I may become permanently infertile if I used contraceptive methods. I knew that is not the case, but

I did not try to reason with him and tell him about benefits and side effects of contraceptive methods. Then he might think I am someone who ate the country [had become too worldly]," Vinitha explained while squatting by the well, washing her son's dirty diapers, her eyes constantly running to the front of the shop to see whether any customers were approaching.

When she was at the FTZ, Dinithi talked about the need for equal partnership within marriage. She also gathered much knowledge from reading tabloids such as *Priyadari*. However, her married life is far from the picture she imagined while dating her husband. "*Ane* miss, it was only after marriage I learned what it is to live with a man who drinks alcohol. He forgets all good qualities when he drinks. If I try to talk to him about not drinking, this man insults me by accusing me of bad behavior while I was at the Zone. How could I not get pregnant when I sleep with a drunkard?" Dinithi said. "Now his parents and even neighbors are on my side and they sympathize with me. But if I show that I know of contraceptives and sexual health and stuff, I would even lose their support," she responded after I asked whether she talked to her husband or his family about contraceptives and family planning.

When I talked to Vasanthi in March 2004, she had not conceived despite being married for about three years. "I am so worried that people will soon insinuate that my immoral lifestyle while at the FTZ is responsible for my not having children. Once I was watching this TV health program with my in-laws and some neighbors. I was so upset when the doctor started talking about infertility caused by abortions. I was almost squirming on my chair. On another day, someone asked about the sex and abortion stories at the FTZ. I told her that I never knew anyone who had sex or abortions. You know that is not the truth. *Ane* truly miss, I hate it when I have to pretend that I am a stupid, ignorant fool during conversations about even simple health issues. I really don't want people to think that I led a fast life at the FTZ. I just hate living like this," she lamented. As can be expected, none of the women had discussed sexual pleasures with their husbands, and only two of them said that their husbands are concerned about their wives' pleasure.

These women are now isolated in different households, and the oppositional consciousness they had cultivated in the FTZ is rendered almost meaningless. In one woman's words, "It all feels like a fragrance that was in a dream." As I showed earlier, they were adept at strategizing their actions in a way that most benefited them and they took pride in the way they managed to fool their families and later their husbands and in-laws. Many times after pretending ignorance and shyness, Vasanthi or Dinithi whispered in my ear, "This man/woman swallowed my lie." Even though the others did not express themselves so bluntly, their facial expressions and body language showed that they took a certain pleasure in knowing that they were fooling those around them. The staged and performative nature of their conformity shows how subversive in character their behavior was.

However, it also became clear that the women resented having to suppress their new knowledge and silence many aspects of the new selves they developed in the urban FTZ. Performing different selves through verbal and visual narratives is a strategy used by people suffering social, cultural, and political repression. When they visited their villages on vacations while working at the FTZ, the women protested by smuggling FTZ knowledge through magazines and audiotapes to younger village women. Now living in new villages with in-laws and nonrelated people, women found it difficult to transfer such directly transgressive knowledge to younger women. They still managed, though, to create room to maneuver through their conscious pretenses to being conforming women.

Knowledge Flows, Networking, and Gendered Spaces

The previous discussion seems to suggest that the social and political possibilities enabled by the modern, urban transnational space of the Katunayake FTZ are limited to a certain space and phase in these workers' lives. However, a careful consideration of my observations in their post-FTZ lives shows that, despite their display of ideal womanhood, these women still hold their FTZ experience close to their hearts and exercise the oppositional consciousness developed there, albeit cautiously, in appropriate places and with appropriate audiences.

As other women have done in oppressive social contexts, these former FTZ workers engaged in subtle everyday resistance. These acts of resistance clearly differed in intensity and effectiveness from their patterns of group resistance at the FTZ. When I first inquired, almost all the women said that how they felt about certain issues and how they felt they should fight for their rights and defy unrealistic demands on their lives by powerful groups was a distant dream and that they did not have the time or the opportunities to pursue that dream while in the village. However, what they did not tell me was how they pursue that dream every day through their strong encouragement of younger village women to take up jobs in FTZ factories.

Even though having babies thwarted their attempts to start income-generating activities, the women also found that the intense scrutiny on their behavior lessened once they became pregnant. This, coupled with their overtly conforming behavior, allowed them time with younger, nonmigrant women without much supervision from suspicious elders.

All seven women I studied at length had a regular following of younger women who visited them almost every afternoon from 2:00 P.M. until about 5:00 P.M. While the elderly relatives napped inside the house, the women sat outside the kitchen and combed each other's hair or helped with household work, such as cleaning rice or green leaves, as they chatted. Many young women actively prompted the former workers to relate stories from the FTZ, and the former workers seemed more than happy to oblige. The former workers related stories of fashions, rituals, love, sex, violence, and resistance, but they always made sure that they were portrayed in a "good light." The narrator never engaged in anything transgressive in any of the stories I listened to. Even while explaining incidents in which I was also a part, the women did not hesitate to exaggerate liberally and emphasize the joyful and satisfying aspects of the incidents. The need to be wise and not forget good values was emphasized to explain away the stories dealing with sex, abandonment, and violence. But the former workers were relentless in encouraging the younger women to try out the FTZ.

"There are so many university graduates working at the FTZ. Women like you, who barely passed their Advanced Level exam, look for status jobs and lead shameless lives like parasites on your parents income," Vinitha once admonished a young woman, who said FTZ work had no status. "It is because of these attitudes that women are suffering like this. Why? Because they hesitate to earn an income at the FTZ. That is okay, but these attitudes also turn women who are brave enough to be independent and who try to earn some money to help their families into prostitutes," Vinitha continued in a rare impassioned tone, using the scholarly Sinhala term for attitudes, *akalpa.*

The younger women were also encouraged to try the Colombo FTZ (Katunayake) or any other FTZ (Biyagama or Koggala) rather than isolated village factories. The former workers invariably romanticized the Katunayake FTZ, saying that the others were also situated in somewhat rural areas while Katunayake was full of life and was a bustling urban center. Kishali explained the new subculture created by FTZ workers by saying, "It is the world of garment girls." I frequently heard the phrase, "You need to see for yourself." In their enthusiasm to get some of the younger women (and, in some cases, even older, married women who were having marital and financial problems) to go to the FTZ, the former workers sometimes even actively discouraged women from migrating to Middle Eastern countries to work as housemaids, which was the only other avenue of escape available for rural women. In such moments, the former workers, especially Dinithi, Vasanthi, Vinitha, and Kishali, tried to explain the difference between the two employment av-

enues in terms of possibilities for developing oppositional consciousness, both feminist and proletarian.

"There is no difference between a housemaid in a Middle Eastern
country and a housemaid in Colombo. They live alone and have no
crowd support. The FTZ is different. In the factory, in the boardinghouse, or in the Averiwatthe area nobody can get away with hurting one
of us. We all fight together and see that justice is done," Dinithi once
told some young women who were gathered around a basket of green
leaves leisurely picking the stems off. All seven former workers related
stories of factory strikes and everyday resistance in order to make their
point. Many former workers seemed to have genuinely forgotten that
there were many times that they were unable to see that justice was done
and that there were some acutely frustrating moments when they felt
like running back to their villages. However, they clearly valued the oppositional consciousness they developed in the FTZ and wanted other
women to experience it as well.

Moreover, former workers actively helped younger workers get jobs in
FTZ factories and find better boardinghouses. They wrote to their
friends still at the FTZ for information on new vacancies and sent letters
of reference to boarding aunties, even to the ones they had despised. All
of them seemed to take much pleasure in relating stories in which they
were instrumental in finding other village women jobs and boardinghouses. Amila was one such former worker who had fulfilled her dream
of attaining middle-class status through her rich, businessman husband
but found life boring in rural Rathnapura except when she engaged in
networking to help a poor village woman get a job and a place to stay in
the FTZ. Considering the elite status of her husband's family in the village, I suspect that she never advertised her own stint at the FTZ. But she
managed to help two women get accommodation at the boardinghouse
her father operated at Katunayake. Even though this increased the danger of her being exposed as a former worker, the pride and joy she experienced in using networks of friendship and kinship to help those in
need and then receive their gratitude seemed to be too attractive for her
to resist.

When I visited her village, Amila took pains to send messengers and
get some of the village women to come to her house. Although the
women were called so that they could have a discussion with me, it was
obvious that she also wanted me to see how highly these women regarded her. They called her "*Sudu Menike* [fair lady]" with reverence and
waited on her and fussed over her needs. "I just sent Dayani's resume to
Sanuja sir asking him to show her special preference," Amila said, pointing to a timid young woman whom she sent to the kitchen to bring her
a glass of water. "Her family is very poor. It will be such a good thing to

get her a job. I will also arrange for her to stay at my parents' house," she continued in obvious delight at her ability to provide such services.

This enthusiasm for networking was also evident in Malani's post-FTZ life. She is now married to a home guard and lives with him in her mother's house. Malani uses her network of friends among the low-level factory officers to help village women find jobs. It is possible suspect that Malani, who seemed to have developed into a worldly and even crafty young woman, obtained some financial or other benefits for the services she rendered these women.

Even though these women were cautious not to associate themselves with FTZ transgressions, their enthusiastic stories seemed to have an effect on young women who visited them. I asked the seven women I studied whether they expected to see the stigma associated with FTZ work diminish if many more young women became former FTZ workers. They all thought the greater number of workers would help in this regard, but at least four noted that the numbers would not lessen the stigma unless women from middle classes started working in the FTZ. I also noted that young women from middle-class village families did not come to these afternoon storytelling sessions at the former workers' homes. The women who did attend seemed to be women from poor, marginalized families who were already somewhat inclined to find employment in the FTZ and needed moral support to make the decision and ground support to see it happen.

"*Ane* miss, these women from 'good families' are not even educated as we are, but they wait until government jobs fall into their laps," Vasanthi once said. Dinithi noted that middle-class women would choose jobs with status over jobs with better salaries and benefits. "Savithri is from a good family in the village, but we are kind of close. She keeps telling me that she sometimes feels like throwing her village health worker position[6] aside and going to work in an FTZ factory. She gets paid only Rs. 2,500 a month, but she needs to wear saris to work and live a certain way. You know, keep the image. Rs. 2,500 is not enough for all that," Dinithi said somewhat disparagingly. But Dinithi was realistic and noted, "She will never go to the FTZ. It will be easier for her parents to arrange a good marriage if she is a health worker."

Even though they were not able to make an impact on rural middle-class women, these storytelling sessions enabled former workers to assume the role of change agents via a somewhat circuitous route. Although they did not flaunt their changed attitudes and new knowledges, they exposed other women to the possibility of developing these new attitudes and knowledges by encouraging them to take jobs in the FTZs.

Although each village had a few former FTZ workers (who had

worked at different FTZs or factories), they did not share confidences. "*Apoi* miss, it is good for my marriage that I do not get too close with all those women. If we get close, we will talk about everything and the details will get out to the village," Vasanthi said, hunching her shoulders together for emphasis.

"There are several in this village, too. I wonder what is up with them because they want to be friends but do not want to share confidences. I don't want such friendships," Dinithi angrily commented about other former workers in her village. When she denigrated these women for being secretive, she seemed to have forgotten that she also kept some aspects of her FTZ life (parties, trips, dancing, flirting, and reading pornography) to herself. Kishali actively sought these former workers' friendship by blurting out her life story and was irritated that the others did not reciprocate. However, she seemed to still enjoy a good friendship with several of those women.

The other women mentioned busy schedules as the reason for the lack of communication and unity among former FTZ workers residing in the same village. While these are valid reasons, I suspect—given some workers' reluctance to let me visit them in their villages—the most significant reason was to avoid exposing one another's FTZ past in petty quarrels that could occur between close friends. Menike, another Suishin worker, who was close to me during my research in 2000 and was overjoyed to meet me at the Averiwatthe junction in 2003, prevented me from visiting her in the village in 2005 without explaining her reluctance. But in a letter to Dinithi she explained that she feared that my presence in the village would arouse speculation about her past life at a time when the stigma of FTZ life was finally fading away thanks to her new baby.

Even though these former workers were not united within their villages, most kept in touch with their FTZ friends who lived in other villages. Dinithi, Vasanthi, Vinitha, Sujatha, Rena, and Menike kept regularly in touch with each other through mail. They sometimes met at weddings and funerals of mutual friends. Twice they arranged to meet at the Averiwatthe junction, but they found that only a few could manage the time and the finances to engage in luxuries such as a "girls' day out."[7] However, their letters showed that they still tried to relive the pleasurable memories of the FTZ through letters. They exchanged gossip about factory officers and other workers they knew and were sad when they got to know that Sanka left Suishin to follow a textile management course. "Suishin would not be as fun anymore," both Dinithi and Vasanthi mused. The information that seemed to have provided them with the most happiness was the news that Pushla also had to leave Suishin employment to take care of her baby. Showing me a letter from

Vasanthi that informed her about Pushla's fate, Vinitha said, "She couldn't wait to get rid of us, but see what happened to her." Normally calm and reasonable, Vinitha had a smug smile on her face when she said this. The fact that Pushla's departure was hastened by rumors about an extramarital relationship did not inspire solidarity among women who seemed to fear continually that such a rumor might destroy their good reputation within marriage. Rather, they were happy that their immediate tormentor at the factory seemed to have left the factory amid humiliating circumstances.

The letters from FTZ friends usually had a pride of place in former workers' own little corner in the house: their *almirahs*. The letters were arranged in empty chocolate boxes or in beautifully decorated cardboard boxes and were displayed to me with joy. Only Dinithi, Vasanthi, and Kishali offered the letters for me to read. Some of the contents surprised me in that the writers seemed much more open about their FTZ escapades than they would ever dare to be in their villages. In one letter, after sharing news about some of the others from Suishin, Menike asked Vasanthi whether Nishan sir writes to her in the village. Considering the special relationship Vasanthi and Nishan had while she was at Suishin and the lengths that Vasanthi went to cultivate a good image for the sake of her in-laws, it appeared that keeping such a letter with her was risky. It also became clear that Vasanthi still holds the memories of her days as Miss Suishin very close to her heart and in particular valued the special attention Nishan, a manager, paid her. Although she talked about Nishan, Sanuja and Sanka at our Averiwatthe meeting, she did not talk about these men while at her village. The letters were the space in which the suppressed desires and unfulfilled dreams were expressed and the women were not inclined to deny the pleasure of holding onto these letters.[8]

Their promotion of FTZ work to younger women and the way they kept their FTZ memories alive through letters showed that the former workers were forced to be cautious and that they selected the appropriate spaces and appropriate audience to raise their voice. Dinithi told me that after her pregnancy she became friendly with the village health worker and helped her organize and keep records of the monthly mothers' meeting. Once the health worker invited Dinithi to give a talk about the FTZ situation at the village meeting. Dinithi declined and in no uncertain terms explained to me that if she revealed everything about her life in the FTZ to everyone, she might as well say good-bye to her marriage and hopes for a better life.

The stigma of FTZ work was the underlying factor in former workers' actions, and they continually feared for their precarious reputations. However, at the village it was very hard to discern that such stigma existed. In fact, the power of the stigma seemed to flow exactly from this subtlety and the invisibility of its maneuverings. When I talked to the relatives and neighbors of former FTZ workers, none of them spoke disparagingly about FTZ work. Rather, I received many comments about how admirable it is that these young women endured hardships to help their families in the villages. While everybody touched on the well-publicized stories about premarital sex and unwanted pregnancies, they were also quick to qualify that it was only a few who were responsible for such acts and that even such women were victims of circumstances beyond their control. A few people blamed rapid globalization and the resultant new forms of cultural flows for the moral degradation associated with the FTZ. As one elderly man said, "Look at what they show on television. They are trying to make us all American. The tourists bring all the garbage of the world to our villages. How can we blame these young girls who are all alone in the city for taking the wrong path when all they can see around them is bad."

In this way, the villagers expressed how they connected notions of a pristine nation, powerless and sexually naïve women, and the evils of globalization to come to an understanding that they could live with. Knowing that the decaying rural economy forced women into FTZ work, villagers had to find a way to reconcile existing ideals of moral conduct and the former FTZ workers among them. Although the villagers blamed global cultural flows and labeled women as naïve, ignorant, and easily manipulated, we have seen that women were, to some extent while in the FTZ and to a lesser extent in the village, agents of their lives. In the FTZ, workers clearly challenged such narratives of nonagency by creating new cultural practices and other cultural and political maneuverings. I assert that in the villages where the space for action was severely restricted, they protested the stigma and the nonagency by consciously disciplining their bodies, voices, and actions.

According to Ong (1987), Malay FTZ workers tried to create an alternative subjectivity to the existing image of workers as westernized, wasteful, and pleasure-seeking women by embracing an ascetic Islamic attitude toward life and through self-regulation (186). The former workers' presentation of self in the village seems at the outset somewhat similar to the Malay women's attempts to construct an identity based on a cult of purity, sexual repression, and self-sacrifice (191). The difference lies in the fact that the women are conscious that they are manipulating norms to make life easier, while still holding onto the memory of their transgressions and encouraging other village women to try that fun life. The networking and the letter writing show that the changes the women experienced within the FTZ have had lasting impressions and positioned them differently from other young rural women who never migrated. In that sense, even though FTZ employment has not enabled them to achieve sustainable livelihoods or set them on a path toward social empowerment, their everyday responses to power relations showed that they still played cultural politics within such restricted spaces. Although they are forced to select appropriate spaces and appropriate audiences even to cautiously raise their voice, they are not totally silenced. In that sense, FTZ employment cannot be considered a transitional space with no effect on existing structures once the workers leave the FTZ. More research is needed to draw a more comprehensive picture of the way former FTZ workers negotiate their lives within increasingly globalizing Sri Lankan villages.

Notes

1. "Suishin" is a Japanese word that means progress. I chose this word for the factory's name because the factory's real name is a Japanese word that means another closely related term prevalent in development discourses. Names of people, places, and factories have been changed to protect confidentiality.

2. Workers and staff both used the Japanese honorific "san" at the end of managers' names while identifying them or addressing them. While the Japanese managing director was called "Ando san," two Sri Lankan managers, Gamini and Kasun, were addressed with "sensei" at the end of their names ("sensei" was slightly higher in respect than "san"). Throughout Chapters 3 and 4 I will use these honorifics to identify the managers.

3. The only restriction that Suishin management put on my research was that I not divulge information about the companies they sewed garments for. When I took photographs of the assembly lines, they instructed me to make sure that the labels would not be visible, and I honored their wishes.

4. This also helped in another way, by providing my knees, already weakened by pattelo-femoral syndrome, a little respite from long stretches of standing and walking around the line.

5. According to *A Review of Free Trade Zones in Sri Lanka*, published by the Dabindu Collective, the availability of "well disciplined and obedient women workers who can produce more in a short time" was used as bait to attract investors to Sri Lanka's FTZs (1997:17).

6. The majority of Sri Lankans are Sinhala (74 percent). While 5 percent of the Sinhala are Christians (principally Catholic), most Sinhala (69 percent) are Buddhist by religion. The Tamil minority (18 percent) is mostly Hindu (15 percent), with some Christians (3 percent). Muslims (7 percent) and small communities of other ethnic groups such as Burghers and Chinese also live in the country (Mann 1993:59).

7. For a detailed account of the ethnic conflict and analysis of its causes, see DeVotta 2004.

8. According to another BOI official, the garment factories that opened in the East, where Muslims and Tamils are concentrated in large numbers, are also having trouble recruiting Tamil and Muslim women from the region. This could possibly be a local protest against an oppressive government while also indicating more-rigid gender norms within the two minority ethnic groups.

9. According to the BOI document "Industrial Factor Costs," skilled Sri Lankan workers are paid between Rs. 2,500 and Rs. 3,250, while nonskilled workers are paid Rs. 2,000 to 2,500. The basic salary of an FTZ worker is Rs. 2,250 (about US$25) per month, but workers could earn about Rs. 3,000 to 4,000 by working overtime and not taking their annual leave. Workers suffer from various ailments caused by difficult work and living conditions and are sexually harassed on their way to and from work (Smith 1993; Dabindu Collective 1997). Many legal and practical barriers to organizing trade unions within the FTZ exist, but NGOs have managed to help somewhat by providing legal advice and opportunities for workers to get together to share experiences (Rosa 1982; Fine and Howard 1995).

10. "Juki" is the brand name of a Japanese industrial sewing machine used in FTZ garment factories. "Juki pieces [*Juki keli*]" combines the word "Juki" with the Sinhala word used in factories to refer to the pieces of clothes women workers assemble using Juki machines. The label strongly conveys the way the garment workers are objectified based on their work.

11. The corresponding Sinhala term is *Ahinsaka*, which means harmless. However, when it is used in the context of young women's reputation it means nonknowledge of sexual matters. In the local English, *Ahinsaka* is translated as innocent, and I chose to use this locally relevant term while noting that "innocent" could have other meanings even within local English usage.

12. Obeyesekere (1970) uses the term "protestant Buddhism" to refer to emergent traditions of Sinhala Buddhism, which were configured by incorporating "Victorian-Protestant ethical ideas" (46). Obeyesekere notes that sexual morality, monogamous marriage ideals, and divorce rules are several such ideas adopted from Protestantism. See Chapter 2 below for more on this configuration.

13. Several studies on women factory workers in transnational or local factories have influenced this study. In addition to the work of Kondo, the works of Fernandez-Kelly (1983), Ong (1987), Lamphere (1987), Wolf (1992), Pena (1997), Lee (1998), Rofel (1999), Mills (1999), and Salzinger (1997; 2003) deserve special acknowledgment.

Chapter 2

1. Factories usually start the workday at 8:00 A.M. or 8:30 A.M. Work usually ends at 5:00 P.M. or 9:00 P.M. Many factories operate work shifts from 6:00 A.M. to 2:00 P.M. and from 2:00 P.M. to 10:00 P.M. Crossing the highway was easier during these times given the vast number of workers who crossed together. At times, I felt like my efforts to exercise my freedom of movement by walking alone and during "untimely hours" only made me waste time at pedestrian crossings.

2. *Slaves of Free Trade Zone: Camp Sri Lanka* (San Francisco: Labor video project, 2000), video.

3. Newspapers, textbooks, and other media usually identify the characteristics of the ideal woman using interchangeable terms, such as ideal Sinhala Buddhist woman, Sri Lankan woman, or Asian or oriental woman.

4. My account of these discursive constructions draws from Malathi De Alwis's insightful analysis of the construction of an image of a sanitized, moral, and religious Sinhala Buddhist woman (1998).

5. Some accounts contradict these dominant views, such as the works of Hugh Boyd (1800) and Fedrick Jobson (1862).

6. Dharmapala's political career as a Sinhala Buddhist nationalist and how his anticolonial campaign became an antiminority one had been analyzed by many other authors (Obeyesekere 1979; Amunugama 1991).

7. Writings of Christian missionaries such as Chapman (1892), Langdon (1890), and Cummings (1892), shows that women were a major factor in keeping their men from converting to Christianity (as quoted in Harris 1994). This suggests that the woman was the protector of the spiritual domain even before the nationalists relegated the task specifically to her.

8. I use the term "state culture" to encompass the ruling parties' performance of culture at various state functions. These performances and expressions reflected Sinhala Buddhist characteristics and was one reason for the discontent felt by other ethnic and religious groups.

9. Today it is common to see women in western attire touting commercial products on television. At the same time, however, an image of the beautiful, sari-clad wife and mother serving the family with various commercial products is also prevalent.

10. In 1998, writing about the fifty years of Sri Lankan cinema, Abeyesekera (1998a) again notes that Sinhala movies continue to portray the village as "good" and the city as "bad" while at the same time portraying women as victimized by the intrusion of city lifestyles into the villages (5).

11. In Sinhala Buddhist homes, children, especially girls, are socialized into norms of shame-fear from an early age. Although differences in the intensity of this socialization exist based on social class, in schools and Sunday schools children from all social classes receive standard instruction on proper behavior befitting Sinhala Buddhist men and women.

12. Even though Katunayake is situated almost one hour away from Colombo, many villagers I talked to in different parts of the country referred to that FTZ as "Colombo garment factory" or "Colombo FTZ."

13. Both *Dabindu* and *Niveka* magazines critiqued the Garden of Love as unnecessary. *Niveka* published several workers' opinions on the garden and almost all of them lamented the image created about them by the very existence of the Garden of Love.

14. For an account of this process, see Hewamanne (forthcoming).

15. By contrast, in their creative-writing journals and in anonymous contributions to two marginalized magazines, FTZ workers did express sexual desire and aggression.

16. It must be noted, however, that many of the contributors on both sides are men. Throughout this debate I read only two opinions written by women.

17. In addition to brief news clips, other television documentaries have been done on the Katunayake FTZ and its female workforce. Most programs were made to promote worker recruitment or to provide political clout to the existing government. One program, titled *Liyathambara* (Women Flowers), was an exception to this in its more complex presentation of women's lives.

18. Ironically, another article, which appeared on the same page as the *Dabindu* movie review, focused on a suicide death of an FTZ woman who "came to the city a charming rural woman" and "became a cancelled coin" in the hands of a married lover.

19. With 3,000 employees, RAC is one of the biggest factories in the FTZ. I was able to secure an invitation to attend their annual New Year party on January 15, 2000.

20. Nalini had originally thought that I was "a tiger girl [*koti kella*]" representing

the Tamil separatist group the Liberation Tamil Tigers of Eelam (LTTE) and had come to Colombo to detonate a bomb at the party.

21. This is a common term used by management, factory staff, and workers to talk about garment factory workers. People use *ape lamai* (our children) to denote workers of one's factory and *anik lamai* or *wene lamai* (other children or different children) to denote workers in other factories. When managers speak in English they, however, use the word "girls" rather than "children."

22. Incidentally, this attitude was extended toward me, too. Mr. Perera was older than the other managers and had the look and demeanor of one who commands respect not only for his high position but also for his advanced age. I was often a willing audience for his monologues on industrial problems, ethnic conflict, and Buddhist values. He was a devout Buddhist who observed *sil* on all *poya* days, read *Pali* texts, and practiced meditation. He reconciled Buddhist values with the contradictory capitalist values mostly through his patriarchal concern for protecting women's sexual "innocence."

23. These officers were in charge of measuring efficiency rates for each assembly line and proposing ways to improve efficiency.

24. The parents who came, however, expressed displeasure with the management for the way they treated their daughters and extended support to their daughters' struggle (*Dabindu* April 2000).

Chapter 3

1. The factory had approximately 550 workers, about 75 of whom were male. Most men worked in the stores and cutting, ironing, and finish sections; only a few (about five or six at a given time) were employed as machine operators.

2. *Matome* is a Japanese word meaning "finishing touches."

3. Workers were expected to be back at their stations within five seconds after the music signaled the end of breaks. While no one directly transgressed this disciplinary measure, they subverted it by not using the restroom during tea breaks, thereby saving a few more minutes for socializing. They then used factory time to use the restroom.

4. Workers liked to pin some of their hair up in what they called a "bump," a center piece of hair that was combed back and then pinned at an angle on the head.

5. It should be recalled here that early colonial writings represented Sri Lankan rural women as talkative and undisciplined (see Chapter 2). Japanese culture focuses on restraint and discipline and there were intricate rules for male and female behavior as well as the role of each person in hierarchical relationships (Kondo 1990). It would be fascinating to investigate these managers' thoughts on Sri Lankan women's behavior vis-à-vis Japanese women and the managers' reasons for introducing these gendered markers.

6. After a few weeks, I started sitting with the junior executives and they integrated me easily into the group.

7. For example, workers with long hair sometimes wore the head scarves as an accessory and let the hair fall down under the scarf. Although this did not comply with cleanliness and safety rules, the show of deference usually satisfied the supervisory staff.

8. Workers formed groups to socialize with after they finished lunch. All workers belonged to a group, which met at a preselected place every day to share snacks and gossip.

9. The valorization of fair skin among the Sinhala carries similar racist and class connotations as in other postcolonial societies. Among the Sinhala, it relates to an understanding of the Sinhala as an "Aryan" race with fair skin and the Tamils as belonging to the "Dravidian" race with darker skin. (Interestingly, however, Tamil people too valorize fairness of skin among themselves.) This mistaken racial and color construction has superimposed itself onto class divisions, and fair skin is now commonly understood as a sign of belonging to the middle class.

10. The female supervisor, Pushla, did not receive such kindness. On the contrary, she suffered many resentful jibes from the workers. However, after she announced that she was pregnant with her first child, the workers' behavior, if not their attitude, toward her changed. Many workers made an effort not to shout back at her because it was considered reprehensible to be cruel to a pregnant woman.

11. The workers showed their sense of belonging by referring to Line C as "our line" and the production assistant as "our production assistant." Although they fought with supervisors and bickered among themselves, when criticism was voiced from outside, many workers instantly defended the personnel on their line.

12. The officer's name is changed from a previously used pseudonym to minimize the probability of him being identified.

13. Chakrabarty (1989) writes that Indian workers developed a religious and spiritual relationship with their work tools (89). Kondo (1990) also notes that Japanese workers developed a special relationship with their machines.

14. They brought in Buddhist salvation ideals and folk beliefs to make sense of their lives as industrial workers.

15. A *pirith* chanting ceremony is a Buddhist ritual ceremony performed to bless premises and people as well as to drive away evil spirits.

16. Workers whose machines were in close proximity formed strong friendships among themselves, and these groups usually spent their breaks socializing together. Groups typically had one or two workers who could be informally identified as leading characters, and they led their groups in differently understanding their work conditions and identities.

17. Madhu lobbied hard for Sanka, Pushla, and me not to join the trip. She was saddened and acted betrayed when we said we would join the trip. When the trip was cancelled because we could not get the day off, Madhu openly rejoiced. At the last minute, when the leave crisis was solved and we were able to take the trip, Madhu expressed a grudging satisfaction that at least Pushla did not join the trip

18. Several experienced, skilled workers declined offers of promotions citing their reluctance to shout at fellow workers.

19. Entertaining an inferiority complex because she does not have a boyfriend, Indika used to make veiled references to nonexistent boyfriends and several suitors. Whenever she came to the line, Amila prompted her to talk about these suitors, making her the line's laughingstock. This emphasis on Indika's unsuccessful love life made most workers downplay her other achievements in education and career choices and instead took pride in their own positions as girlfriends even in abusive relationships.

20. Buddhists pay respect to elderly relatives, teachers, and powerful people as they would to Buddhist monks by holding the palms together and kneeling at the person's feet with the forehead touching the feet. Such worshiping of

people was not looked down on (unless it was a nonrelated peer); instead, it was valorized by many as a sign of tradition and virtue.

21. The day I bid the workers good-bye to return to the United States they presented me with a gold pendant and a set of pillowcases. Vasanthi later informed me that Kishali was again in charge of the contribution list and that they all participated in choosing the gifts.

22. In February 2001, Kishali had an accident, which left her with a permanently disabled leg. After two months of medical leave, she had to resign from the factory because of her disability. In a letter to me, she lamented that only seven Line C workers came to see her in the hospital and even though she organized farewell gift lists for others nobody returned the favor for her.

Chapter 4

1. I faced a dilemma in identifying some activities as more political and strategic than other everyday activities. Activities such as linguistic strategies and manipulation of sentiments were so tightly interwoven into workers' everyday lives that it was after much consideration that I decided to include such activities in this chapter on political activism. The major deciding factors were the expressed or perceived intentionality and the effect on building solidarity for short- or long-term struggles.

2. Although the activities presented in this chapter were part of worker struggles, their dividing line from everyday activities was not rigid or finite.

3. Supervisors could complain to the human resources office about workers who were consistently insubordinate, and these complaints could result in warning letters and even the loss of one's job. Reports about workers who were fired based on supervisors' complaints appeared frequently in *Niveka* and *Dabindu*. Suishin, however, made much effort to hear the workers' perspectives on many issues. As the workers jokingly acknowledged, Suishin had lower courts, higher courts, appeal courts, and even a "fourth floor" (referring to the dreaded Sri Lankan Central Intelligence Department's interrogation center). These labels referred to inquiries conducted by Sanuja, Jayantha (factory manager), Perera, and then a panel of several officers.

4. As noted earlier, workers made alliances with different parties, looking for ways to maximize individual and group benefits. Line C workers sought alliances with me as a way of enhancing their bargaining power with the officers. They subtly pressured me to take their grievances to the human resources manager, thereby saving some of their bargaining chips for the future. My efforts to help them once got the whole line, including the supervisors, in trouble. They had one dirty plastic bottle to fill with water for the whole line and workers constantly complained about being thirsty. I once provided Madhu with an empty plastic bottle and then proceeded to provide any worker who asked for one with an empty plastic bottle, which they could fill. This made the use of water bottles visible to the deputy managing director and all the bottles, including the dirty old bottle, had to be thrown away!

5. In one such incident, a machine operator was fired from her job for making a sorcery threat against her supervisor and her supervisor's husband.

6. Burawoy (1979) writes about how the labor process at an agricultural equipment factory he studied was structured to manufacture consent rather than rebellion (77–94).

7. In an earlier reading of this chapter, Gananath Obeyesekere once asked why, if workers are developing class consciousness, is there no active organization geared toward collective transformative politics among the workers even though the FTZ had been in existence for more than twenty years by 1999? It is the intersecting strains of consciousness together with the particular structure of the FTZ ("forcing" workers out of the factory work after few years of employment, thus removing the threat of experienced and increasingly politically conscious workers) that made it impossible for workers to organize for collective transformational politics.

8. Rural Sinhala women from certain areas have almost no opportunity to meet Tamil people, and the FTZ did not have many Tamil workers. I came across a *Dabindu* article on a workshop conducted at a rubber estate where the majority of workers were Tamil women. According to the report, a group of FTZ workers were taken to this estate and they were deeply touched by the stories of labor and sexual oppression that the Tamil workers related. Sinhala FTZ workers shed tears along with the Tamil women; the article was appropriately titled, "Sinhala or Tamil, There is no Difference in Sorrow and Tears." I met several FTZ workers who participated in this workshop, and they eloquently expressed the need for more such opportunities to get to know Tamil women. They went on to explain how women of all groups similarly suffer from family, institutional, and state patriarchal forces.

9. "Do you think we are machines?" is an angry question that was commonly hurled at supervisors when workers were asked to work long overtime hours or produce at an impossible target rate.

10. Many times, however, I saw factory officers taking naps or just sitting on beds socializing. The secretive nature of these quick breaks was evidence of how harsh the factory discipline was even for executives. Several times I was invited to clandestine socializing at the medical center in which the three female executives along with the nurses sat on the beds and shared food or looked at photo albums.

11. In the United States, measles and chicken pox are considered childhood diseases and are not particularly dreaded. In Sri Lanka, however, these diseases are feared, so parents protect children from contracting them. As a result, any time an outbreak occurs many adults face the danger of contracting the diseases.

12. Line C workers' prominent role in the labor strike affected my relations with management and junior officers in subtle ways for a short time. The next day at breakfast Ranjan jokingly suggested, "I wonder whether it was you who fanned the unrest," and another junior officer concurred, "Yes, she aroused it and quietly stayed away." Although these comments were delivered in a playful manner, I felt uncomfortable looking at the top management table. I thought they also were suspicious of me. However, the perceived hostility from the managers and officers proved to be mere imagination because relations were just as cordial as before when I returned after the long vacation.

13. These shaming episodes appeared to be the informal punishment meted out to strikers by their immediate supervisors. What compelled the supervisors to shame women workers seemed to be their surprise at "male-like behavior" (striking, shouting slogans, collective disobedience) displayed by the women.

14. This worker, Lilani, had long been a controversial figure at Suishin because of her combative attitude toward supervisors and her fierce sense of justice. She had been transferred from line to line in a bid to accommodate

supervisors' wishes and to keep the other workers from following her. During my research, she worked on Floor 2 and thus escaped my attention until the labor strike in which she reportedly played a major part. She worked on Line C before being transferred to Floor 2, and she joined several Line C social activities. On one such occasion, I asked her why she chose to be the greeter. She said she felt uncomfortable with the silence and thought, "Even an enemy should not be ignored when he greeted you and bid you a happy New Year." I understood how she felt; I also found it difficult to remind her about the gender and class symbolism of these rituals without indirectly shaming her. Although I wanted to explore that aspect, I decided not to because of my own internalized rules of politeness.

15. The only writing by a Suishin worker that I found published was about a romantic relationship.

16. Whether they felt that way or not, other FTZ workers and NGO officials usually identified women as workers from a particular factory (i.e., as Suishin workers). The factories initiated and maintained intensification rituals that reiterated this belongingness. The factory-sponsored annual events such as the New Year party or the trip provided workers grounds on which to talk about their factory in contrast to other factories. Symbolically reiterating this belongingness, the Suishin workers were given a ceramic mug with "Suishin 2000" scripted on it to commemorate the fifth anniversary of Suishin.

17. Michael Burawoy (1979) describes how workers give consent to the exploitation of surplus labor when production relations are obscured through mechanisms such as incentives and competitions (77–94).

18. Once when I briefly visited another line, its production assistant requested that I come and study them. "My girls like to talk to you, too. It is wrong to favor only one line," he said. When the production assistant and the workers asked me to give my reasons for spending so much time with Line C, I replied that they talk much and actively sought my friendship from the beginning. But they challenged this by reminding me that it was because the table (the one I used to write my notes between work) was near them that Line C had a chance to show their interest in the first place. When I was about to leave, one worker, in a sad voice, said, "If we had a bit more space, we would have put a table here and got you to come and watch us, too."

Chapter 5

1. The creation of the FTZ brought many changes to neighboring villages. In addition to boardinghouse income, women in the area found it lucrative to provide cooked breakfast and other snacks or to sew dresses for workers. These informal economic activities surrounding FTZ employment contributed to a lifestyle change in the neighborhoods as people started to depend on FTZ workers for their primary income. In addition to economic changes, neighboring villages also saw significant social cultural change after the inception of the FTZ. Though the new economic activities increased their workload at home, women were able to achieve a certain power over family decision making by becoming co-owners of the boardinghouses. Given that the expected way to communicate with unrelated women was via women, men had to depend on their wives and mothers to play a significant role in the day-to-day running of these boardinghouses. Some mothers, however, lamented that their boy children were not in-

terested in education anymore and instead aspired to start economic activities catering to FTZ workers. Saman, in whose boardinghouse all these women stayed, and his siblings belonged to a generation that was raised in the new social cultural milieu surrounding the FTZ.

2. The women workers call the wives of the boardinghouse owners "auntie," but they pronounce it "Anti." Using the correct pronunciation shows a certain class position. I choose to use "Anti" to avoid the misrepresentation of class affiliations.

3. Groups of workers who were from the same area, got together to arrange private vans when they went home for their long vacations in April and December. These vans, unlike public transportation, picked up workers from their boardinghouses and dropped them off at their homes. Most important, the vans also transported the big pots and pans and boxes by securing them on the vehicle's roof.

4. There were areas around the FTZ in which all the houses had attached boarding rooms and small shops. Quite a few such cluster areas had specific names.

5. I rarely felt guilty about not paying Saman. But when he asked my help to find sponsors for a trip to India, I put him in touch with several companies and felt a bit relieved. Saman did not meet my friends but became more accepting of my presence thereafter.

6. I frequently accepted their invitations to eat with them. I reciprocated this by treating them to pastries or ice cream. My normal meal, however, came from the Liyanagemulla boardinghouse where I was officially a resident. The boardinghouse owner's wife supplied my lunch and dinner for a fee. I collected my lunch packet in the morning and brought it to Saman's to eat with the shift workers who were still there.

7. These conditions, common to many boardinghouses, were well-known and widely reported in the mainstream media. Health officials, however, conveniently turned a blind eye and made no routine checks on the boardinghouses.

8. I chose to refer to such words as "rough terms (*ralu*)" to delineate them from other forms of address considered more refined. Women who used these terms were especially looked down upon by the middle class as women without shame-fear.

9. Dharmapala's (1898) "The Daily Code for the Laity" included thirty rules about how women should conduct themselves, and it discouraged women from unsanitary practices at home and before others (Guruge 1963). While Anti's expectations seemed to come from these internalized protestant Buddhist ethics, the workers' playful resistance to undertaking what they thought was the landlord's obligations clearly marks a break with these teachings as well as an affiliation with individualistic capitalist ethics.

10. At first I was saddened by the way Saman and his friends invaded the women's privacy. I was also angered if a man intruded when I was at the well. But over time, I got used to the way the boardinghouse owner and the boarders playfully handled these actions. However, near the end of my stay women showed how angry they were with Saman for these intrusions. I had already brought a rented camcorder to the boardinghouse when Saman refused me permission to videotape the boardinghouse. When I told the residents about Saman's refusal, they got angry and told me to go ahead and use the camcorder because the boardinghouse belonged to them as well. Several women stationed themselves at regular intervals from the front of the house to the kitchen to alert me if

Saman was approaching and I started taping. After I finished taping the rooms, the kitchen, the well, and the toilet area, they got Saman to come to the kitchen so that I could tape the front part of the house and the boutique. Later I realized that my actions violated research ethics. But at the moment it seemed adventurous and subversive. I also did not have the heart to refuse this little satisfaction to women whose lives were daily intruded on by Saman. I could not help feeling a certain sense of justice while performing this act.

11. At the time of my research, Premasiri's boardinghouse had been featured on two television documentaries. Quite different from Saman, Premasiri not only let me take photographs and videotape his boardinghouse but actually organized and enthusiastically participated in these events.

12. The matron, her visitors, and the officers of the labor organization did not have to comply with this rule.

13. Although she did not say so, her preference was also related to staying fair. I discussed skin-color preferences briefly in Chapter 3 and discuss it further in Chapter 6.

14. Rural men and women wrote to several alternative newspapers about violence between married couples and between parents and children, suggesting that such violence was prevalent in rural areas, especially in the North Central Province.

15. Silva and Eisenberg (1996), in their study of premarital sex among Sri Lankan youth, also refer to such sexual activities, especially among Sri Lankan university students, that safeguard virginity while providing sexual gratification (6).

16. Brides were usually given a white sheet at the marriage ceremony to put on the bed and family members from both sides later inspected this sheet for the supposed "sign of purity," a red stain. Although the inspection habit is fading away among middle-class Sinhala Buddhists, the idealization of virginity at marriage does not show signs of waning.

17. Lynch (2000) writes that her conversations with workers, factory officers, and villagers about real-life incidents as well as teledramas convinced her that the "concepts of rape and consensual sex are blurred" (173). FTZ workers, however, carefully delineated the two concepts as well as the difference between abduction and rape, and date rape. Lynch's assertion could be a misreading of the Sinhala words *vinasa kala* (destroyed) and *anatha kala* (made destitute) that many women later used to identify the abandonment by their consensual sex partners.

18. The scholarly term was rarely used in popular media and sounded alienating even to me. Once I read a one-page article in the leading Sunday newspaper about two FTZ workers who committed suicide together after writing a letter about leaving the "world which does not understand our love" (*Silumina*, May 2, 1999:3). The writer skillfully conveyed the idea of a romantic relationship between the two women without ever using a specific term.

19. Hoppers are a type of crispy crêpe with a soft center made using a batter.

20. Jyoti Puri (1999) discusses how her middle-class informants were empowered by the use of the English language in discussing intimate details of their sex lives and wondered if they would have been able to express ideas on some matters if they had only used Hindi.

21. Other youth groups, including university students, also engaged in such group communication at the beginning of relationships. When I attended the university in the late 1980s and early 1990s, there was as much direct communication as group communication. It should be noted here that although occupy-

ing a "respectable public space," the majority of university students also come from rural areas.

22. Elsewhere I analyze in detail how this engagement, while being critical and transgressive, also ensures the continuation of both sexual and labor exploitation (Hewamanne, 2006).

23. Once when I was visiting another boardinghouse, a resident's family members started beating her for having an unsuitable boyfriend. She fell to the floor and her brother kept kicking her unconscious body. Thoroughly shaken, I hurried toward Saman's boardinghouse and spent the whole evening commiserating with my friends.

24. An "army deserter" is a man who has deserted his post with the armed forces and is in hiding.

25. After Kamani's third abortion, however, I was overcome with a desire to help them acquire knowledge on contraceptive methods. Knowing they resented the implications of ignorance as well as of premarital sex—and this happened whenever they were given educational material on contraceptive methods—I left such material in several rooms as if by accident. The next day most were returned to the Pollonnaruwa room where I stayed and at least two workers told my roommates to ask me to mind my own business. Thankfully the tension quickly subsided.

26. According to stories published in alternative newspapers, resorting to the excuse of being a "hypnotic medicine victim" was a common cultural explanation for seemingly "unexplainable" and severe transgressions of sexual norms.

27. Sri Lanka has one of the highest suicide rates in the world. According to Jeanne Marecek (1998), many suicides and attempted suicides resulted from matters involving love affairs. The mainstream media routinely talked about FTZ worker suicides resulting from "unwise relationships." Although women somewhat lightly threatened to commit suicide for a variety of reasons, neither workers nor NGO personnel were able to put me in touch with friends or family members of an FTZ suicide victim. This situation provides grounds to speculate whether the FTZ experience offers alternatives not available to nonmigrant, nonworking men and women in the villages.

Chapter 6

1. There is a Sinhala saying that no matter where a male child goes or whatever he does, he could take a bath and return clean. Growing up, we were told that a woman's reputation once tarnished could not be salvaged. Looking at the way men singled out garment workers for harassment, I could not help but wonder whether this symbolized a communal punishment for women who transgressed. Especially with the memory of being sprinkled with holy water at Saman's boardinghouse fresh in my mind (Chapter 5), I wondered how closely this supposedly playful activity resembled that cleansing ritual.

2. The discussions I had with the few urban, low-income shantytown dwellers during previous research showed how they tried to identify themselves with dominant middle-class values and tastes. Sheeran (1997) also reports similar tendencies among Colombo's shantytown dwellers. The few Suishin workers who were from low-income communities in Katunayake or Colombo tried to create a difference between migrant FTZ workers and themselves by more firmly embracing middle-class tastes.

3. After some time with them, I asked eight workers at Suishin and twenty residents in Saman's boardinghouse to write in a journal what they thought of me and my activities among them. We sometimes shared notes and, at the end of my stay, twelve women gave me photocopies of their notes.

4. On Sundays many peddlers visited boardinghouse areas and women bought various items such as plastic flowers, brass vases, and gold-colored "welcome" signs—items that middle-class people would not consider buying.

5. Sangeetha is a famous female movie star.

6. Miller (1993; 1995) holds that gift giving is a major instrument for enacting and furthering a commitment to family and community. Workers also bought gifts for family members and for the family home and perceived this simultaneously as an indication of their commitment to their families as well as their value as good village daughters.

7. Because many factories operated on a work-shift basis, some women remained at boardinghouses at any given time and they favored the railroad tracks to the hot, crowded boardinghouses.

8. On an average Sunday, at least ten food vendors visited, selling popsicles, fruits, sweets, fried snacks, and pickles. While all the other fun activity providers charged a little money, the NGO singers performed for free.

9. The movie *Titanic* was showing in Sri Lankan theaters at the time, and the dress mimicked the period dresses worn by western high-society women of the early twentieth century, such as that worn by the character portrayed by the female lead of the film. The dresses had a low, round neckline; a high waist; tiny sleeves, and criss-crossed ribbons in the back. The length was modified by shortening the dresses to flow just below the knee.

10. Workers constantly commented on my clothes and playfully admonished me to get some colorful clothes. In one journal note, the author used the word "mud-colored shirts" and continued that those "made it hard to decide whether they were just dirty or highly fashionable." This was an appropriate way to describe my ambivalent position in Sri Lanka: an unmarried woman, who had migrated temporarily, although to a prestigious destination, the United States.

11. Another remarkable preference was to use black nailpolish on their toes. Prior to this, I had never seen Sri Lankan women paint their toenails black.

12. The day I last visited Suishin, Line C workers presented me with a gold pendant as a farewell gift. Seeing that I felt guilty over their spending money on me, they proceeded to tell me in hushed tones that I should not feel so guilty because the pendant did not cost them that much money as its red stone is actually glass.

13. Flower-girl dresses are knee-length dresses made of pastel satin or charmeuse material. Until they start to wear saris to weddings, rural young women wear bigger versions of dresses worn by flower girls at Sri Lankan weddings. The shiny material as well as puffed sleeves, frills, beads, and embroidered flowers characterize such dresses. I heard such dresses referred to as "flower-girl dresses" only once, but I thought it was a fitting characterization, especially considering the poetic use of the term "flower" to denote virgins and what the progressive change from flower-girl dresses to FTZ dresses signified for their crafting of new subjectivities for themselves.

14. *Niveka* (August 2001) carried an article written by a member of a major advertising company who belonged to a group that toured FTZ factories promoting beauty products. The workers' refusal to be swayed by these influences

marked a local response to modernity and global practices that were sweeping the middle class off their feet.

15. Jayamanne (1992) broadly identified these two strains as generic cinema and films that blur the simple binary oppositions that characterize generic cinema (57).

16. Diehl (1998) reports that Tibetan refugees of all ages were torn by their enthusiastic consumption of Indian pop music and that even the Buddhist monks secretly craved popular music (317–18). Similarly, Sri Lankans belonging to all classes demonstrate intense, conflicted feelings about enjoying *baila*. Although it is still derided because it threatens cultural purity, *baila* music has been incorporated into leisure activities as "party time music"—that is, as a harmless source of enjoyment as long as one does not forget the "true culture."

17. Sheeran (1997) also notes that many express a preference for soft classical music to save face (233).

18. For example, one of her songs translates as follows: "O, Krishna, in this beautiful bed I am like a she-bear who has lost her cubs. Even the river Yamuna is shaken thinking about our former sexual games. . . . Harassed by the king of physical desire, the youthful body does not allow any rest." The whole song is written in scholarly and metaphoric Sinhala and Sanskrit, perhaps a prudent ploy, considering that the song would have been banned if it were written in everyday Sinhala. Although the song conveyed a message close to their hearts, none of the FTZ workers was able to decipher the erotic content, and the song failed to catch on. It was also important to notice that this song was used for Sinhalacized *bharatha natyam* (Indian classical dance), which was popular among middle-class young women. When these young women expressed sexual frustrations through sanitized movements and lyrics on national television and in prestigious theaters, it was applauded as high culture. However, FTZ workers are reviled for expressing the same emotions through *baila* at their factory parties.

19. The song was heavy with symbolic meaning in that the *sari*, introduced and maintained as a mark of respectability, is torn by the protagonists to use as curtains—perhaps to cover the sexual activities that followed their elopement. One wonders if the woman is ridiculing the middle-class categories of respectability and promiscuity by pointing out the ways in which this respectable costume has been used to cover up lapses in ideal behavior.

20. This information is based on conversations with the vocalist. I am grateful to Nirmala Herath for providing me with several opportunities to talk to Nanda Malini.

21. This is important because middle-class women were apprehensive about men appropriating and parodying the song. I thank Rohinie Kularathne and Shamila Asiri for reporting two such incidents related to a university pleasure trip and an office trip.

22. This was the only time I visited the RAC workers. Nalini could well have been attempting to save the reputation of RAC and its workers. It is also noteworthy that Nalini's reasoning that the female dancer was "crazy" (that she forgot how to behave) closely resembles the hypnotic medication explanation given about the extreme sexual transgressions at Saman's boardinghouse.

23. All three of these dance forms followed themes that depicted typical female activities and, in the case of *bharatha natyam*, stories that focused on stereotypical women's roles. Low-country dancing usually included dance sequences featuring paddy work, transporting water, and so on. An advanced student in

low-country dancing must learn dances associated with healing rituals (*balithovil* and *shanthi karma*) that required more unrestrained movement. Though the dances were highly choreographed, they did not have as much prestige as the other forms.

24. Although the parties provided opportunities to transgress, no worker reflected on the way the factories structure their leisure time by organizing these parties and trips. When asked, the workers did not identify factory parties as a capitalist strategy or think the activities might hinder their efforts to resist exploitation.

25. More opportunities to do such pushing and forcing occurred when FTZ workers went on trips. The few men workers and the women usually danced precariously balanced on the floor of the bus. Whenever a sharp turn was taken or brakes applied hard, which was often, men and women laughingly bumped into each other and men held women a little longer even after the bus steadied. The women's blushing cheeks and happy laughter, as well as the men's straying hands, demonstrated that they approved of the rough driving.

26. Obeyesekere (1978) asserts that the increasing popularity of the fast-paced erotic-ecstatic *kavadi* dancing (religious dancing in honor of god *Skanda*) results from the sexual frustrations in modern Sri Lanka. According to Obeyesekeve, the prevalent sexual repression and the internalization of aggression have led to a widespread hysterical disposition among Sri Lankans (473). Although Obeyesekere states that in 1978 *kavadi* dancing was enormously popular among people of all classes (475), by 2000, *kavadi* had been replaced by western and *baila* musical shows.

27. A Thai Buddhist missionary group was attempting to reach FTZ workers and they provided transportation to attend religious meetings in a Negombo tourist hotel and treated the workers to a delicious Thai meal. During my research, residents of one boardinghouse attended three such meetings. They laughingly admitted, though, that it was the opportunity to socialize and enjoy the free trip and lunch that made them attend the meetings.

28. *Bodhi puja* (bodhi tree worship), includes bathing the *bodhi* tree (*ficus religiosa*) with water and offering flags, flower garlands, and gold necklaces.

29. Stirrat (1992) found that the devotees of popular Catholic shrines belonged to disparate social backgrounds such as the urban upper middle classes, urban slum dwellers, and people from impoverished rural areas. It should be noted that Sri Lanka has seen enormous social and cultural change after Obeyesekere's work (and even after the work of Seneviratne and Wickramaratne and Stirrat). It would be interesting to look at whether the people they studied still follow *bhakthi* devotionalism or are also responding to changes in the economy and the media and perhaps developing similar tastes as the FTZ workers. I suspect that while, as young, working-class people living in urban areas, they develop similar preferences at a general level, the special location of FTZ workers as migrant women (not quite urban, not quite rural, and certainly not male) shapes their tastes and preferences differently from the male, urban proletariat that Obeyesekere studied and the urban, middle-class youth that Seneviratne and Wickramaratne focused on.

30. They, in fact, made vows at any place with religious significance or famed for miraculous powers, including Catholic churches and Hindu temples.

31. In the 1980s and 1990s, many Buddhist temples, including some ancient temples, became commercialized around a monk or some other symbol. Nikaveratiya and Dolukanda, both ancient temples, were two among several that were

reputed for miracles. Women talked about these temples in their boarding-houses and planned, but failed, to visit them.

32. The three-wheeler taxi driver who drove Sujani and me to a famous shrine (*devale*) in Negambo told us that he took garment workers to this shrine every-day and that they called it the "garment *devale.*" There were many women wait-ing to see the ritual specialist that day and, except one, they were all either FTZ workers or workers from garment factories in the vicinity.

33. Rumors circulated also about middle-class women committing sexual transgressions with Buddhist monks as well as with male laity through their "re-spectable temple activities."

34. Although at the two Katunayake temples a significant portion of the laity consisted of FTZ workers, no member represented them in the Lay Trustees' Council or in women's societies.

Chapter 7

1. Goffman (1959) asserts that when people *give off* impressions of themselves in a particular way they can select an appropriate *front* from several available to them. When an actor uses a certain front in a performance, it might or might not be intentional or conscious (18). Although the sisters' actions seemed well designed to create a particular impression, I was not sure whether they planned these actions beforehand. Although some of their actions may have been habit-ual acts associated with a certain environment, their involving me as a "prop" in their performance certainly seemed well designed.

2. The city woman had been portrayed in films (and in many other sources) as a short-haired, trouser-wearing, loud-mouthed person, while the village woman was portrayed as one who is dressed in simple clothes, wears her hair in a knot, and displays shy smiles and downcast eyes (Abeysekera 1989; 1998).

3. I visited several workers' villages in the Southern, North Western, and Cen-tral provinces and discerned similar symbolic changes of clothing and hairstyle. During earlier research, I found that returned Middle Eastern migrants also used clothes to express their resistance and accommodation. When migrant re-turnees wore the long black garments they received from their Middle Eastern employers at home, it registered their new status and showed defiance to the es-tablished norms of attire (Hewamanne 1997). FTZ workers' reluctance to chal-lenge village norms seemed to result from their status as young, unmarried women who had to come back to get married to village men. Given the impor-tance accorded virginity and reputation, the young women had to keep up ap-pearances at least until they could contract a good marriage.

4. I have noted an incident similar to this in which a young, unmarried Mid-dle Eastern migrant wore an old school uniform to signal her unchanged "pure innocence." This action pacified the elders, males, and elites who were nervous about how she might contaminate the village. Her action, however, brought her much admiration and allowed her more space to maneuver her newfound wealth and knowledge (Hewamanne 1997; 2000).

5. According to Bourdieu (1977), habitus is a system of lasting transposable dispositions that integrates past experiences to become present nature. It pro-duces thoughts, expressions, actions, and practices that are common to all within the same habitus (72–95). Village women who migrated have confronted other structures and, as a result, started to question the former habitus. While

they were back in the village, though, they performed according to the shared worldview of the group, thereby easily conforming to the practices already generated by the habitus.

6. It should be noted here that I got to know Mala and Karuna at Saman's boardinghouse and that I had never seen them at their work environments. During my visit to the village, I was pleasantly surprised to see Leela's understanding and accepting attitude toward some transgressions that her daughters related when no one else was present.

7. Although I did not see them dancing, both of them showed me photographs from previous parties in which they appeared in dancing poses while dressed in all their FTZ finery.

8. I have never told them anything to this effect.

9. According to Bourdieu (1977), one way the dominant classes accumulate symbolic capital is by collecting luxury goods that attest to the taste and distinction of their owner (197). My show of this one luxury item, however, was necessitated by practical reasons, especially given the village's close proximity to the border with the war-torn Eastern Province.

Chapter 8

1. Another worker, whose house I visited in Weligama, explained that she usually threw away the color-faded underwear rather than bring it to the village. Women in her house hang their underwear outside the house, although it is hidden behind a thatched fence that covers part of the kitchen. She, therefore, worries about the higher cut of the panties she bought in the FTZ bazaar with phrases such as "kiss me," "I love you," or "You belong to me" printed on them.

2. Gananath Obeyesekere via personal correspondence, reminded me that Dharmapala's prescription of white as the appropriate color for women's attire did not catch on because it was considered the traditional color of mourning. The overwhelming preference for pastel colors in women's everyday wear seems to be a compromise that many could accept as befitting the spiritual, restrained, newly independent women active in the public sphere. This becomes even more telling when considering the vibrant and colorful choices available to women on the Indian subcontinent.

3. The empowerment I felt and recorded while among the workers was not an absolute sense of empowerment that makes them authors of their own lives (assuming such a condition is even possible). Rather, it consists of what they have achieved through their encounter with global cultural flows as opposed to the opportunities they would have had if they had not migrated for FTZ work.

4. These letters are written in Sinhala. The translations are mine.

Epilogue

1. *News Hour with Jim Lehrer*, http://www.pbs.org/newshour/bb/economy/july-dec03/textile9–23.html (accessed September 23, 2003).

2. At this woman's request, I changed the previously used pseudonym to minimize the risk of her being identified.

3. At this woman's request, I changed the previously used pseudonym to minimize the risk of her being identified.

4. She said this in June 2005; in July 2006, she gave birth to a son.

5. In October 2005, I received a letter from Sujatha announcing that her parents had found a suitable husband for her and that they would marry on November 21, 2005. In November 2006, she informed me that she was six months' pregnant with their first child.

6. The health worker was attached to a project jointly organized by the Health Ministry and an NGO.

7. They were, in fact, grateful to me for two meetings at the junction before I started the research. Because their husbands and in-laws knew about me, it was easy for them to get permission to leave home.

8. It seems that the women had sole access to the *almirah*, which usually they brought to the marital residence as part of the dowry. All five of the married women kept the key with them, while two even went so far as to hide it.

Bibliography

Abeysekera, Sunila. 1989. Women in Sri Lankan Cinema. *Framework* 37:49–58.
———. 1998. Women, Sexuality, the City, and the Village. *Pravada* 5(4–5):39–42.
———.1998a. Fifty Years of Cinema in Sri Lanka: Looking Back, Moving Forward. *Options* 13(1): 2–6.
Abu-Lughod, Lila, and Catherine, Lutz. 1990. Introduction: Emotion, Discourse, and the Politics of Everyday Life. In *Language and the Politics of Emotion*, ed. Catherine Lutz and Lila Abu-Lughod. Cambridge: Cambridge University Press.
Amunugama, Sarath. 1979. Ideology and Class Interest in One of Piyadasa Sirisena's Novels: The New Image of the "Sinhala Buddhist" Nationalist. In *Collective Identities: Nationalism and Protest in Modern Sri Lanka*, ed. Michael Roberts. Colombo: Marga Institute.
———. 1991. A Sinhala Buddhist "Babu": Anagarika Dharmapala (1864–1933) and the Bengal Connection. *Social Science Information* 30(3):555–91.
Appadurai, Arjun. 1990. Topographies of the Self: Praise and Emotion in Hindu India. In *Language and the Politics of Emotion*, ed. Catherine Lutz and Lila Abu-Lughod. Cambridge: Cambridge University Press.
———. 2000. Grassroots Globalization and the Research Imagination. *Public Culture* 12(1):1–19.
Bartholomeusz, Tessa. 1994. *Women under the Bo Tree: Buddhist Nuns in Sri Lanka*. Cambridge: Cambridge University Press.
Binning, Robert. 1857. *A Journal of Two Years Travel in Percia, Ceylon*. London: William Allen and Company.
Blackburn, Robin, and Michael Mann. 1975. Ideology in the Non-Skilled Working Class. In *Working Class Images of Society*, ed. M. Blumer. London: Routledge.
Board of Investment of Sri Lanka. N.d. Document series. Columbo: Board of Investment of Sri Lanka.
Bourdieu, Pierre. 1977. *Outline of a Theory of Practice*. Cambridge: Cambridge University Press.
Boyd, Hugh. 1800. *The Miscellaneous Works of Hugh Boyd with an Account of His Life and Writings by Lawrence Dundas Campbell*. London: T Cadell, Jr., and W. Davies.
Brochman, Grete. 1993. *Middle East Avenue: Female Migration from Sri Lanka to the Gulf*. Boulder, Colo.: Westview Press.

Brow, James. 1996. *Demons and Development: The Struggle for Community in a Sri Lankan Village.* Tucson: University of Arizona Press.

———. 1999. Utopia's New-Found Space: Images of the Village Community in the Early Writings of Ananda Kumaraswamy. *Modern Asian Studies* 33(1):67–86.

Burawoy, Michael. 1979. *Manufacturing Consent: Changes in the Labor Process under Monopoly Capitalism.* Chicago: University of Chicago Press.

Chakrabarty, Dipesh. 1989. *Rethinking Working-Class History: Bengal, 1890–1940.* Princeton, N.J.: Princeton University Press.

Chatterjee, Partha. 1993. *The Nation and Its Fragments: Colonial and Post Colonial Histories.* Princeton, N.J.: Princeton University Press.

Comaroff, J. 1990. Goodly Beasts and Beastly Goods: Cattle and Commodities in a South African Context. *American Ethnologist* 17:195–216.

Cordiner, James. 1807. *A Description of Ceylon.* London: Longman, Rees and Orme.

Cravey, Altha J. 1998. *Women and Work in Mexico's Maquiladoras.* Lanham, Md.: Rowman and Littlefield.

Cummings, Constance. 1892. *Two Happy Years in Ceylon.* London: William Blackwood.

Dabindu Collective. 1989. *Prathiba.* Boralesgamuwa: CRC Press.

———. 1997. *A Review of Free Trade Zones in Sri Lanka.* Boralesgamuwa: CRC Press.

Davy, John. 1821. *An Account of the Interior of Ceylon.* Dehiwala: Tisara Prakasakayo.

De Alwis, Malathi. 1995. Gender, Politics and the "Respectable Lady." In *Unmaking the Nation: The Politics of Identity and History in Modern Sri Lanka*, ed. Pradeep Jeganathan and Qadri Ismail. Colombo: Social Scientists' Association.

———. 1997. The Production and Embodiment of Respectability: Gendered Demeanors in Colonial Ceylon. In *Sri Lanka Collective Identities Revisited*, ed. Michael Roberts. Colombo: Marga Institute.

———. 1998. Maternalistic Politics in Sri Lanka: A Historical Anthropology of Its Conditions of Possibility. Ph.D. diss., University of Chicago.

De Certeau, M. 1988. *The Practice of Everyday Life.* Berkeley: University of California Press.

Deleuze, Gilles, and Felix Guattari. 1983. *Anti Oedipus: Capitalism and Schizophrenia.* Minneapolis: University of Minnesota Press.

Devaraja, Lorna. 1991. The Position of Women in Buddhism with Special Reference to PreColonial Sri Lanka. Manuscript.

DeVotta, Neil. 2004. *Blow Back: Linguistic Nationalism, Institutional Decay and Ethnic Conflict in Sri Lanka.* Stanford, Calif.: Stanford University Press.

Diehl, Keila M. 1998. Echoes from Dharmasala: Music in the Lives of Tibetan Refugees in North India. Ph.D.diss., University of Texas.

Dublin, Thomas. 1981. *Farm to Factory: Women's Letters, 1830–1860.* New York: Columbia University Press.

Enstad, Nan. 1999. *Ladies of Labor, Girls of Adventure: Working Women, Popular Culture and Labor Politics at the Turn of the Twentieth Century.* New York: Columbia University Press.

Fantasia, Rick. 1988. *Cultures of Solidarity: Consciousness, Action and Contemperory American Workers.* Berkeley: University of California Press.

Fedric Ebert Stiftung. 1997. *Diriya Diyaniyo.* Colombo: Fedric Ebert Stiftung.

Fernandes, Leela. 1997. *Producing Workers: The Politics of Gender, Class and Culture in the Culcutta Jute Mills*. Philadelphia: University of Pennsylvania Press.

Fernandez-Kelly, Maria Patricia. 1983. *For We Are Sold, I and My People*. Albany: State University of New York Press.

Fine, Janice, with Matthew Howard. 1995. Women in the Free Trade Zones of Sri Lanka. *Dollars and Sense* November/December:26–27, 39–40.

Forbes, Jonathan. 1841. *Eleven Years in Ceylon*. London: Richard Bentley.

Foucault, Michel. 1973. *The Birth of the Clinic: An Archaeology of Medical Perception*. New York: Vintage.

———. 1978. *The History of Sexuality, Volume 1*. New York: Vintage.

———. 1979. *Discipline and Punish: The Birth of the Prison*. New York: Vintage.

Gamburd, Michele. 2000. *The Kitchen Spoon's Handle: Transnationalism and Sri Lanka's Migrant Housemaids*. Ithaca, N.Y.: Cornell University Press.

Gilroy, Paul. 1993. *The Black Atlantic: Modernity and Double Consciousness*. Cambridge, Mass.: Harvard University Press.

Goffman, Erving. 1959. *The Presentation of Self in Everyday Life*. New York: Doubleday.

———. 1963. *Stigma: Notes on the Management of Spoiled Identity*. Englewood Cliffs, N.J.: Prentice Hall.

Gombrich, Richard, and Gananath Obeyesekere. 1988. *Buddhism Transformed*. Princeton, N.J.: Princeton University Press.

Gramsci, Antonio. 1971. *Selections from the Prison Notebooks of Antonio Gramsci*. New York: International Publishers.

Grossholtz, Jean. 1984. *Forging Capitalist Patriarchy: The Economic and Social Transformation of Feudal Sri Lanka and Its Impact on Women*. Durham, N.C.: Duke University Press.

Gunasekera, Manisha. 1994. The Splintering of Aladdin's Myth: Education, Occupational Mobility and the Social Context. *Options* 2:17–20.

Guruge, Ananda. 1963. *Dharmapala Lipi*. Colombo: Government Press.

———. 1965. *Anagarika Dharmapala: Return to Righteousness*. Colombo: Government Press.

Hall, Stuart. 1986. Gramsci's Relevance for the Study of Race and Ethnicity. *Journal of Communication Inquiry* 10(2):5–27.

———. 1995. Fantasy, Identity and Politics. In *Cultural Remix: Theories of Politics and the Popular*, ed. Erica Cater, James Donald, and Judith Squires. London: Lawrence and Wishart.

———. 1996. The Question of Cultural Identity. In *Modernity: An Introduction to Modern Societies*, ed. Stuart Hall, David Held, Don Hubert, and Kenneth Thompson. Oxford: Blackwell.

———. 2000. Introduction. In *Questions of Cultural Identity*, ed. Stuart Hall and Paul DuGay. London: Sage.

Hall, Stuart, and Tony Jefferson, eds. 1975. *Resistance Through Ritual: Youth Subcultures in Post-War Britain*. London: Hutchinson.

Haney, Peter. 1999. Fantasia and Disobedient Daughters: Undistressing Genres and Reinventing Traditions in the Mexican American Carpa. *Journal of American Folklore* 112:437–49.

Harris, Elizabeth. 1994. *The Gaze of the Colonizer: British Views on Local Women in 19th Century Sri Lanka*. Colombo: Social Scientists' Association.

Hayley, F. A. 1923. *A Treatise on the Laws and Customs of the Sinhalese, Including Portions Still Surviving Under the Name of Kandyan Law*. Colombo: Cave and Company.

Hebdige, D. 1988. Object as Image: The Italian Scooter Cycle. In *Hiding in the Light*, ed. D. Hebdige. London: Routledge.

Hettiarachchi, T. 1991. Some Aspects of Social Problems Related to Export Promotion. *University of Colombo Review* 10:42–59.

Hewamanne, Sandya. 1997. Migration as Resistance to Paternalistic Control: Recovering the Lost Voice. Master's thesis, University of Texas at Austin.

———. 2000. Resistance, Contradictions and "Agency" among Sri Lanka's Migrant Housemaids. *Asian Women* 11:109–36.

———. 2002. Uneasy Alliances: Sri Lankan Factory Workers' Writings on Political Change *SAGAR* 8:1–7.

———. 2003. Performing Disrespectability: New Tastes, Cultural Practices, and Identity Performances by Sri Lanka's Free Trade Zone Garment Factory Workers. *Cultural Dynamics* 15(1):71–101.

———. 2006. Pornographic Voice: Critical Feminist Practices among Sri Lanka's Garment Factory Workers. *Feminist Studies* 32(1):125–54.

———. Forthcoming. City of Whores: Nationalism, Development and Female Garment Workers of Sri Lanka. *Social Text*.

Hewamanne, Sandya, and James Brow. 1999. "If They Allow Us We Will Fight": Strains of Consciousness among Women Workers in the Katunayake Free Trade Zone. *Anthropology of Work Review* 19(3):8–13.

Jayamanne, Laleen. 1992. Hunger for Images, Myths of Femininity in Sri Lankan Cinema 1947–1989. *South Asia Bulletin* 21(1):57–75.

Jayawardena, Kumari, and Swarna Jayaweera. 1986. *A Profile on Sri Lanka: The Integration of Women in Development Planning*. Colombo: Women's Education Center.

Jayaweera, Swarna. 1990. Women and Development: A Reappraisal of the Sri Lanka Experience. In *The Hidden Face of Development: Women, Work and Equality in Sri Lanka*, ed. Center for Women's Research. Colombo: Center for Women's Research.

Jeganathan, Pradeep. 1997. After a Riot: Anthropological Locations of Violence in an Urban Sri Lankan Community. Ph.D. diss., University of Chicago.

Jobson, Fedrick. 1862. *Australia; With Notes by the way, On Egypt, Ceylon, Bombay and the Holy Land*. London: Hamilton, Adams and Company.

Kaplan, Fred. 1987. *Sacred Tears: Sentimentality in Victorian Literature*. Princeton, N.J.: Princeton University Press.

Knighton, William. 1854. *Forest Life in Ceylon*. London: Hurst and Blackett.

Kondo, Dorinne. 1990. *Crafting Selves: Power Gender and Discourses of Identity in a Japanese Work Place*. Chicago: University of Chicago Press.

———. 1997. *About Face: Performing Race in Fashion and Theater*. New York: Routledge.

Lamphere, Louise. 1987. *From Working Daughters to Working Mothers: Immigrant Women in a New England Industrial Community*. Ithaca, N.Y.: Cornell University Press.

Langdon, Samuel. 1890. *My Happy Valley*. London: Charles H. Kelly.

Lee, Ching Kwan. 1998. *Gender and the South China Miracle: Two Worlds of Factory Women*. Berkeley: University of California Press.

Limón, José E. 1989. Carne, Carnales, and the Carnivalesque: Bakhtinian Batos, Disorder, and Narrative Discourses, *American Ethnologist* 16(3):471–86.

Little, David. 1994. *Sri Lanka: The Invention of Enmity*. Washington D.C.: United States Institute of Peace Press.

Lynch, Caitrin. 1999. The "Good Girls" of Sri Lankan Modernity: Moral Orders of Nationalism and Capitalism. *Identities* 6(1):55–89.

———. 2000. The Good Girls of Sri Lankan Modernity: Moral Orders of Nationalism, Gender and Globalization in Village Garment Factories. Ph.D. diss., University of Chicago.

Malalgoda, Kitsiri. 1976. *Buddhism in Sinhalese Society 1750–1900.* Berkeley: University of California Press.

Mann, Richard. 1993. *International Investor Guide to Sri Lanka.* Ontario: Gateway.

Marecek, Jeanne. 1998. Culture, Gender and Suicidal Behavior in Sri Lanka. *Suicide and Life-Threatening Behavior* 28:69–81.

Marshall, Gordon. 1983. Some Remarks on the Study of Working Class Consciousness. *Politics and Society* 12(3):263–301.

Martin, Biddy, and Chandra T. Mohanty. 1986. Feminist Politics: What's Home Got to Do with It? In *Feminist Studies/Critical Studies,* ed. Teresa Delauretis. Bloomington: Indiana University Press.

Mayol, Pierre. 1998. Living. In *The Practice of Everyday Life,* ed. M. De Certeau, L. Giard, and P. Mayol. Minneapolis: University of Minnesota Press.

McClintock, Anne. 1995. *Imperial Leather: Race, Gender and Sexuality in the Colonial Conquest.* New York: Routledge.

McNay, L. 1994. *Foucault: A Critical Introduction.* Cambridge: Polity Press.

Miller, David. 1993. Christmas against Materialism in Trinidad. In *Unwrapping Christmas,* ed. David Miller. Oxford: Oxford University Press.

———. 1995. Consumption and Commodities. *Annual Review of Anthropology* 24:141–61.

Mills, Mary Beth. 1997. Contesting the Margins of Modernity: Women, Migration and Consumption in Thailand. *American Ethnologist* 24(1):37–61.

———. 1998. Gendered Encounters with Modernity: Labor Migrants and Marriage Choices in Contemporary Thailand. *Identities* 5(3):301–34.

———. 1999. *Thai Women in the Global Labor Force: Consuming Desires, Contested Selves.* New Brunswick, N.J.: Rutgers University Press.

Moore, Mick. 1985. *The State and Peasant Politics in Sri Lanka.* Cambridge: Cambridge University Press.

Morris, Rosalind. 1995. All Made Up: Performance Theory and the New Anthropology of Sex and Gender. *Annual Review of Anthropology* 24:567–92.

Narayan, Kirin. 1993. How Native Is a Native Anthropologist? *American Anthropologist* 95(3):671–87.

Nash, June. 1979. *We Eat the Mines and the Mines Eat Us: Dependency and Exploitation in Bolivian Tin Mines.* New York: Columbia University Press.

Nash, June, and Maria Fernandez-Kelly, eds. 1983. *Women, Men and the International Division of Labor.* Albany: State University of New York Press.

Nissan, Elizabeth, and R. L. Stirrat. 1990. The Generation of Communal Identities. In *Sri Lanka: History and the Roots of Conflict,* ed. Jonathan Spencer. London: Routledge.

Obeyesekere, Gananath. 1963. The Great Tradition and the Little in the Perspective of Sinhala Buddhism. *Journal of Asian Studies* 22(2):139–53.

———. 1970. Religious Symbolism and Political Change in Ceylon. *Modern Ceylon Studies* 1(1):43–63.

———. 1975. Sorcery, Premeditated Murder, and the Canalization of Aggression in Sri Lanka. *Ethnology* 14(1):1–23.

———. 1978. The Fire Walkers of Kataragama: The Rise of Bhakti Religiosity in Buddhist Sri Lanka. *Journal of Asian Studies* 37(3):457–76.

———. 1979. The Vicissitudes of the Sinhala-Buddhist Identity through Time and Change. In *Collective Identities: Nationalism and Protest in Modern Sri Lanka*, ed. Michael Roberts. Colombo: Marga Institute.

———. 1981. *Medusa's hair: An Essay on Personal Symbols and Religious Experience*. Chicago: University of Chicago Press.

———. 1984. *The Cult of the Goddess Pattini*. Chicago: University of Chicago Press.

Ochs, Elinor, and Lisa Caps. 1996. Narrating the Self. *Annual Review of Anthropology* 25:19–43.

Ong, Aihwa. 1987. *Spirits of Resistance and Capitalist Discipline: Factory Women in Malaysia*. Albany: State University of New York Press.

———. 1991. The Gender and Labor Politics of Postmodernity. *Annual Review of Anthropology* 20:279–309.

Peiris, Ralph. 1956. *Sinhalese Social Organization*. Colombo: Ceylon University Press.

Peiss, Kathy. 1986. *Cheap Amusements: Working Women and Leisure in Turn of the Century New York*. Philadelphia: Temple University Press.

Pena, Devon. 1997. *The Terror of the Machine: Technology, Work, Gender and Ecology on the U.S.-Mexico Border*. Austin: University of Texas Press.

Percival, Robert. 1803. *An Account of the Island of Ceylon: Containing Its History, Geography, Natural History with the Manners and Customs*. London: Baldwin.

Perera, Nirosha Priyani. 1995. Girl of the Zone. *Dabindu*. June: 5.

Prieto, Norma. 1997. *Beautiful Flowers of the Maquiladora: Life Histories of Women Workers in Tijuana*. Austin: University of Texas Press.

Puri, Jyoti. 1999. *Woman, Body, Desire in Post-Colonial India: Narratives of Gender and Sexuality*. New York: Routledge.

Rajasingham-Senanayake, Darini. 1997. The Sinhala *Kaduwa*: Language as a Double Edged Sword and Ethnic Conflict. *Pravada* 5(2):15–20.

Reagon, Bernice Johnson. 1983. Coalition Politics: Turning the Century. In *Home Girls: A Black Feminist Anthology*, ed. Barbara Smith. New York: Kitchen Table Women of Color Press.

Reed, Susan A. 1998. The Politics and Poetics of Dance. *Annual Review of Anthropology* 27:503–32.

Risseeuw, Carla. 1988. *The Fish Don't Talk about the Water: Gender Transformation Power and Resistance among Women in Sri Lanka*. Leiden: E. J. Brill.

Rofel, Lisa. 1999. *Other Modernities: Gendered Yearnings in China after Socialism*. Berkeley: University of California Press.

Rosa, Kumudhini. 1982. Problems Facing Organizations Working within the Free Trade Zone in Comparison to Those Working Outside the Free Trade Zone Area. *Voice of Women* 4:8–9.

———. 1990. Women Workers' Strategies of Organizing and Resistance in the Sri Lankan Free Trade Zone (FTZ). *South Asia Bulletin* 10(1):33–43.

Rutnam, S. C. K. 1899. *Race Antagonism in Christian Missions*. Colombo: Star Press.

Salaff, J. 1981. *Working Daughters of Hong Kong*. Cambridge: Cambridge University Press.

Salzinger, Leslie. 1997. From High Heels to Swathed Bodies: Gendered Meanings under Production in Mexico's Export Processing Industry. *Feminist Studies* 23:549–71.

———. 2003. *Genders in Production: Making Workers in Mexico's Global Factories*. Berkeley: University of California Press.

Samaraweera, Vijaya. 1978. The "Village Community" and Reform in Colonial Sri Lanka. *Ceylon Journal of Historical and Social Studies* 8:68–75.

Sandoval, Chela. 1991. U.S. Third World Feminism: The Theory and Method of Oppositional Consciousness in the Postmodern World. *Genders* 10(Spring):1–24.

Savigliano, Martha. 1995. *Tango and the Political Economy of Passion.* Boulder: Westview.

Schiller, Herbert. 1989. *Culture Inc.: The Corporate Takeover of Public Expression.* Oxford: Oxford University Press.

Schrijvers, Joke. 1988. Blueprint for Undernourishment: The Mahaweli River Development Scheme in Sri Lanka. In *Structures of Patriarchy: State, Community and Household in Modernising Asia,* ed. Bina Agrawal. London: ZED.

Scott, James. 1985. *Weapons of the Weak: Everyday Forms of Peasant Resistance.* New Haven, Conn.: Yale University Press.

Seizer, Susan. 2000. Roadwork: Offstage with Special Drama Actresses in Tamilnadu, South India. *Cultural Anthropology* 15(2):217–59.

Selkirk, James. 1844. *Recollections of Ceylon After a Residence of Nearly Thirteen Years.* London: J. Hatchard and Sons.

Selvadurai, A. J. 1976. Land, Personhood and Sorcery in a Sinhalese Village. *Journal of Asian and African Studies* 11(1–2):82–101.

Seneviratne, H. L., and Swarna Wickramaratne. 1980. Bodhi Puja: Collective Representations of Sri Lanka Youth. *American Ethnologist* 4:734–43.

Sheeran, Ann. 1997. White Noise: European Modernity, Sinhala Musical Nationalism, and the Practice of a Creole Popular Music in Modern Sri Lanka. Ph.D. diss., University of Washington.

Siddiqi, Dina. 1996. Women in Question: Gender and Labor in Bangladeshi Factories. Ph.D. diss., University of Michigan.

Silumina. May 2, 1999, p. 3.

Silva, K. Tudor, and Merrill Eisenberg. 1996. Attitude Towards Pre-marital Sex in a Sample of Sri Lankan Youth. Paper presented at the National Convention on Women's Studies, Center for Women's Research, Sri Lanka.

Siriwardene, Kalinga. 1996. Sri Lankan Women Get a Raw Deal. *Third World Net* January 16.

Siriwardene, Reggie. 1990. The Choice before the Intelligentsia—Jathika Chintanaya or Multi-Culturalism. *The Island* January 14.

Sirr, Henry Charles. 1850. *Ceylon and the Cingalese.* London: William Shoberl.

Smith, Helen. 1993. Health Survey of Women Workers in the Katunayake Free Trade Zone. *Voice of Women* 4(13):7–11.

Spivak, Gayatri. 1988. Can the Subaltern Speak? *Marxism and the Interpretation of Cultures,* ed. C. Nelson and L. Grossberg. Urbana: University of Illinois Press.

Striffler, Steve. 1999. Wedded to Work: Class Struggle and Gendered Identities in the Restructuring of the Ecuadorian Banana Industry. *Identities* 6:91–120.

Stirrat, R. L. 1988. *On the Beach: Fishermen, Fishwives, and Fish Traders in Post-Colonial Sri Lanka.* Delhi: Hindustan.

———. 1992. *Power and Religiosity in a Post-Colonial Setting: Sinhala Catholics in Contemporary Sri Lanka.* Cambridge: Cambridge University Press.

Tambiah, Stanley. 1992. *Buddhism Betrayed? Religion, Politics and Violence in Sri Lanka.* Chicago: University of Chicago Press.

Tarlo, Emma. 1996. *Clothing Matters: Dress and Identity in India.* Chicago: University of Chicago Press.

Thompson, Edward. 1963. *The Making of the English Working Class.* New York: Vintage.

Toren, C. 1989. Drinking Cash: The Purification of Money in Ceremonial Exchange in Fiji. *Money and the Morality of Exchange*, ed. M. Bloch and J. Parry. Cambridge: Cambridge University Press.

Umble, D. 1992. The Amish and the Telephone, Resistance and Reconstruction. *Consuming Technologies*, ed. R. Silverstone and E. Hirsch. London: Routledge.

Visweswaran, Kamala. 1994. *Fictions of Feminist Ethnography*. Minneapolis: University of Minnesota Press.

Voice of Women. 1982. Women in the Free Trade Zone. *Voice of Women* 4(July):5–7.

Willis, Paul. 1993. Symbolic Creativity. *Studying Culture: An Introductory Reader*, ed. A. Gray and J. McGuigan. London: Edward Arnold.

Wolf, Diane. 1992. *Factory Daughters: Gender, Household Dynamics, and Rural Industrialization in Java*. Berkeley: University of California Press.

Index

Acknowledgments

Many people have contributed to the publication of this book. I am immensely grateful to them all, but several need special mention. Foremost of this group is Kirin Narayan, who encouraged me to write the book I would most love to read. In September 2005, she sent me an e-mail containing six gems of advice, an enlarged copy of which still adorns my office wall and will inspire and guide me through much academic writing in the years ahead. I am most grateful to Kirin for her support, encouragement, and inspiration throughout this project.

I have always been fortunate to have been guided by great mentors who continue to support me. I owe much to James Brow for believing in me and providing unfailing support throughout. For intellectual inspiration, insight, and generosity, I will always be immensely grateful. But my biggest debt to James is for showing me how to be a great scholar, teacher, and mentor. I owe special thanks to Kamala Visweswaran, Polly Strong, Kamran Ali, and Siri Hettige for intellectual inspiration and guidance. I am grateful to Polly and Kamran for many years of support and friendship.

I am privileged to have had Gananath Obeyesekere, the doyen of Sri Lankan anthropology, as a reader, and this book is much better thanks to his valuable suggestions. I am humbled by his kindness, generosity, and support throughout my career.

Most of all, I am hugely indebted to all the FTZ women workers in the Suishin factory and boardinghouses for accepting, supporting, and tolerating me during 1999–2000 when I did my field research. Many still welcome me to their homes whenever I return to Sri Lanka. To protect confidentiality I refrain from naming these women, who have become close friends and extended me kindness, friendship, and affection in ways that I never expected when I first began my research. I had a fantastic time participating in their everyday lives and I will always treasure the memories. To them all, I extend my heartfelt gratitude and appreciation.

I am also thankful to boardinghouse owners, Katunayake neighbors, workers' families, and village neighbors for welcoming me into their homes and spending time with me. I am grateful to the managing director and human resources manager of the Suishin garment factory for allowing me to conduct research within the factory. To them and all other Suishin managers and staff I extend a big thank-you for the warm welcome and support extended to me. I am especially grateful to Jeevaka Senanayake for negotiating with Suishin and arranging for my research there. This book would never have been realized without his intervention. I am also grateful to Rajiv Fernando for facilitating my repeated visits to Suishin.

I am indebted to the members and staff of Dabindu and Mithurusevene who took me into their offices and included me in their activities. I especially appreciate Samanmali and Chamila, who always welcomed me with open arms. Himali, formerly at Dabindu, has enthusiastically supported my work. Milla, Jayanthi, Vijee, Kumar, and Ranjan at Mithurusevene continued to help me get in touch with workers and boardinghouse owners during my subsequent research trips. Sudharshan Gunawardene was always willing to discuss gender and transnational production, and I benefited from his grass-roots activist perspectives. I am also grateful to Group Captain Vijitha Gunaratne, the commanding officer of the Katunayake Air Force Camp, for meeting with me to discuss matters relating to FTZ workers' romances with military personnel.

Colleagues and students at the Department of Sociology, University of Colombo, provided much intellectual stimulation during my research and after I returned from the United States to teach. I am most grateful to Professor Siri Hettige for his constant encouragement throughout my career.

Dayalal Abeysekere and I. V. Edirisinghe continue to provide me with intellectual homes during my frequent research visits to Sri Lanka. Miguel Gomez, Itty Abraham, Patrick Ollivell, Alaka Basu, Sajeda Amin, Jeanne Marecek, Ritu Khanduri, Andrew Causey, Calla Jacobson, and H. L. Seneviratne have provided support during crucial times in my career.

I owe much to Peter Agree and his staff at the University of Pennsylvania Press. I am grateful for their support throughout the publishing process. I am also grateful to all my colleagues in the Department for the Study of Culture and Society at Drake University—especially Janet, Sandi, Vibs, Karl, and Joseph for their support and encouragement. Sandi and Imani certainly make life in Des Moines easier.

For financial support, I am grateful to the Fulbright Foundation, the Ford Foundation, the Social Science Research Council, and the University of Texas Population Research Center for various fellowships and summer research grants and the University of Texas at Austin for a generous writing fellowship. The one-year field research was funded by a Wenner Gren fellowship. A Wenner Gren research fellowship enabled me to extend my research among former FTZ workers in 2005–6 and some of the material collected during this period is included in this book. I extend my heartfelt gratitude to all these organizations. Earlier versions of parts of this book appeared in *Cultural Dynamics* 15, 1 (2003):71–101 (copyright Sage), and *Journal of Third World Studies* 23, 1 (2006):51–74 (copyright Association of Third World Studies).

I thank my family for their support. When I did my research during 1999–2000 all six siblings were in Sri Lanka, and I continually complained about family obligations interfering with my fieldwork. As I write this acknowledgment six years later, my family is dispersed over three continents with my dearest brother Kamal having left us and the world behind. Globalization haunts me in a different vein as I now scramble to visit my diaspora-residing siblings and in-laws. In this changing world, I am extremely grateful to my mother and to my brother, Anura, for providing a warm, cozy place in Sri Lanka for me to call home. I am also grateful to my aunts Nirmala and Asoka and my cousins Manel, Anula, and Anuradha for enveloping me with their love and care.

Most of all I am deeply grateful to Neil for his love, patience, and understanding. His intellectual insights and fine editing skills helped immensely when writing this book. It is to Neil, for all that he is to me, that I dedicate this book.

Stitching Identities in a Free Trade Zone

CONTEMPORARY ETHNOGRAPHY
Kirin Narayan, Series Editor

A complete list of books in the series is available from the publisher.